Spanish and Mexican Land Grants and the Law

Edited by Malcolm Ebright

For Harry Kelsey
Happy Birthday 1989!
Sincerely,
Iris Engstrand

ISBN 0-89745-120-1

From the July 1988 *Journal of the West,* with one additional article.

Sunflower University Press®
1531 Yuma (Box 1009), Manhattan, KS 66502-4228 USA

Spanish and Mexican Land Grants and the Law

Edited by Malcolm Ebright

ERRATA

p. 29 — col. 2, para. 3, line 5: change Neuva to Nueva.
p. 32 — caption: change caroa to canoa; change annoyo to arroyo.
p. 35 — fn 6, line 1: change leves to leyes.

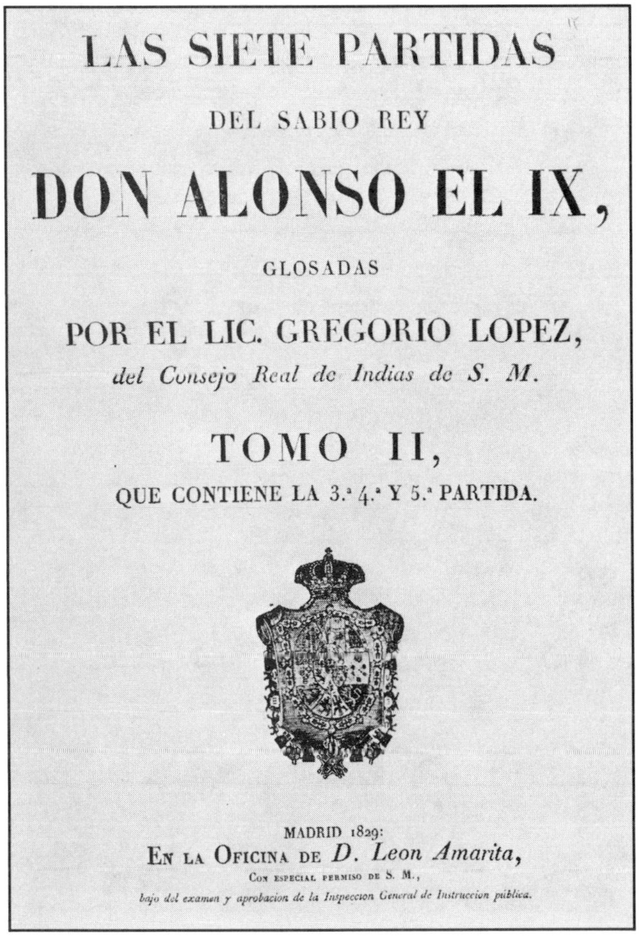
LAS SIETE PARTIDAS
DEL SABIO REY
DON ALONSO EL IX,
GLOSADAS
POR EL LIC. GREGORIO LOPEZ,
del Consejo Real de Indias de S. M.
TOMO II,
QUE CONTIENE LA 3.ª 4.ª Y 5.ª PARTIDA.
MADRID 1829:
EN LA OFICINA DE *D. Leon Amarita,*
CON ESPECIAL PERMISO DE S. M.,
bajo del examen y aprobacion de la Inspeccion General de Instruccion pública.

Title page of ***Las Siete Partidas****, Madrid, 1829.*

Introduction:
Spanish and Mexican Land Grants and the Law

Malcolm Ebright

THIS is the second special edition of the *Journal of the West* on the subject of Spanish and Mexican land grants. The first was published as the July 1980 issue,[1] and was republished in book form as *Spanish and Mexican Land Grants in New Mexico and Colorado*.[2] The introduction to that volume provided a good general background to the scholarly study of land grants and pointed out several areas that needed further study. One of the areas listed was the legal aspects of Spanish and Mexican land grants and their administration.[3] This special issue concentrates on that subject matter, hence its title: *Spanish and Mexican Land Grants and the Law*. We are also expanding the geographical areas of concern beyond Southern Colorado and New Mexico to also include California, Central Mexico, and Castilian Spain.

Spanish law is like a great river, made up of numerous tributaries each contributing to the whole, but, like a continuously flowing waterway, difficult to pin down. To start with, let us jump into that river a good distance downstream from the first rivulets in the mountains where Spanish law's origins are found in prehistoric Spain. Since the first article in this volume deals with sixteenth-century Castile, that is a good place to start.

In sixteenth-century Spain, the law that applied to the Indies was the law of the kingdom of Castile.[4] Although the Spanish kingdoms of Castile and Aragon were united by the marriage in 1469 of their respective monarchs, Ferdinand and Isabella, each kingdom retained separate laws, institutions and political identities. Since it was Queen Isabella alone who sponsored the initial voyages of Columbus, it was the law of Castile that governed the territories Columbus discovered.[5]

Castilian law had several very different components, including codified law covering the entire kingdom, law codes covering local regions or municipalities, and customary law. Among the great comprehensive law codes were the *Fuero Juzgo*, *Las Siete Partidas* and the *Nueva Recopilación de todas las leyes de Castilla*. Then there were the local and regional *fueros* (local codes or ordinances applying to just one municipality or region). Hopeless conflict and confusion existed among these local *fueros*, and between the local *fueros* and the more comprehensive codes. When unwritten local customs were added to the mix, the result was chaotic.[6]

This confusing state of Spanish law was capitalized on by the lawyers in sixteenth-century Castile, who could always find a law to cite in support of their clients. These lawyers helped spawn a litigation explosion in Castile,[7] symptomatic of the weakening of traditional bonds of loyalty in a society that was experiencing rapid economic growth.

Litigation in sixteenth-century Castile was much different than it was in eighteenth- and nineteenth-century New Mexico. The legal system through which a Castilian litigant had to pick his way was exceedingly complex. First of all, there were three types of lawyers: the *abogado* (advocate), the *procurador* (attorney), and the *solicitador* (solicitor). Each had different functions, and they often fought among themselves regarding their overlapping duties. The *abogado* researched the law that applied to a particular case, wrote the briefs required, and orally presented the legal arguments of his clients to the judge. The *procurador* had direct contact with the client from the time he took a case and was given authority to represent his client in court. This attorney did most of the leg-work in preparing the case, including the interviewing of witnesses and the preparation of routine documents.[8]

Finally there was the *solicitador,* whose functions were not clearly spelled out in the documents. This may have been because some of those duties were illegal, such as arranging for bribes and other payoffs intended to further the client's case. The *solicitador* had to be aware of everything that might affect the case, such as changes in royal policy, impending legislation, and just plain court gossip. He was not unlike a modern-day influence peddler whose job was to keep the complex machinery of litigation well oiled, even if he had to grease a few palms to do so.[9]

Faced with this bewildering array of lawyers and laws, whose complexity served to raise the cost of litigation, the litigant in sixteenth-century Castile also had to confront a court system comprised of a proliferation of officials whose income depended largely on the fees paid by the litigant. Besides the magistrates themselves, who often vied with one another to get jurisdiction over as many cases as possible, the royal courts included a retinue of scribes, notaries, accountants, assessors, receivers, constables, and porters. Most of them had purchased their offices, so they expected to receive a reasonable return on their investment.[10]

Of course not all litigation in sixteenth-century Castile was this complicated. Courts in rural areas were more streamlined with fewer court officials, but on the whole the legal system in Spain was far more complex than it was in Spain's overseas possessions. This comparison is particularly extreme if one looks at the legal systems in New Spain's frontier provinces of New Mexico and Upper California.

The flow of Spanish law that arrived in the provinces of New Mexico and California had been subjected to many influences in the course of a series of invasions of the Iberian peninsula. The Visigoths brought a Germanic influence in their *Fuero Juzgo* code, the Roman influence was strongly present in *Las Siete Partidas,* and the Moorish influence on the course of Spanish jurisprudence is also felt in New Mexico and California. It was Moorish institutions, more than Arabic laws, that left their mark in the Southwest. The administration of water distribution is a prime example.

***Canoa** (flume) still in use at Las Trampas. This part of the irrigation works carries the water in the **acequia** over the highway. (Courtesy Historic Preservation Division (OCA), State of New Mexico.)*

Most Spanish names for irrigation works like *acequia* (irrigation ditch) and *atarque* (diversion dam), have Moorish origins, and the customary irrigation practice that traveled from Spain to the New World was influenced by Moorish practices.[11]

The office of *alcalde* also had Moorish origins. This locally elected rural official acted as both mayor and judge in rural villages that did not have the full panoply of legal officials and lawyers found in the larger municipalities. The *alcalde* was much in evidence in New Mexico and California and was often the only official available to administer the functions of local government. As the local judge, the *alcalde* did not follow a fixed set of legal rules or law codes. Rather, his decisions were most often based on ethical and practical considerations and on local customs. The *alcalde's* judgments seldom referred to specific laws, or even to his own prior legal decisions or those of other alcaldes. If a litigant was unhappy with the decision of an *alcalde*, his usual recourse was an appeal to the provincial governor. But even the decisions of the governors often lacked any reference to specific laws or to prior decisions.[12]

This is not to say that there was no pattern to the decisions of the *alcaldes* and governors in the frontier provinces. A reading of these decisions does yield a structure from which general rules can be stated. These rules are in the nature of customary law, a largely unwritten law usually not found in the law codes. It was customary law that largely governed the settlement of disputes and the granting of land in New Mexico and California.[13] The antecedents of this customary law are found in sixteenth-century Castile.

Customary law was made up, not only of the decisions of *alcaldes* and governors in litigation, but also of the acts of these officials in response to petitions for land. Customary law was the totality of what was actually done in response to a conflict or a petition, not what was supposed to be done. Sometimes the laws and the customs coincided and there was no conflict between the two. But many times there was a conflict, often because the local authorities did not know about the law in question.[14]

The use of customary law, both in Spain and in New Spain, was partly in response to the high cost of litigation and the excessive time spent in its pursuit. The complex and contradictory laws and the labyrinthine legal system cried out for a simpler method of dispute resolution.

The Treaty of Guadalupe Hidalgo and international law made it necessary for nineteenth-century U.S. lawyers and judges involved in the litigation and confirmation of Spanish and Mexican land grants to apply Spanish and Mexican law to the land grant cases they were faced with. It was much easier for these American lawyers and judges to buttress an argument or legal decision with quotations from one or two Spanish codes, or commentators on those codes, than it was to research what the customary law was that applied to the dispute. The injustice that was done in the adjudication of Spanish and Mexican land grants was mostly a result of American lawyers taking advantages of the earlier confused state of Spanish and Mexican law. It was not that American lawyers and judges trained in the common law of England did not understand the legal concepts of the civil law tradition of Spain. The basic legal concepts to be applied were part of the history of both legal systems. For example, the institution of common land ownership was found in England, as well as France, and most of the rest of Europe.[15] The fundamental cause of the injustice was the failure to understand and apply customary law as it related to the issues in conflict.

Scene of typical Hispanic village life in the spring. Many of the materials used in these activities are from the common lands. (Original painting by Glen Strock.)

Several of the articles in this volume illustrate the kinds of source materials that are used to determine customary law. Both David Vassberg and Daniel Tyler, for instance, rely heavily on archival records of early lawsuits in Spain and New Mexico, respectively, as well as on other archival documents. It is the outcome of these lawsuits that is most important, not what laws (if any) are cited in the lawsuit. Since Vassberg's article and Tyler's article each focus on common lands, one in sixteenth-century Castile the other in nineteenth-century New Mexico, it is interesting to compare the two articles.

The issues of common land ownership and use were perplexing enough before they were interpreted by American courts. By that time the river of Spanish law had traveled quite a ways towards the ocean of the present. It is at the point where Spanish law begins to be interpreted by courts in the United States that the waters become quite muddied.

Ever since the United States Supreme Court decided the case of *U.S. v. Sandoval*[16] the historical question of ownership of the common lands has become further clouded. In *Sandoval,* the Supreme Court held that the common lands of a community land grant were owned, not by the individual land grant, but by the government (of Spain or Mexico) that made the grant. Under this theory, when a community grant, such as San Miguel del Bado, was made by the Mexican government, the government theoretically transferred title to the grantees only of the land within the individual allotments, and it retained title to the common lands. The effect of this theory of ownership upon U.S. land-grant adjudication was that after *Sandoval,* the U.S. government rejected land-grant claims for common lands, approving only the private allotted lands. They did this on the theory that since the governments of Spain and Mexico had retained title to the common lands, the United States acquired that title as successor sovereign.

Applied to the San Miguel del Bado grant, the community grant involved in the *Sandoval* case, this theory meant that of the 315,300 acres surveyed to be within the grant, only a little more than 5,000 acres were confirmed to the grantees. The remaining 310,000 acres was held to be U.S. public domain. The same result was repeated with every community land grant that came before the Court of Private Land Claims after 1897, so that millions of acres of common lands once claimed by community land grants in Northern New Mexico wound up as government land administered by the U.S. Forest Service in the Carson and Santa Fe National Forests.

Sandoval was an immensely important case as it related to land-grant claimants, because it was upon their common

San Miguel church at San Miguel (del Bado). (Courtesy Historic Preservation Division (OCA), State of New Mexico.)

lands that New Mexican communities depended for the resources they needed to survive. But *Sandoval's* reasoning left much to be desired. The opinion by Chief Justice Fuller cited only two authorities, which provided a very shaky underpinning for that important decision.[17] While the articles by Vassberg and Tyler do not provide simple or easy answers to the questions of common land use and ownership, they do provide a richness of detail in their examination of archival cases dealing with common land ownership, giving us immensely more information and authority than was included in *Sandoval*. It is upon such research that a better reasoned decision as to ownership of the common lands can be based in further litigation.

Professor Vassberg found that there was a high degree of confusion over the types of common lands in sixteenth-century Castile. Theoretically, *tierras baldías* were the only

Lush grazing land and abundant woodlands, all used in common, provided essential resources necessary for the survival of Hispanic villages. Acquisition of land grant common lands by the U.S. Forest Service often made land, once part of a land grant, unavailable to local residents because of restrictions imposed by the Forest Service on the use of the land. (Photo by U.S. Forest Service, Neg. no. 59006. Courtesy Museum of New Mexico.)

true public-domain lands at the absolute disposition of the sovereign, and *tierras concegiles* were common lands owned by municipalities. The general codified law provided protection of the *tierras concegiles* from encroachments by nobleman or commoner, as well as by other municipalities. But when the king himself cast a covetous eye on the money-making potential of these common lands, there was little that could be done to stop him. Vassberg uses the concept of eminent domain to describe the crown's perogative of power. The king could limit or impose conditions on a property right as long as he was careful not to go too far. For if an institution with substantial popular support was completely done away with, the monarch might have a rebellion on his hands. Note that, with the sales of the common lands in the 1590s, King Philip II did not completely eliminate the institution of common lands, as happened in France and England with the Enclosure Acts.[18] He was instead requiring payment for the continuation of common land usage.

Professor Tyler found the same confusion as did Professor Vassberg, between the public domain of the sovereign (*tierras baldías* or *tierras realengas*) and the common lands of communities (*ejidos* or *tierras concejiles*). As in Castilian Spain, this confusion was due in part to an imprecise use of language, as where common lands of the community would be called *realengas*,[19] or public domain lands would be called *ejidos*. The blurring of the distinction between the two types of land was also due to the similarity of use of the two types of land, both in Spain and in New Mexico. As Professor Tyler points out, although everyone had a generalized right to use the public domain (*baldías* or *realengas*) in common, communities and community land grants had an overriding right to use the public domain surrounding their community in preference to others. In addition to this sphere of influence in the public domain, a community generally had its own common lands (*ejidos*) that were for the exclusive use of the community unless permission was given to outsiders to also use these lands. The fact that the boundaries between the *ejidos* lands and the *baldío*/*realengo* lands were not always clearly marked was an additional reason for the confusion between the two types of lands. But it seems clear from Professor Tyler's article that the *ejido*, or common lands of a community land grant, belonged to the land grant and were not public domain. Based on this interpretation *Sandoval's* holding was clearly wrong.

Other articles in this volume deal more directly with specific land grants, how they were made, and how they were adjudicated. All of the articles in this volume raise questions that will not necessarily be resolved here. Some of those issues are:

1. The relative importance of customary law versus codified law in the Spanish legal tradition, especially on the northern frontier of New Spain.
2. The ownership and use of common lands.
3. The extent to which the Spanish civil law tradition was in conflict with the Anglo-American common law tradition.
4. The extent to which any conflict between Spanish civil law and Anglo common law was the cause of some of the unjust decisions of the U.S. courts.

The article by G. Emlen Hall raises the last two issues in his study of New Mexican Pueblo Indian lands. In particular, Hall traces the way three successive sovereigns dealt with Santa Clara Pueblo and the extent to which the individual farm tracts worked by individual Pueblo members were private property that could be sold. There was a change of law on this point in the Mexican Period that allowed sales of Pueblo land to non-Indians, but other than this temporary aberration, the three sovereigns were fairly consistent in barring sales of Pueblo land to non-Indians. The point that Professor Hall's article makes so well is that, despite a fairly uniform prohibition against sales of Indian land, such land was sold, and this issue returned again and again to confront the Spanish and American judicial authorities.

It was not so much that the successive sovereigns disagreed about the law, but that the Pueblo itself was divided on the question, as Hall demonstrates. When one faction lost a decision, even the legal principle of *stare decisis* did not stop that faction from raising essentially the same issue again in a slightly different guise.

The issue of the importance of codified law is dealt with in Joseph McKnight's article on Spanish law books. Professor McKnight points out that in the areas of the Hispanic frontier, such as New Orleans, where Spanish law books were readily available, Spanish law took firm root and was influential even after the U.S. acquired sovereignty. In other areas where there were few Spanish law books, like Florida, the law was rapidly Americanized after the U.S. occupied the region.

Since Iris Engstrand's article deals with California land grants and several other articles deal with land grants in New Mexico, it will be useful to compare land grant procedures in New Mexico with those in California.

The procedures involved in making a land grant were similar in New Mexico and in California. Both provinces were subject to the Colonization Law of 1824,[20] and to the Regulations of 1828,[21] but these laws did not cover every detail of land grant procedure, and the gaps were filled by customary practice. The custom and practice in California sometimes differed from that in New Mexico. In both places, the person or persons seeking the grant would direct a petition to the governor, requesting a grant, describing the land sought, listing his or her qualifications for receiving a grant and stating that here were no claims by third parties to the land petitioned for. In both places the description of the land requested was by natural landmarks. It later turned out that many of these landmarks were difficult to locate, causing endless problems in the adjudicatory process.

The landmarks of the Mora grant as described in Clark Knowlton's article are a good example. The petition requested a tract of land bounded on the north by the Ocate River, on the south by the mouth of the Sapello River where it empties into the Mora River, on the east by the Aguaje

Main Street in Mora, c. 1900. (Courtesy Historic Preservation Division (OCA), State of New Mexico.)

(spring) de la Yegua, and on the west by the Estillero. While the northern and southern boundaries, being well-known rivers, were relatively easily located, the eastern and western boundary calls were to become the source of much consternation. When the Surveyor General of New Mexico attempted to locate the western and eastern boundaries, the witnesses could not agree as to where these landmarks were, and it took a series of surveys, followed by protests, and then by resurveys, to finally locate the eastern and western boundaries of the grant, as Professor Knowlton points out.

The problem of vague and indefinite boundary calls in land grant petitions was not as acute in California as it was in New Mexico. While one seldom, if ever, sees a map accompanying a petition for a land grant in New Mexico, in California such maps, called *diseños,* were not uncommon. Professor Engstrand points out in her article that professional surveyors were not unknown in Mexican Period California, as some experts had previously thought. In particular, she mentions the work of Jasper O'Farrell, whose *diseños* of California ranchos were often submitted to the California Board of Land Commissioners, set up to adjudicate land grant claims in that state. A testament to the accuracy of O'Farrell's work is that in most cases where one of his surveys was submitted with a petition for confirmation, the grant was confirmed by the Land Commissioner's Board with little argument.[22] Besides O'Farrell, there were several others with varying amounts of training doing surveys and drawing *diseños* in California.[23]

The next step in the granting procedure after the petition was usually a request by the governor to the local *alcalde* for a report on the petition. This request was usually written in the left-hand margin of the petition. The *alcalde's* report generally discussed whether there were any claims to the land by third parties or whether the making of the grant would prejudice anyone in any way. To make this determination, the *alcalde* would often announce to the community that the land was being sought by the petitioner(s) and allow a certain time within which objections to the proposed grant could be made.

Sometimes the petition for the grant would be directed to the *alcalde* initially and would then be forwarded to the governor with the *alcalde's* recommendation.[24] Often the *alcalde* would provide a rather terse report, basically recommending that the grant be made and stating that the making of the grant would not harm anyone. Sometimes the *ayuntamiento* (town council) would be consulted and would render a more detailed report. In the case of the Tierra Amarilla grant, the *ayuntamiento* of Abiquiu reported that the land petitioned for had abundant pasture, water, and firewood, and was capable of supporting 500 families.[25]

Normally the next step would be the making of the grant by the governor, but there could be additional proceedings before the petition reached the governor's desk. Again the Tierra Amarilla grant is a case in point. After the *ayuntamiento* made its report to the governor, the petitioner, in a rare move in the annals of land-grant procedure, filed a protest to the *ayuntamiento's* report. Then the governor did what every good bureaucrat would do under the circumstances: he appointed a commission to report on the protest. The commission overruled the protest, recommending that the grant be made, and listing specifically the recommended terms of the grant. The governor adopted the commission's report and made the grant with the same terms recommended by the commission.[26]

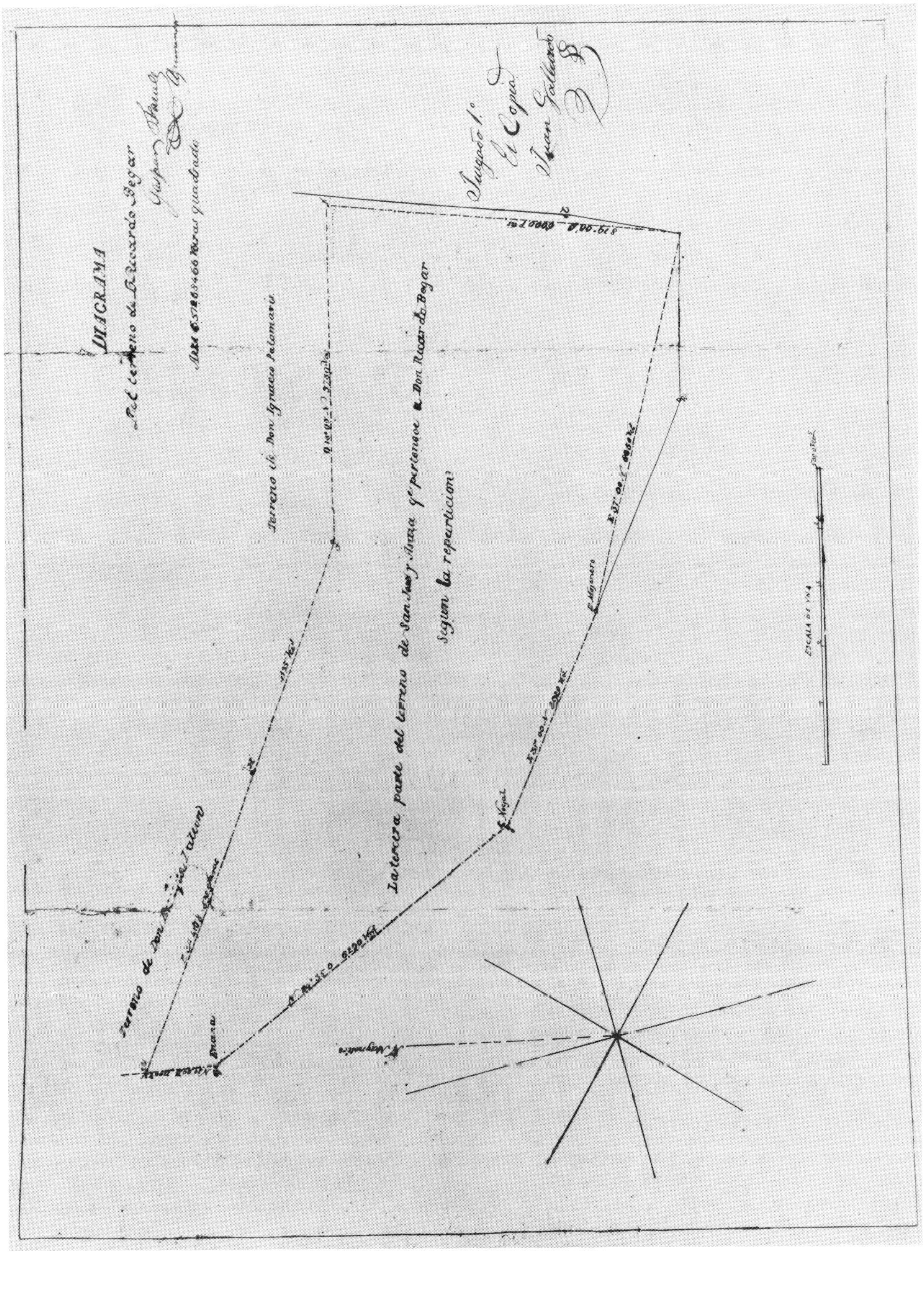

Diagram of Jasper O'Farrell's 1846 survey of the partition of the Rancho San Jose in California. This was one of the few accurate surveys to be made in Mexican Period California. Not a **diseño**, this is a precise, mathematically based survey of a tract of land, showing courses and distances, as well as boundary markers (**mojoneros**). If more land grants had had the benefit of surveys like this, subsequent land grant litigation would have been greatly reduced. (From **California Rancho Diseños: Designs on the Land** by Robert H. Becker. Courtesy the Book Club of California, San Francisco.)

The third step in the grant-making procedure was the grant by the governor, but it was not the end of the process. The grant by the governor was directed back to the local *alcalde* for the final step in the process: the delivery of possession of the land. Generally, in New Mexico, the governor would list some of the standard conditions of the grant and the *alcalde* would expand on and add to them in his act of possession. Among the conditions often found in typical land grants and acts of possession are the following:

1. That the grant not prejudice or cause harm to any third party.
2. That the grant be occupied by the grantee within a certain minimum time (often six months), and that the grantee occupy the land continuously for another minimum period (often four years).
3. That the grantee could not sell the land until the minimum possession period had been met.

In the case of community land grants, more detailed conditions about the use of the land would also be included. A community grant was made to a group of settlers (usually ten or more) who received private allotments of land for their homes, gardens and fields. They used the rest of the grant in common for grazing their animals, gathering firewood, collecting building materials such as timbers and rock, fishing, hunting, and gathering other resources from the land such as herbs and acorns. Some of the provisions that might be added to the grant documents in the case of a community grant are the following:

1. Allotment of private tracts of land to each individual settler, often along a river.
2. Notification of the grantees that any unallotted land was reserved for other settlers who might join the community in the future, and that the remaining land within the grant was to be used in common by all the settlers in the grant.
3. Directions to fence the farm plots (which was rarely done) and to keep the grazing animals some distance from the cropland.
4. Directions to arm themselves with firearms against Indian attack. (Those who did not have firearms at the time the settlers were inspected by the *alcalde* could be ordered to leave the community.)
5. Directions to furnish all the labor necessary for such projects as digging and cleaning the *acequia,* building a church, and other tasks deemed necessary for the common welfare.

The delivery of possession was probably the most important step in the land-grant procedure. It was important because it was physical and direct, in a culture which valued the tangible above the abstract. This was the time when the grantees went to the land itself with the *alcalde* and neighboring landowners, set the boundary markers, and performed a ceremony that signified, in a very concrete way, their ownership of the land.

Scene of typical Hispanic village life in the winter. Many of the materials used in these activities are from the common lands. (Original painting by Glen Strock.)

There was wide variation in the fixing of boundaries, from one extreme of a formal and fairly accurate survey, to the other extreme of no survey or attempt to mark the boundaries at all. In New Mexico surveys were extremely rare, especially if there were no adjoining land grants. Often the grantees were told to mark their boundaries, and that was that. Until, of course, the problem surfaced later as it did in the Mora grant discussed by Professor Knowlton. Locating boundaries is still a problem in Northern New Mexico where much of the land has still not been surveyed.

While a few rudimentary surveys were done in Southern New Mexico, in California the documents reveal greater detail about how surveys were made at the time of the delivery of possession. The documents for the Rancho Corral de Piedras at San Luis Obispo show than in 1842 a survey was performed by the local *jues de pas* assisted by two *cordeleros* appointed by the justice "for want of a skillful surveyor." The *cordeleros* were mounted on horseback, each carrying a pole. The poles were connected to one another by a measuring rope (*cordel*), 50 *varas* in length (a vara is 33 inches). The justice began at the first landmark by establishing the proper compass direction. Then the first *cordelero* rode forward the length of the cord, stopped and placed the tip of his pole on the ground. The second *cordelero* then rode past him the length of the cord, and so on until the magistrate directed them to change course. In this way the perimeter of the grant was traversed. Although the landmarks used in this California survey were no more precise than those used in New Mexico, the surveying party for the Corral de Piedras grant did mark the corners of the grant with stakes, providing an additional means of retracing the survey.[27]

Once the grant was surveyed with the approval of the adjoining landowners and the grantees were instructed in their duties in regard to the land, the final step in the act of possession was when the local official notified the grantee that he was now the legal owner of the land. In response, the grantee pulled up grass, threw rocks (in the four directions some say), and cried *''Viva el Rey!''* or during the Mexican Period *''Viva el Presidente y la Nación Mexicana!''*

The making of a land grant resulted from a combination of handwritten legal documents required by the law and by custom, and the tangible, concrete relationship to the land that took place during the act of possession. After the grant was made that relationship with the land continued (if it did not, the grantee could lose the land by abandonment). The legal documents that have survived help us piece together the story of the land grants. But it is well to remember that these documents are just the tip of the iceberg. The rest of the iceberg is the day-to-day living on the land in a self-sufficient manner giving rise to a strong attachment to the land. This connection is on the visceral rather than the legal level. It is this feeling for the land in the heart and in the gut that guarantees that the legal history of land grants in the Southwest is not just something from the dim, dark past. Land grants and the law are as current as today's news, and will continue to be so as long as there are people who remember the land, and who remember their ancestors who received title to the land by means of a *merced de tierra*.

NOTES

1. *Journal of the West,* 19 (July 1980).
2. *Spanish and Mexican Land Grants in New Mexico and Colorado* (Manhattan, KS: Sunflower University Press, 1980).
3. John R. Van Ness and Christine M. Van Ness, ''Introduction,'' *ibid.,* 11.
4. Castile was only one of the several kingdoms comprising sixteenth-century Spain. Besides the kingdom of Castile, there were the kingdoms of Aragon and Navarre. David E. Vassberg, *Land and Society in Golden Age Castile* (Cambridge, England, 1984), 3.
5. *Recopilación de Leyes de Las Reynos de las Indias* (Madrid, Spain: Ivlian de Paredes, 1681), Book I, Title 1, Law 2.
6. Richard L. Kagan, *Lawsuits and Litigants in Castile: 1500-1700* (Chapel Hill, NC, 1981), 22-32.
7. *Ibid.,* 3-20.
8. *Ibid.,* 52, 60-61.
9. *Ibid.,* 53-56.
10. *Ibid.,* 35-38.
11. Thomas F. Glick, *The Old World Background of the Irrigation System of San Antonio, Texas* (El Paso, TX, 1972), 3-4; Malcolm Ebright, ''New Mexican Land Grants: The Legal Background,'' in *Land, Water, and Culture* (Albuquerque, NM, 1987), 16-17. According to one scholar, however, the Moorish influence was a ''minor accretion to the body of Spanish irrigation practice that had flourished from the days of the Romans,'' Marc Simmons, ''Spanish Irrigation Practices in New Mexico,'' *New Mexico Historical Review,* 57 (April 1972): 135-136.
12. Marc Simmons, *Spanish Government in New Mexico* (Albuquerque, NM, 1968), 67-68; David J. Langum, *Law and Community on the Mexican California Frontier* (Norman and London, 1987), 30.
13. An excellent example of the use of this method to establish what the law was in California during the Mexican Period (1821-1846) is David J. Langum, *Law and Community on the Mexican California Frontier.*
14. Custom and customary law are defined in *Las Siete Partidas,* Samuel Parsons Scott, translator (Chicago, 1931), Partida I, Título 2; see also John Leyba and Joseph Sena, ''Customary Law in New Mexico,'' in *Land, Law, and La Raza,* presented for a seminar in comparative law, University of New Mexico School of Law, Fall Semester 1972, under Professor Theodore Parnall.
15. For England see, E.C.K. Gonner, *Common Land and Inclosure* (London, 1966), *passim;* for France see, Marc Bloch, *French Rural History,* (Berkeley: 1966), 219-221; for the rest of Europe see, John R. Van Ness, ''Hispanic Village Organization in Northern New Mexico: Corporate Community Structure in Historical and Comparative Perspective,'' in Paul Kutsche, ed., *The Survival of Spanish American Villages* (Colorado Springs, 1979), 22-24.
16. *U.S. v. Sandoval,* 167, U.S. 278 (1897).
17. Elizondo's *Practica Universal Forense* and Frederic Hall's *Mexican Land Laws.*
18. See note 15.
19. Arroyo Hondo grant, New Mexico Land Grants — Private Land Claims (NMLG-PLC), microfilm roll 33, case 5, New Mexico State Records Center and Archives, Santa Fe, NM.
20. Manuel Dublán and José María Lozano, *Legislación Mexicana,* 2 vols. (Mexico, 1876), I, 712; for a translation see Hall, *The Laws of Mexico* (Mexico, 1893), 148-149.
21. Francisco de la Maza, *Código de colonización y terrenos baldíos . . . publicado según acuerdo del Presidente de la República 1541-1892* (Mexico, 1893), 237-240; for a translation see Hall, *The Laws of Mexico,* 150-153.
22. Geoffrey P. Mawn, *''Agrimensor y Arquitecto:* Jasper O'Farrell's Surveying in Mexican California,'' *Southern California Quarterly,* 61 (Spring 1974): 1.
23. Robert H. Becker, *Diseños of California Ranchos: Maps of Thirty-seven Land Grants: 1822-1846* (San Francisco, CA: The Book Club of California, 1964), *passim.*
24. Alcalde José Miguel Tafoya to Governor Alberto Maynes, Taos, 27 Mar. 1815; Arroyo Hondo Grant, NMLG-PLC, roll 33, case 5.
25. Ayuntamiento of Abiquiu to Governor Santiago Abreu, Abiquiu, 15 May 1832; Malcolm Ebright, *The Tierra Amarilla Grant: A History of Chicanery* (Santa Fe, NM: Center for Land Grant Studies, 1980), 34-35.
26. *Ibid.,* 36-41.
27. Becker, *Diseños of California Ranchos,* xiv-xvii.

Malcolm Ebright, who lives in Guadalupita, New Mexico, is an attorney and historian. He is president of the Center for Land Grant Studies, and has written numerous articles on land grants in New Mexico. His books include *The Tierra Armarilla Grant: A History of Chicanery and Essays on Land Grants and Lawsuits in Northern New Mexico*, soon to be published by University of New Mexico Press.

The town of Lebrija [LEBRIXA] (Seville province), with surrounding fields and olive groves. Many small fields are shown walled, for protection from grazing animals. From Georg Braun, ***Civitatis orbis terrarum****, vol. 2, no. 5 (Cologne, 1576-1618). (Photo courtesy of The Harry Ransom Humanities Research Center, University of Texas at Austin.)*

The Spanish Background:
Problems Concerning Ownership, Usurpations, and Defense of Common Lands in 16th Century Castile

David E. Vassberg

The Communitarian System

THE *conquistadores* who shaped the institutions of Spanish America came from a land where the tradition of public landownership was a pervasive influence. In fact, Castile's complex system of common property rights played a profound role in forging the mentality that enabled Spain to become the world's most powerful nation in the sixteenth century.

The tradition of public property ownership in Spain can be traced back to pre-Roman times. But it was during the centuries-long Christian Reconquest of Spain from the Moslems that it developed its distinctive modern characteristics and its legal framework. Because the Reconquest was sponsored by the monarchy, the rulers of Castile were able to assert a powerful claim to the right of eminent domain over all the property in their kingdoms.[1]

The Castilian kings attracted settlers to the vulnerable, newly conquered zones along the Moslem frontier by offering generous grants of land to nobles and commoners who would move there. Thus both large and small private landholdings were created from portions of the royal domain. All lands that were not apportioned through royal grant remained theoretically the property of the crown and were called crown lands (*tierras realengas*). The monarchs, eager to promote colonization, generously allowed the public to have free access to these lands for hunting, fishing, pasture, forest products, and even agriculture. This led to the development of a strong popular feeling that the crown lands, although vaguely subject to royal control, were commons in the public domain. The people usually called them *tierras baldías,* or simply *baldíos*.

From the very beginning, the ownership of the *baldíos* was problematical, for no one held legal title to them. The monarchs claimed ultimate ownership, but this claim often seemed remote to those who were freely using the lands, paying rent to no one. Furthermore, the crown tacitly per-

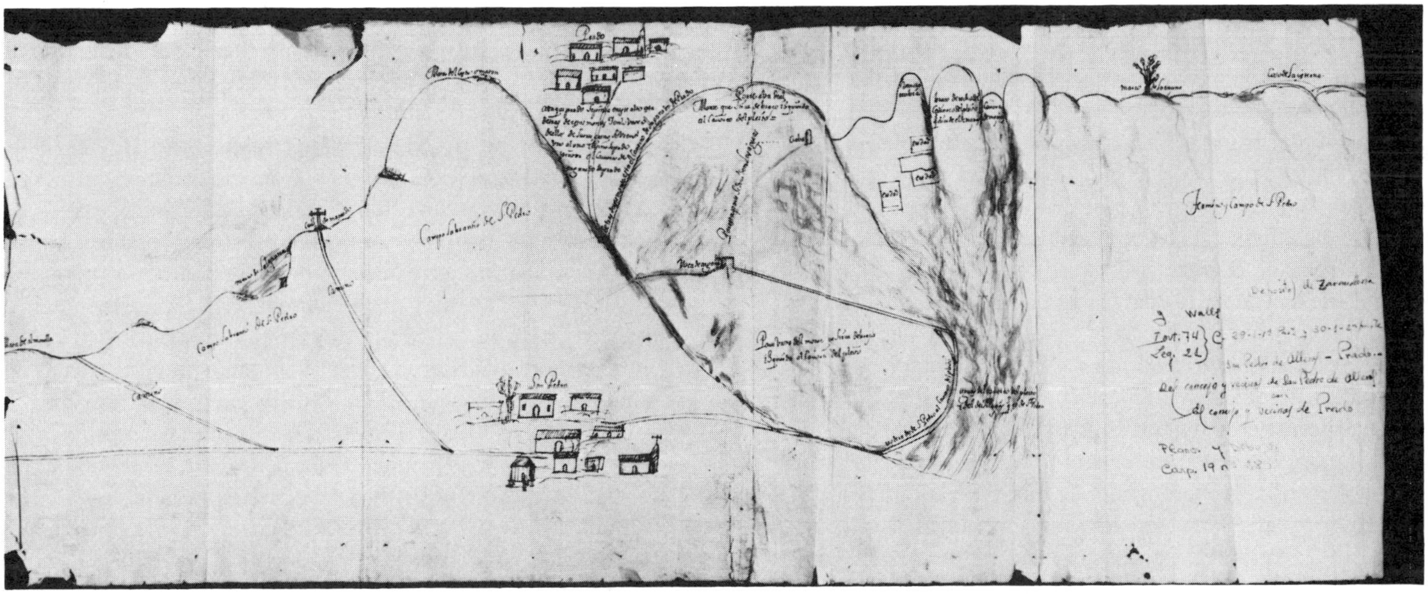

Simple map submitted as evidence in a suit (1592-1653) between San Pedro de Olleros and Prado (both in León province) over the ownership of a ***monte*** *situated between the two villages. (Photo courtesy of Archivo de la Chancillería de Valladolid, Planos y Dibujos 19, no. 280.)*

mitted municipal governments to exercise their authority over the *tierras baldías* under their jurisdiction, making municipal control the normal order of the day.[2]

The question was all the more complex because the monarchs also made munificent land grants to municipalities. Virtually every Castilian city, town, and village came to own property that was set aside for the benefit of its own inhabitants. Typically, these royal cessions simply granted the municipality a certain portion of the local *baldíos*, as municipal property (*tierras concegiles*). And often the municipalities merely appropriated for themselves whatever they wanted of the local *baldíos*, using only their own authority, without royal permission. Small wonder, then, that there was the vaguest distinction between *tierras baldías* and *tierras concegiles* (lands of the town council). Sixteenth-century Castilians often used the terms interchangeably.[3]

The precise juridical status of much of the property of the Castilian municipalities was uncertain. Some property had been purchased, or acquired through royal grant, or through bequests from patriotic citizens. But when the origin was centuries old, and when the documentary proof had been lost (or had never existed), ownership might be based upon "possession from time immemorial," a formula usually acceptable in Castilian courts.[4]

Municipally owned property fell into two distinct juridical categories: commons, which were set aside for the free use of the local citizenry; and *propios,* which were normally rented out, with the proceeds going into the municipal treasury for projects in the public interest. Both could include pasture, woodlands, and arable land. There were also commons of an intermunicipal character — property of the same type which was shared by two or more towns. Castilians of the day had a strong conviction that municipal property should be inviolable. The noted sixteenth-century authority Castillo de Bobadilla asserted that neither the king nor the seigniorial lords had any proprietary right to such lands.[5]

In brief, the Castilian tradition included common rights to crown lands, or *baldíos,* in addition to municipal and intermunicipal commons (or *tierras concegiles*). But that was not all. According to a venerable Castilian custom, even private property was available for free public use through the *derrota de mieses,* a custom allowing the public to graze their animals on the stubble of privately owned grain fields after harvest. This converted virtually the entire territory of a village — until the next planting — into a continuous common pasture.[6]

The Castilian customs regarding common rights applied to lands under seigniorial jurisdiction, as well as those directly subject to royal authority. All Castilians, regardless of jurisdictional status, considered the traditional common privileges to be an inalienable right. Thus, when the crown established new seigniorial jurisdictions, it carefully stipulated that the señor was not to abridge the people's common rights.[7]

The responses to royal questionnaires sent to all towns in Castile in the late 1570s demonstrate that the communitarian system was a vital part of the socioeconomic structure of Castilian society. Virtually all towns reported that they had common property, and the consensus was that it was of great benefit to the people, especially to the poor.[8]

Usurpations of Commons

The communitarian system, then, was widespread and important; it was universally praised by the peasants; it was actively encouraged by the municipalities and the crown; and it was protected by local and royal law. Nevertheless, during the sixteenth century the system was under continual attack, and this had been going on for centuries. The attacks came from the nobility, the municipalities, the crown, and even from the peasants who supposedly were the prime beneficiaries of communitarianism. The problem of the usurpation of commons was aggravated by the fact that legal ownership of many of these lands was questionable. Moreover, the existing local and national laws about common privileges were often vague or conflicting.

The most frequent and persistent usurpations of commons came from the peasants who were using them. It is understandable that an individual who used a certain common plot year after year could ultimately come to believe that his right to the plot should extend beyond a mere temporary occupancy. Consequently, the customs which allowed individuals to use common lands produced a strong tendency to usurp those lands and to transform them into private property. Accordingly, throughout Castile the various types of commons gradually tended to become privatized, as peasants illegally appropriated portions of them for their own exclusive use.[9] With the passage of time, the holders of these usurped commons were able to accumulate legal documentation in support of their claims, as the plots changed hands through sale, inheritance, or in dowries.[10]

Members of the Castilian nobility, and other powerful persons (*personas poderosas*), were also guilty of usurping the commons to add to their estates. Typically they accomplished this by having their servants surreptitiously move their land markers (*mojones*) gradually into the adjacent *baldíos*, so as not to attract attention. But sometimes the usurpations involved brazen seizures by wealthy and influential people who were able to cow the local authorities into acquiescence.[11] Such "powerful persons" also allowed their animals to graze illegally on restricted common pastures and even on the grain fields of their neighbors, avoiding prosecution because of their influence in the local government.[12] And some arrogant landowners felt strong enough to attempt to abrogate the *derrota de mieses*, denying their weaker neighbors the traditional pasture rights on their grain stubble.[13]

A confusion between the rights of seigniorial jurisdiction and land ownership caused another form of noble interference with common privileges. Seigniorial jurisdiction did not in itself confer land ownership. But many powerful lords were also large landowners, and their influence and prestige were so great that they were able to arrogate to themselves the right to control the *tierras baldías* and other commons under their jurisdiction. Thus, in all parts of the kingdom we find examples of lords illegally granting permission for private parties and municipalities to clear forests, to plow pastures, and to plant orchards, gardens, and vineyards on common lands. This was almost invariably a prelude to the privatization of ownership.[14]

Although municipal governments generally defended the communitarian system, that was not always the case. The towns often gave their citizens permission to take parts of the local *tierras baldías* for use as private property. This was of dubious legality, but until the second half of the 1500s the Castilian monarchs seldom interfered. In any case, these municipal grants of the *baldíos* usually involved plowing for the first time lands that traditionally had been treated as common pasture. And it contributed to the rapid depletion of the country's forest (*monte*) resources.[15]

Another type of municipal usurpation was for local governments to appropriate lands from the commons to add to their *propios*. Town officials usually cited financial difficulties to justify the imposition of fees, or rent, for the use of lands that had formerly been common. Upon occasion this was done with the monarch's consent, especially when the proceeds were to enrich the Royal Treasury.[16]

A far more widespread abuse of common property was its temporary loss due to misconduct by municipal officials. Administrative officers (*regidores*) sometimes were guilty of using their positions to monopolize portions of the commons for themselves or for the benefit of friends and relatives.[17] The advantages of a seat on the local government council led many wealthy individuals to purchase such positions. And there is evidence that some seigniorial lords manipulated municipal elections to ensure that the local government would tolerate their despoliations of the commons.[18]

The crown, like the municipalities, generally defended communitarian institutions. But the rulers of Castile were chronically short of funds, and could not resist the temptation to use their privilege of eminent domain to exploit the money-making potential of the commons under their jurisdiction. Early in his reign, Philip II (1556-1598) experimented briefly with selling privileges of enclosure (*acotamientos, cerramientos*), abrogating the *derrota de mieses* on those particular fields. But he soon abandoned the project after discovering that revenues were disappointingly small, and that there was strong resistance from the Cortes (national assembly) and from other powerful interests.[19]

A far more important royal disruption of Castilian communitarianism came when the monarchy developed a revenue-raising scheme involving the *tierras baldías*. Begun in 1557, this scheme exploited the fact that many individuals and municipalities held lands with defective (or nonexistent) titles, having been originally usurped from the *baldíos*. These *baldío* occupiers were willing to pay handsomely for a royally approved title conferring full legal ownership. The crown claimed the right to sell all *tierras baldías concegiles* to which the occupiers did not have "good" title. And royal lawyers could usually find some pretext to invalidate previous royal grants, either on the basis of "defects" in the original grants, or on the basis of illegal land use in the interim. Eventually the treasury devised a type of public auction in which *any* part of the *baldíos* — not just illegally occupied areas — could be sold to the highest bidder. Those *baldío* occupiers who refused to bid on their land were likely to lose it, as their neighbors came up with the money. The crown preferred to sell to municipalities, rather than individuals, and many towns that purchased *baldíos* continued to permit the age-old common privileges. Nevertheless, the program of *baldío* sales resulted in a massive privatization of common lands throughout Castile. This sales program turned out to be a major source of revenue for the Royal Treasury,

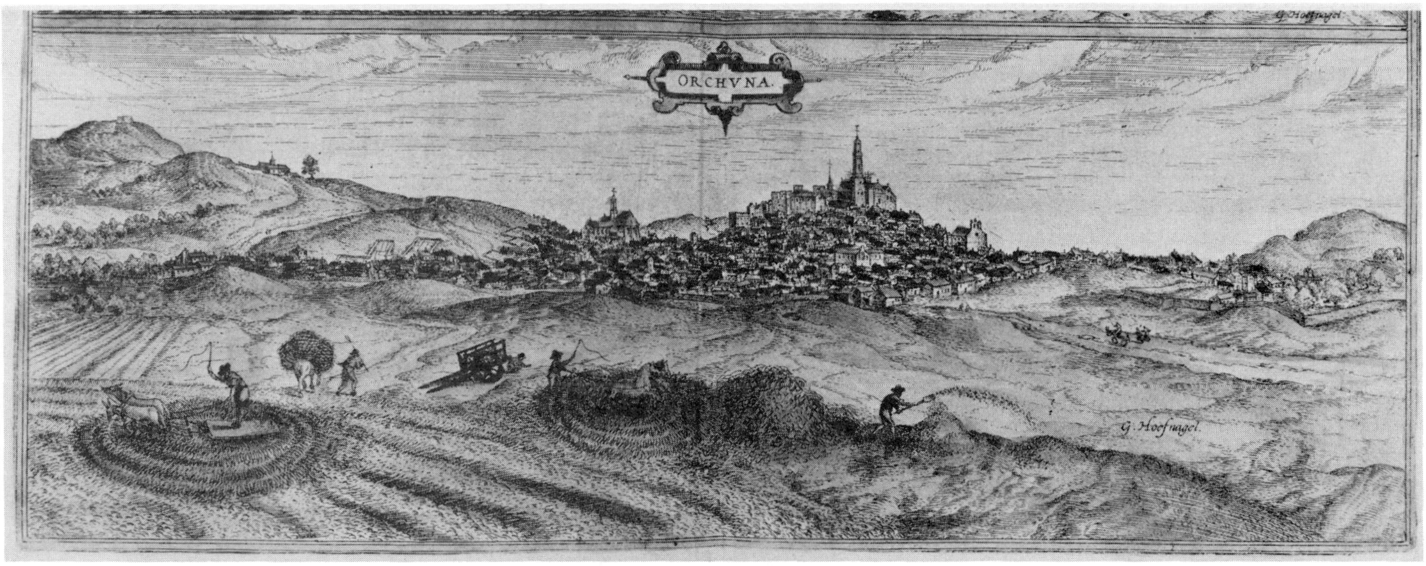

The town of Osuna [ORCHVNA] (Seville province), with a common threshing floor in the foreground. Between 1575 and 1600 the crown made over a thousand sales of ***tierras baldías*** *in Osuna's territory. From Georg Braun,* ***Civitatis orbis terrarum****, vol. 2, no. 3 (Cologne, 1576-1618). (Photo courtesy of The Harry Ransom Humanities Research Center, University of Texas at Austin.)*

reaching its peak in the 1580s, then tapering off after the best lands (both pasture and arable) had been sold.[20]

The *baldío* sales represented a cynical repudiation of previous royal policy, which had generally protected the *tierras concegiles*. The crown in this matter was inconsistent, duplicitous, and unfair. The royal need for revenues simply overcame royal scruples. And the municipalities accepted such abuse with surprising docility, having fallen increasingly under royal domination since the reforms of Ferdinand and Isabella, and particularly after the defeat of the Revolt of the Comuneros (1520-1521). Although the Castilian municipalities generally opposed the idea of the sales, they seldom questioned the crown's right to alienate public lands, unless they were *propios*. The crown, then, did sell municipal commons, and the municipalities generally acquiesced in the sales, even participating in them to purchase their own commons. Nevertheless, the sales were regarded as an unfortunate expedient forced on the country by financial necessity. And both the crown and the municipalities continued to hold the theoretical principal of the inviolability of the municipal commons (*tierras concegiles*).

King Philip II, whose incessant wars kept him continually on the edge of bankruptcy, also sold other types of commons, notably live-oak trees (*encinas*) and bee-hive sites (*colmenares*).[21] Moreover, when it became difficult to collect taxes from an overburdened population in the 1590s, Philip gave the municipalities a blanket authorization to rent common pastures to the highest bidder for plowing and to sell common forests for firewood. The damage to the commons was extensive and often irreparable.[22]

An important underlying cause of the usurpation of commons was rivalry between municipalities competing for the same *tierras baldías*. Prejudice against outsiders was intense, and the officials of one town often preferred to abridge common rights, or even to destroy common resources, rather than allow the inhabitants of a neighboring town to enjoy them. The Chancillería (Supreme Tribunal) archives are full of suits between towns squabbling over grazing rights and other communitarian disputes. Often these disagreements degenerated into violence.[23]

The villages (*aldeas* and *lugares*) under the jurisdiction of larger and more powerful municipalities (*villas* and *ciudades*) complained bitterly about discriminatory laws and arbitrary treatment. Usually their complaints involved the utilization of common lands. Many oppressed villages sought relief by purchasing their municipal autonomy (*villazgo*). During the second half of the sixteenth century the crown sold hundreds of *villazgos,* elevating former subject villages to independent *villa* status. The inhabitants of the new *villas* were land hungry, and proved to be aggressive plowers of common pastures. This provoked indignant reactions from the older municipalities, who were already resentful of the independent ways of their former charges. The result was a proliferation of lawsuits, usually over questions of common rights. The burden of financing these legal battles, added to other municipal obligations, compelled many towns to seek new revenues by augmenting the area of cultivation (often with royal permission), thus further eroding the common pastures.[24]

Defense Mechanisms

In view of the ubiquity, the frequency, and the magnitude of attacks on the communitarian system, one might conclude that the commons of Castile would have been virtually extinguished by the end of the sixteenth century. But that was not the case. The system was battered, and it suffered serious losses, but it remained a vital part of the socioeconomic structure of Spanish society until the disamortizations of the nineteenth century. And remnants of the system can be found even today, particularly in isolated mountain areas. The communitarian system retained its vitality despite its sixteenth-century adversities, because it had been staunchly defended.

The communitarian tradition was protected not only by custom, but also by myriad national and local laws. The national laws, created by royal decree, gave legal sanction and protection to the various communitarian practices of the kingdom. The municipalities operated under royally conferred *fueros* (law codes, or privileges) and municipal charters (*cartas puebla*), which also upheld communitarianism. Additionally, the municipalities adopted their own ordinances, submitted for royal approval, defining the precise local rules for the use of community property. These various laws specified the exact monetary fine, and other penalties, to be levied for each infraction of the rules. From time to time it became necessary to alter the fine schedules, as inflation or other changing conditions made them obsolete.[25]

The municipalities appointed guards (*guardas*) to protect the local commons and *propios,* and to apprehend violators. These guards had authority over private property as well, to enforce the *derrota de mieses* and to keep animals from damaging crops. This was a difficult task, involving great distances and nocturnal as well as daytime patrols. When the guards encountered a violation, they reported it to judicial authorities, who would set a hearing and levy a fine (or other appropriate punishment) against those found guilty. Occasionally the guards could arrest the malefactors on the spot, and bring them to the local jail. But it was more likely for

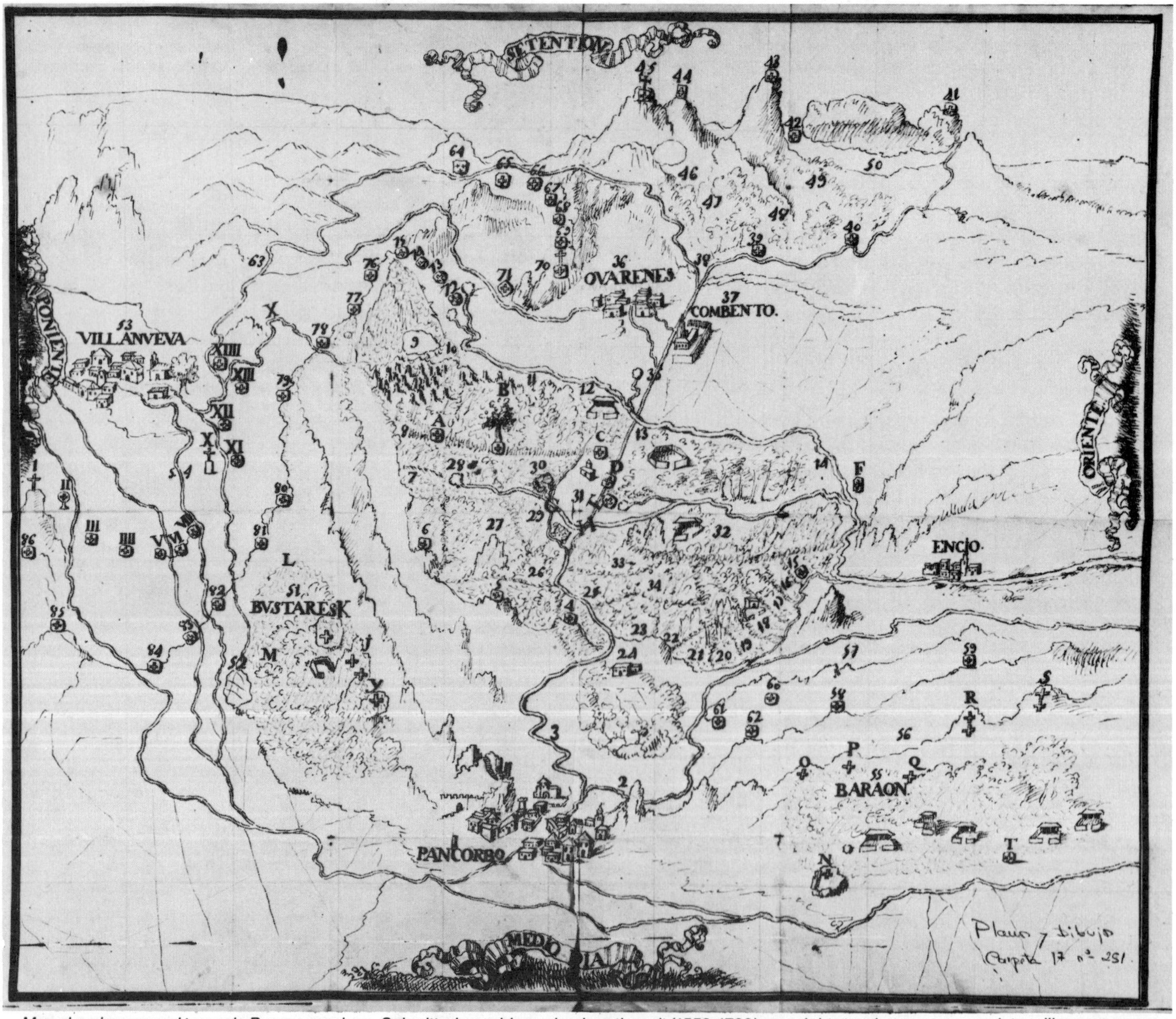

Map showing several towns in Burgos province. Submitted as evidence in a lengthy suit (1552-1729) over rights to what was once an inter-village common ***monte****, to which the new* ***villas*** *were attempting to establish exclusive privileges. Municipal markers and dividing lines are indicated by capital letters and Roman and Arabic numerals. (Photo courtesy of Archivo de la Chancillería de Valladolid, Planos y Dibujos 17, no. 251.)*

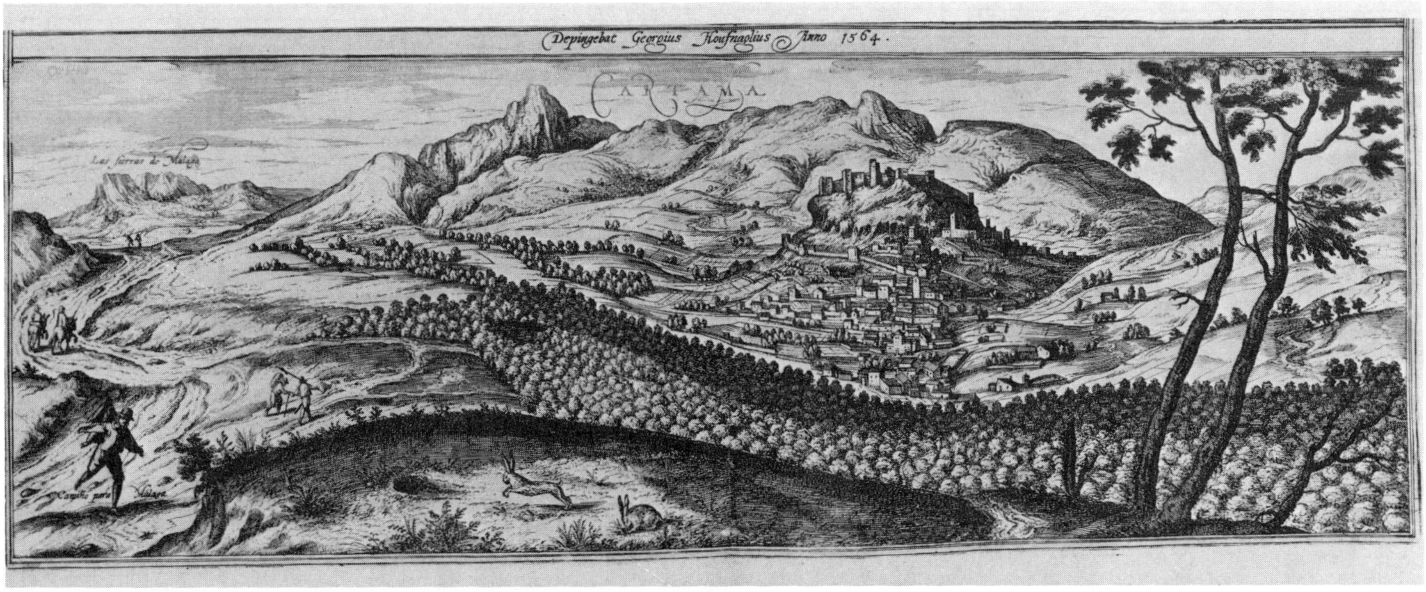

The village of Cartama (Málaga province) in 1564, showing surrounding planted fields, grasslands and wooded areas, all policed by municipal guards. From Georg Braun, ***Civitatis orbis terrarum,*** *vol. 3, no. 11 (Cologne, 1576-1618). (Photo courtesy of The Harry Ransom Humanities Research Center, University of Texas at Austin.)*

them to confiscate some or all of the animals involved in the infraction, and to herd them to the municipal corral to be held as security pending the resolution of the case. Fines levied against guilty parties were assessed sometimes in cash, and sometimes in animals.[26]

To facilitate the task of policing the local fields, many towns organized all the arable land of their territory into compulsory blocks or districts (*pagos* or *hojas*) where every one followed the same planting schedule. Since all the planted fields were grouped together, it was easier to protect crops. It also facilitated herding animals into fallowed fields, which were similarly grouped together. Another widespread practice was to organize the livestock of a town into community herds, which could be more easily watched than many tiny groups of independently wandering animals.[27]

Despite these and other aids, it was impossible for the guards to detect all infractions, and it often proved impossible to ascertain who was guilty of even the grossest violations of the local commons. For example, in the 1570s devastating brush fires swept through the Sierra Morena overlooking Andújar. It was believed that they had been deliberately set by local stockmen seeking to destroy the underbrush in an effort to produce better pastures for their animals. But no one was ever caught in the act, and stockmen blamed beekeepers or hunters for the fires. And sometimes the violators of commons escaped punishment because of temporarily turbulent conditions, as during the civil wars in Extremadura in the late 1400s.[28]

The municipal governments ordered periodic inspection tours (*visitas, de términos* or *de inspección*) of the local commons and *propios*. The committees of inspection normally included two *regidores* and the local *corregidor* (royal supervisory official) or his lieutenant. It was the job of the committee to check for violations of municipal property, and to rectify boundaries, if necessary. There were also periodic joint inspections, by committees from adjacent towns, to check common boundaries, and to inspect their shared commons. These inspections were supposed to be made annually, but most places seem to have held them less frequently. The city of Trujillo, which had an effective year-round system of law enforcement, limited its inspections to every sixth year.[29]

But despite royal and local laws, police efforts, fines, and inspection tours, the usurpation of commons and *propios* continued to be a problem. In the Cortes of Toledo in 1480 the municipalities of Castile asked the crown for special help to deal with the problem. The result was the Law of Toledo (1480), which became the basic instrument of royal protection of public property. This law was designed to make it possible for the towns to recover their lost property, even when "powerful persons" were guilty of the usurpations. The Law of Toledo was to be enforced by *corregidores* and other royal officials, who were empowered to assess severe penalties for convicted offenders. From time to time the law was modified, to strengthen it and to close loopholes. And in especially frustrating situations, the municipalities could petition the crown to dispatch a special royal judge (*juez de términos*) to deal with violators. Nevertheless, the best efforts of municipalities, crown, *corregidores,* and *jueces de términos* could not permanently halt the usurpations of public lands. In the late 1500s Castillo de Bobadilla wrote, "I never saw the penalties of the Law of Toledo . . . carried out, nor did I ever see a place where the rich had not violated that law many times, nor did I ever see anything more commonplace than for each of them to take community property for himself, nor did I ever see such a lack of

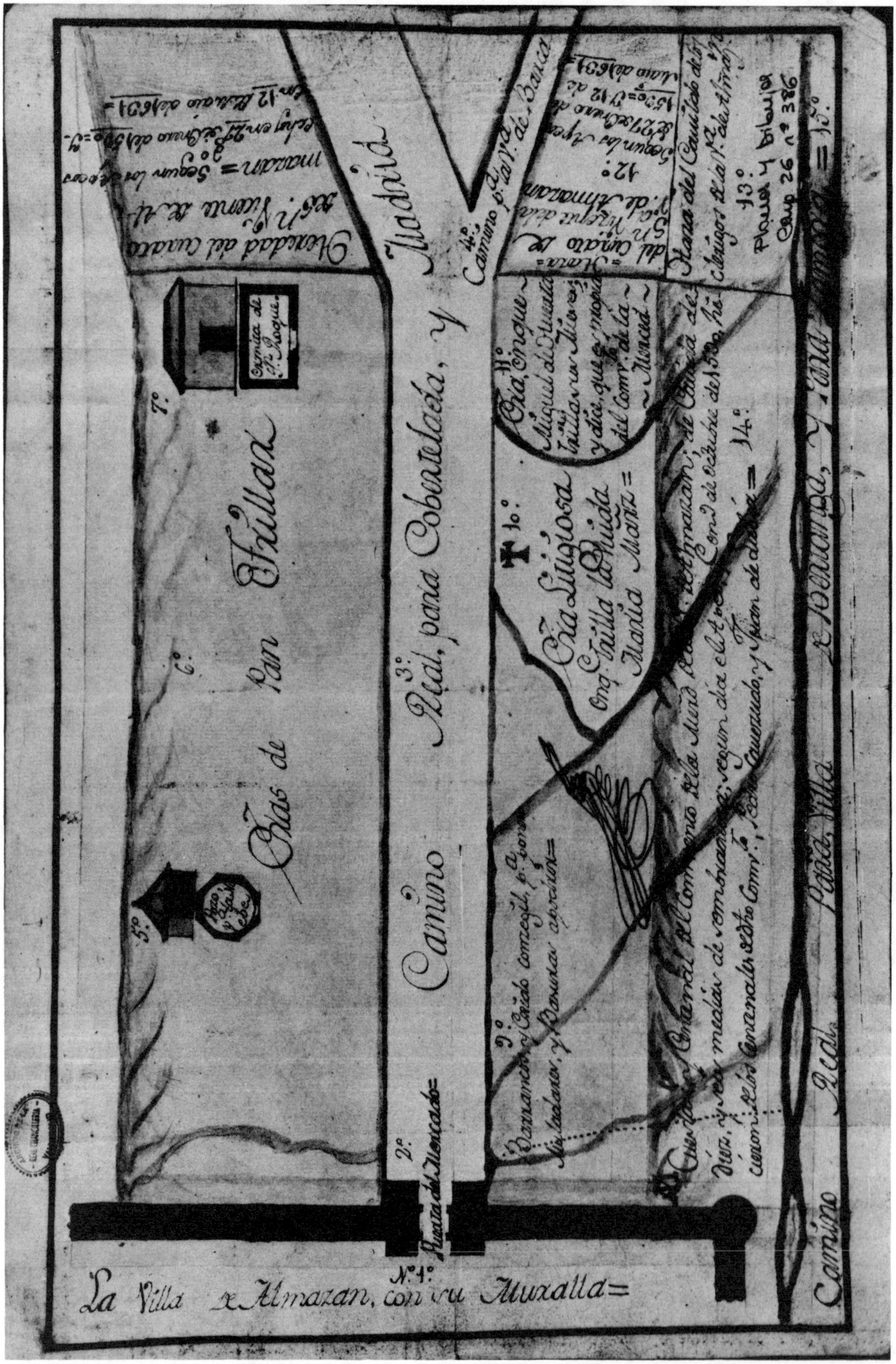

Map of the outskirts of the town of Almazán (Soria province), based upon surveys made in 1590 and 1631. Submitted as evidence in a suit over the use of a threshing floor located along the road to Madrid. (Photo courtesy of Archivo de la Chancillería de Valladolid, Planos y Dibujos 26, no. 386.)

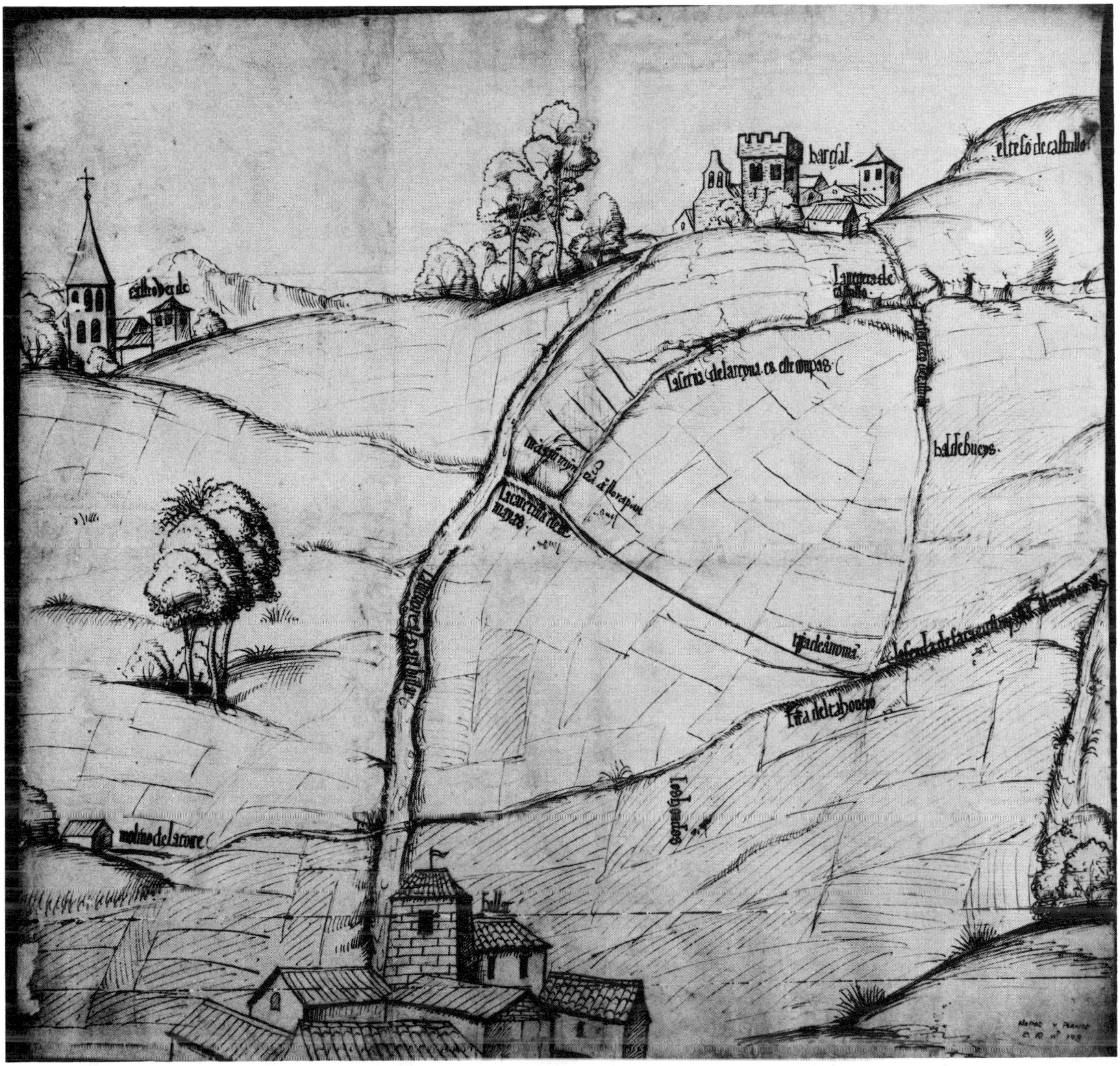

Map showing the countryside between Castroverde de Campos, Villar de Fallaves (both in Zamora province) and Barcial de la Loma (Valladolid province), drawn between 1509 and 1511 as evidence in a suit over land use. (Photo courtesy of Archivo de la Chancillería de Valladolid, Planos y Dibujos 10, no. 143.)

enforcement of the infinite remedies that are provided to deal with the situation."[30]

Among the defenders of the communitarian system, one must mention the royal Mesta (association of livestock owners), although its actions were largely motivated by self-interest. During the Middle Ages the Mesta influenced the crown to grant many special privileges for its migrating flocks and herds. The Mesta's *cañadas* (designated trails) were regarded as commons that could never be plowed. The crown guaranteed the Mesta flocks the right to pasture in the country's *baldíos*. But the towns were usually able to reserve their distinctly local commons (*tierras concegiles*) for local animals. There were conflicting laws about Mesta access to municipal pastures, and the situation in a given locale depended largely upon the strength of the local government, and its willingness to tangle with the Mesta in court. Ferdinand and Isabella, anxious to stimulate lucrative wool exports, increased Mesta privileges. Association members became arrogant and overbearing, and by the early 1500s Mesta flocks were regularly invading local commons that had previously been off-limits to outside animals. It is moot whether this constituted an infringement of communalism, or an attempt to broaden its base.[31]

The intruding Mesta flocks disturbed the local equilibrium

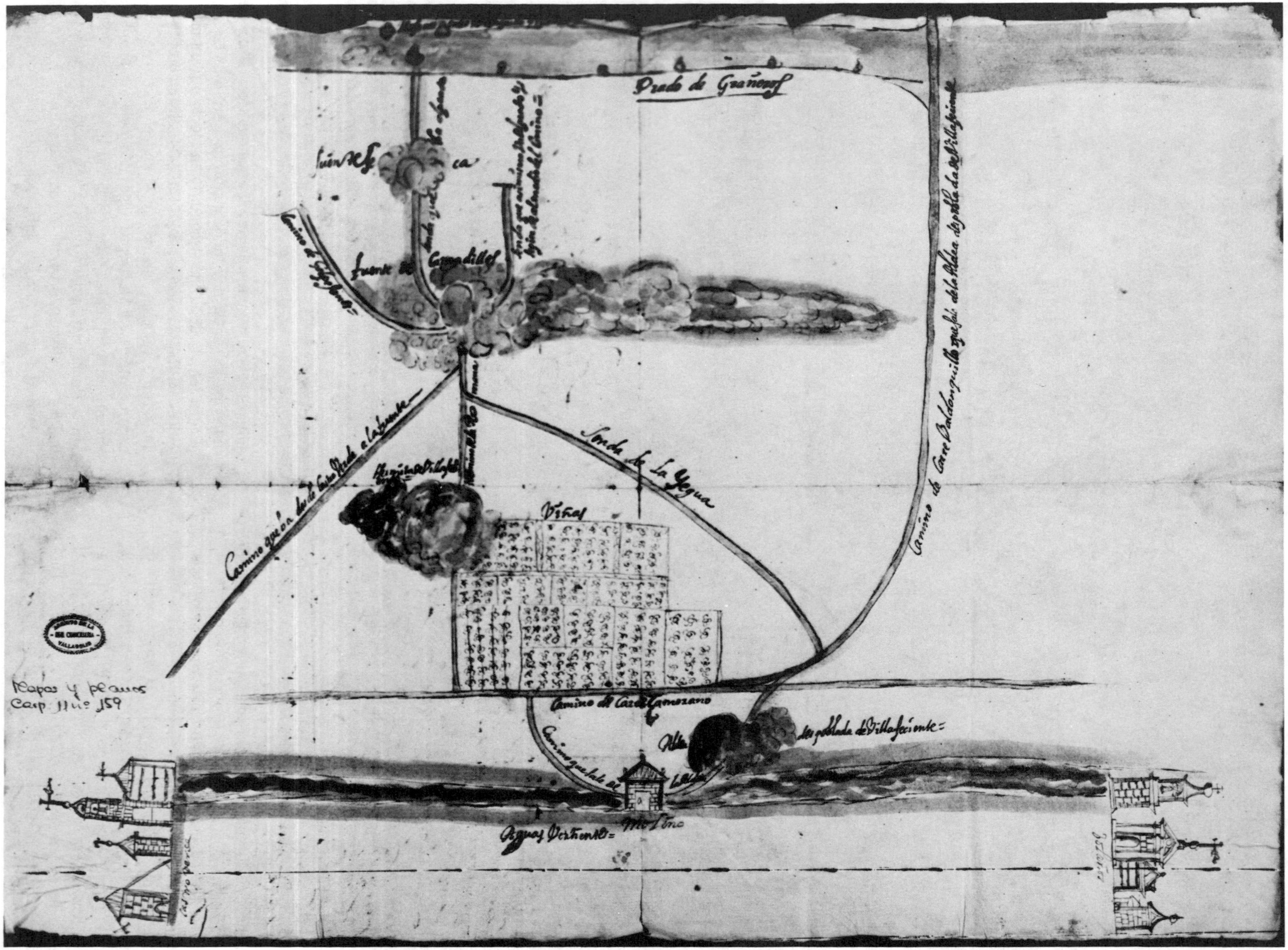

Map drawn c. 1650 showing an area called La Romana, between Castroverde de Campos (Zamora province) and Bolaños de Campos (Valladolid province). This area, in which residents of both towns had common rights, was the subject of litigation between the two. (Photo courtesy of Archivo de la Chancillería de Valladolid, Planos y Dibujos 11, no. 159.)

between arable and pastoral resources. As a result, there was an intense anti-Mesta reaction on the part of local inhabitants. This led to an explosion of litigation over access to common land. By the mid-1500s the Mesta's influence was on the wane. The crown no longer favored the organization, because arable agriculture had become more important than wool. The Cortes became increasingly critical of the Mesta, and the Chancillería rulings now tended to favor arable and local interests. The Mesta continued to defend its traditional privileges, but with diminishing success. Most of the litigation betwen the Mesta and local interests involved the *baldíos* — lands of ambiguous ownership claimed as pasture by local and migratory stockowners, and as potential arable by land-hungry agriculturalists.[32]

The Castilian Cortes, composed in the 1500s of delegates from 18 major cities, was dominated by noble and urban interests. Thus it was not a truly representative body, and it was generally subservient to the monarchs. Nevertheless, the Cortes' power to vote (or deny) taxes and subsidies could influence the crown, and the Cortes could propose measures which became law when given royal approval. Many Cortes delegates were landowners and stockmen who were intensely interested in the fate of the country's public lands. Consequently, whenever there appeared a serious menace to the *baldíos*, the *propios*, or the municipal commons, the Cortes spoke out to alert the monarch to the danger, and to propose remedies. The Law of Toledo was instituted at the request of the Cortes. And the Cortes opposed the crown's *baldío* sales practically from their inception, warning the king that the effect would be disastrous.[33]

Sixteenth-century Castile was a highly litigious society, with hordes of lawyers handling countless lawsuits over every possible cause. Much of this litigation involved the common lands, as municipal governments, the Mesta, and other parties defended communitarian rights against those who would abridge them. The suits often dragged out interminably, requiring great determination and financial sacrifice on the part of town governments and inhabitants. For instance, in the mid-1530s Morón de la Frontera initiated proceedings against the County of Viana. The suit was eventually resolved in the town's favor, but the legal battle took 18 years, and at one point the townspeople were so discouraged that they nearly gave up the struggle. It must have been difficult, and frustrating, to bring suit against wealthy nobles and other powerful parties. The existing national law recognized this, and ordered municipal officials (under pain of loss of office) to defend public property, and to seek justice, even when the usurpers were "powerful persons."[34]

Settling grievances through the courts was so lengthy, expensive, and uncertain that some town governments resorted to violence to achieve quick justice. For example, in 1597 the *alcalde* of Arroyo el Puerto rang the church bells and organized over 150 citizens into a raiding party to destroy fences and vineyards that had been put on lands considered to be commons. The vineyards and fence owners protested vigorously, and brought suit against the town, but in the meantime the lands were returned to common pasture.[35]

Conclusion

The problem of contested land ownership was of transcendental importance in the Spain of the *conquistadores*. A Spanish historian, writing about Badajoz, concluded that the city's entire history "could be summed up in the history of the incessant and tireless struggle between the rival forces of the [municipal] council, resisting the constant despoliations and diminutions [of its lands], and the individual or corporative interests determined day after day and year after year to pluck the richest flowers of the rich and splendid patrimony conceded [to Badajoz] by the munificence of the kings of the Reconquest."[36]

The experience of Badajoz was repeated in other cities, towns, and villages throughout Castile. There was a natural tenseness arising from the coexistence of the growing institution of private property ownership with the Castilian tradition of public ownership. The situation was exacerbated by conflicting laws and customs, the uncertain legal status of many lands, and the opportunistic crown sales of the *baldíos*. Consequently, the Spanish *conquistadores*, government officials, and colonists who came to America brought with them a muddled tradition regarding public property. It included a powerful attitude of respect for municipal lands, but also a tradition of the royal right to eminent domain over those lands. And the Spanish background had in it a long history of municipal, private, and royal attacks on the communitarian landowning system.

These diverse and often contradictory traditions were transported to America, where the colonists embellished them with variations of their own.

David E. Vassberg, a native Texan, received a Ph.D. in history from the University of Texas at Austin in 1971. Since that time he has taught at Pan American University, where he is professor of history. Vassberg's specialty is rural society in sixteenth-century Castile. He is the author of *Land and Society in Golden Age Castile* (Cambridge University Press, 1984), two books published in Spain, and numerous articles in scholarly journals. His latest project is a book on daily life in sixteenth-century Castilian village.

NOTES

1. I have dealt with the origins of public landownership in Castile in David E. Vassberg, *Land and Society in Golden Age Castile* (Cambridge, England, 1984), 5-7; and in David E. Vassberg, "The *Tierras Baldías:* Community Property and Public Lands in 16th Century Castile," *Agricultural History,* 48, no. 3 (July 1974): 383-401.
2. For examples of municipal governments controlling their *tierras baldías,* see the suit *Lora v. El bachiller Gerónimo Maldonado y consortes* (1536-1539), Archivo de la Chancillería de Granada [henceforth ACHGR], 511-2288-1, part 4; and documents relating to the town of Torrelobatón (1588) in Archivo General de Simancas, Expedientes de Hacienda [henceforth AGS, EH], 403. See also Vassberg, "Tierras baldías," 385-386; and *Land and Society,* 7-13.
3. Ferdinand and Isabella provided for the establishment of common pastures in the villages subject to the city of Soria in a *cédula* of 15 Apr. 1497, a copy of which is in the suit *La Mesta v. Pozalmuro,* Archivo de la Chancillería de Valladolid, Pleitos Civiles, Fernando Alonso (Fenecidos) [henceforth ACHVA, PC, FA (F)], 28. See also Vassberg, *Land and Society,* 19-20.
4. The phrase was employed by the city of Medina del Campo, in defense of its land claims, in a letter to the Crown of 1 Dec. 1568, in AGS, Consejo y Juntas de Hacienda [henceforth CJH], legajo 61 moderno (89 antiguo).
5. One may get a glimpse of the benefits that sixteenth-century Castilians received from municipal property from documents relating to the Montes of the Sierra Morena of Andújar (mid-1500s), in AGS, EH, 220. See also the Ordenanzas de Montes de Trujillo (1499), transcribed in Archivo de la Mesta [Madrid — henceforth AM], Ejecutorias, Trujillo, 16 Dec. 1521. A detailed analysis of the various types of commons and *propios* may be found in Vassberg, *Land and Society,* 19-64. For a description of an intermunicipal community, see documents concerning Montánchez (1592), AGS, EH, 323. See also Alejandro Nieto, *Bienes comunales* (Madrid, 1964), 58-60. The Castillo de Bobadilla statement is cited in Carmelo Viñas y Mey, *El problema de la tierra en la España de los siglos XVI-XVII* (Madrid, 1941), 41.
6. The *derrota de mieses* (though not called by that name) is described in the Ordenanzas de Arjona (1537), AGS, EH, 223. See also Vassberg, *Land and Society,* 13-18.
7. See, for example, a Privilegio from King Enrique to Pedro Alfonso de la Cámara (original dated 3 June 1407), in the suit *Trujillo v. Don Juan Alonso de Orellana* (1540-1608), ACHGR, 3-443-3.
8. Noël Salomon, *La campagne de Nouvelle Castille á la fin du XVIe siècle d'après les "Relaciónes topográficas"* (Paris, 1964).
9. For details of peasant usurpations, see David E. Vassberg, "Peasant Communalism and Anti-Communal Tendencies in Early Modern Castile," *The Journal of Peasant Studies,* 7, no. 4 (July 1980): 477-91.
10. This is prominently mentioned in the suit *Córdoba v. Montoro* (1539-1561), ACHGR, 3-1805-1.
11. I could cite dozens of cases of noble usurpations. For classic examples, see *Talarrubias v. El Duque de Béjar* (1588), ACHGR, 3-813-1; Relación de Diego López de Ayala, 21 Aug. 1584, AGS, CJH, 215; *Doña Agueda Cano y sus hijos v. Alcalá la Real* (1563-1569), ACHGR, 3-1228-6.
12. See documents relating to Andujar (1540s-1560s), AGS, EH, 220; the suit *Plasenzuelas v. Núño García de Chaves y consortes* (1546-1551), ACHGR, 3-1643-11; and a report about the village of Santa Cruz, AM, Ejecutorias, Trujillo, 2 June 1586.
13. Miguel Caxa de Leruela, *Restauración de la antigua abundancia de España, or prestantíssimo único y fácil reparo de su carestía presente* (Naples, 1631), 124-125. I shall cite only one of many suits arising from this abuse: *Don Juan de Guzmán v. Salvaleón* (1517-1526), ACHGR, 507-1919-1.
14. For examples, see the suits *El Arahal v. Francisco Ximénez* (1561), ACHGR, 3-996-1; *Don Francisco de Benavides v. Las Navas* (1547), ACHGR, 508-2026-1; and *La Marquesa de Villanueva del Río v. Campana* (1576), ACHGR, 3-417-1; and documents relating to the village of San Martín de Montalbán (1510-1587) in AGS, EH, 400.
15. This often produced suits such as *San Sebastián v. Alcobendas* (1580s-1590s), ACHVA, PC, FA (F), 81; and *Badajoz v. Juan Andrés y consortes* (1551-1552), ACHGR, 3-463-5. Other characteristic examples are cited in a report to the Royal Treasury by Diego de Argote (undated, but apparently from 1583), AGS, Contadurías Generales, 3262; and in documents relating to the town of Montánchez (1589), AGS, EH, 323.
16. Typical cases may be found in documents concerning Torrelobatón (1588), AGS, EH, 403; a bill of sale drawn up by Alonso López de Obregón for the town of Priego, 27 Mar. 1590, AGS, Contaduría de la Razón-7 [henceforth CR-7], 3260; papers concerning El Azebrón (1597), AGS, EH, 209; Diego López de Ayala to the Treasury about lands in Iscar, 21 Aug. 1584, AGS, CJH, 215; *Plasenzuela v. Núño García de Chaves y consortes* (1546-1551), ACHGR, 3-1643-11; and *Don Llorente v. Toribio Moreno* (1574-1575), ACHGR, 3-762-10.
17. See, for example, *Plasencia v. Diego Nieto* (1568-1575), ACHVA, PC, FA (F), 25; *Baeza v. Francisco de Jesús* (1540-1542), ACHGR, 3-1059-8; Venta que Esteban de Gamarra otorgó a Alonso Guirao, 19 Apr. 1583, AGS, CR-7, 3260. Antonio Gil Olcina, *El Campo de Lorca; estudio de geografía agraria* (Valencia, 1971), 92. The problem was mentioned by Jerónimo Castillo de Bobadilla, *Política para corregidores y señores de vasallos en tiempo de paz y guerra* [first publ. 1597], 2 vols. (Medina del Campo, 1608): II, 946.
18. *Juan de Almonte y consortes v. El Duque de Medina Sidonia* (1560-1564), ACHGR, 3-966-4; *Talarrubias v. Puebla de Alcocer* (1575-1588), ACHGR, 3-813-1.
19. Vassberg, *Land and Society,* 169-170.
20. See David Vassberg, "The Sale of *Tierras Baldías* in Sixteenth-Century Castile," *Journal of Modern History* 47, no. 4 (Dec. 1975): 629-654; and my book *La venta de tierras baldías; el dominio público y la corona en Castilla durante el siglo XVI,* trans. David Pradales Ciprés, et al. (Madrid, 1983).
21. I am planning a future article on the Crown sale of *encinas* and *colmenares.* About the former, see *Actas de las Cortes de Castilla,* 45 vols. (Madrid, 1869-1918): XII, 190-192, 234-344; XIII, 183, 268. For the *colmenares,* see a group of documents about the city of Andújar (1567), AGS, EH, 220.
22. *Actas:* XI, 472-476; *San Sebastián de los Reyes v. Alcobendas* (1591), ACHVA, PC, FA (F), 81; *Mesta v. Valdemoro* (1598), ACHVA, PC, FA (F), 70. See also Angel García Sanz, *Desarrollo y crisis del antiguo régimen en Castilla la Vieja; economía y sociedad en tierras de Segovia de 1500 a 1814* (Madrid, 1977), 145; and Caxa de Leruela, *Restauración,* 109.
23. See *Toro v. La Bóveda* (1512-1542), ACHVA, PC, FA (F), 60; and *Campillo de Altobuey v. Paracuellos* (1589-1614), ACHGR, 504-838-1.
24. The Chancillería archives abound in suits arising from municipal jealousies and the consequences of the *villazgos;* see also Vassberg, *Land and Society,* 165-169.
25. National sixteenth-century laws may be found in *Novísima recopilación de las leyes de España,* 6 vols. (Madrid, 1805-1829). Local ordinances from the period may be encountered in municipal archives. For example, I found a set from 1575 in the Archivo del Ayuntamiento de Trujillo [henceforth AAT], 1-2-72, no. 13. And many, such as those of Arjona (1537, AGS, EH, 223), are preserved in the national archives. Spanish Americanists will be interested in a published set for Extremadura (birthplace of many *conquistadores*), edited by Arcadio Guerra, "Ordenanzas municipales de Felipe II a Los Santos de Maimona," *Revista de estudios extremeños* [Badajoz], 8 (1952): 495-534.
26. Vassberg, *Land and Society,* 71-76, includes a detailed section about municipal guards.
27. Town herds and *pagos* are frequently encountered in sixteenth-century documents. The latter are described in Jesús García Fernández, "Los sistemas de cultivo en Castilla la Vieja," in *Aportación española al XX Congreso Geográfico Internacional* (Madrid, 1964?), 142-143.
28. See documents about Andújar (1575) in AGS, EH, 220; and testimony from the mayordomo of Trujillo in 1494, transcribed in *Trujillo v. las villas y lugares de su tierra,* ACHGR, 3-958-1.
29. *Actas:* V, 123-124; Castillo de Bobadilla, *Política para corregidores:* II, 946-949, *Congosto v. Ahumada* (1537) ACHVA, PC, FA, (F), 3; papers relating to Torrelobatón (1588), AGS, EH, 403; and Visita del año 1585, AAT, 1-3-82, no. 54.
30. For the Law of Toledo, see *Novísima recopilación,* libro VII, título, XXI, leyes II, V, VI, VII. A copy of a *juez de término*'s commission may be found in *Juan Ximénez v. Córdoba* (1535-1537), ACHGR, 508-2083-11; and an example of a town's use of the Law of Toledo is in *Arahal v. Francisco Ximénez* (1561), ACHGR, 3-996-1. Castillo de Bobadilla, *Política para corregidores:* II, 947. See also Vassberg, *Land and Society,* 77-79. It is noteworthy that royal officials encharged with selling *tierras baldías* used the records of *jueces de términos* to determine which lands could be sold. See a report to the Crown by Diego de Soto Siliceo, 15 May 1585, AGS, CJH, 228.
31. Julius Klein, *The Mesta; A Study in Spanish Economic History, 1273-1836* (Cambridge, MA, 1920), *passim.*
32. ACHGR and ACHVA abound in suits involving the Mesta. And the Archive of the Mesta, naturally, is essential for an investigation of these conflicts. See also Vassberg, *Land and Society,* 79-83.
33. The minutes of the Cortes have been published as *Cortes de los antiguos Reinos de León y Castilla,* 7 vols. (Madrid, 1861-1903); and as *Actas* (cited above, note 21). References to the

Cortes opposition to the *baldío* sales may be found in my two works cited above, note 20.

34. Papers relating to the Morón suit in Archivo Histórico Nacional [Madrid], Osuna, 82^2, no. 9; and *Novísima recopilación*, libro VII, título XXI, ley III.

35. *Don Alonso de Rivera v. Arroyo el Puerto* (1597-1604), ACHGR, 3-607-10. Another instance of this sort of semi-official vigilantism can be found in *Antonio Hernández v. La Puebla* (1563), ACHVA, PC, FA (F), 67.

36. Esteban Rodríguez Amaya, "La tierra en Badajoz desde 1230 a 1500," *Revista de estudios extremeños* [Badajoz], 7, nos. 3-4 (July-Dec. 1951): 396.

Ejido Lands in New Mexico

Daniel Tyler

ONE of the more difficult problems addressed by surveyors general, land officials, attorneys, politicians and others following the Treaty of Guadalupe Hidalgo concerned the nature of common lands used by New Mexicans since Spanish colonial times. Because ownership of land in common was not typical of land tenure systems in the United States, the concept created difficulties in the courts and in Congress when the time came to validate property rights in the Mexican Cession. As a result, after many years of litigation, some New Mexicans found themselves deprived of the property on which they had depended for their livelihood, even though Article 8 of the treaty guaranteed them the same property rights they had enjoyed as Mexicans.[1]

An example of this tragedy can be seen in the military occupation of Ysleta, Socorro, and San Elizario in 1849 by U.S. forces. In addition to the towns, U.S. troops took possession of the *ejido* lands on the left bank of the Rio Grande which belonged to the residents of towns located across the river. The *ejido's* resources were used by them, as well as by citizens of San Lorenzo and Senecú. Almost immediately, U.S. authorities told the Mexicans that if they tried to cross the river with salt from the "public domain" of the U.S., they would be charged a duty of four *reales* per *fanega*. This was a blow to the townspeople who regarded the grant of *ejidos* a century and a half previously as sacred and inviolable.[2]

Although modified by 250 years of local custom and tradition, as of 1848 the common lands system of New Mexico followed the basic outlines of Spanish law which allowed communities to expand, to graze livestock where grass and water were available, and to enjoy the fruits of the land that nature made available without the intervention of man.[3] Sixteenth-century Spaniards had separated the common lands idea into theoretical use categories, most of which were carried over to the New World: *prados* (a high quality pasture land where grass was allowed to grow or forage crops were planted); *dehesas* (pasture lands that might also be partially under cultivation); and *ejidos* (unplanted, unenclosed areas used for grazing, recreation, a place for stray animals, and a garbage dump).[4] Distinct from the common lands set aside for the free use of nearby citizens were the *propios* or *concegiles* (*tierras concegiles*) which were possessions belonging to the municipalities. These pasture and farming lands were rented out to provide income for the towns. They were different from common lands in that they were legally treated as private property and "were not legally alienable" as were the commons.[5] Even so, confusion existed in New Mexico as to the location and use of these different kinds of lands due to the frontier status of northern New Spain, the abundance of land for settlement, and a shortage of trained officials who understood the intent of the laws.

New Mexicans understood and implemented the common lands concept as an integral part of community land grants, Indian pueblos, and municipalities. They used the word *ejido*, or *exido*, in different ways to convey the idea that certain lands had special status apart from the public domain. But they also used the word loosely, in a more generic sense, to underscore the rights of citizens to wood, water, pasturage and other resources on the public lands.

This essay is an attempt to clarify the *ejido* concept, as it was interpreted by New Mexicans throughout the colonial and Mexican periods, and what they believed to be their rights in the commons at the time the United States became sovereign in 1848. To accomplish this objective, the author has reviewed and interpreted the use of *ejido* in the Surveyor General records (NMLG-SG) and in the Spanish and Mexican Archives of New Mexico (SANM, I; SANM, II; MANM). With a clearer understanding of what Spaniards and Mexicans believed to be their rights in common lands, one can make an effort to deal with the more difficult subject of their water rights in these same *ejidos*.

Ejidos from the Recopilación to the Ley Agraria (1933)

The Iberian background of the *ejido* can be found in the *Recopilación*, Book IV, Title 7, Law 7, which stipulates that land granted for settlement by contract should first be divided up into *solares* (town lots), then into *ejidos* and *dehesas*, and finally into *propios*. The remaining lands were to be divided between the contractor and the settlers to be used as *suertes* (farming lots). Law 13 added that the *ejidos* had to be large enough to accommodate an increasing population, and Law 14 provided for the designation of *dehesas* adjoining the *ejidos* for pasturing animals, with excess lands being divided into *suertes* for irrigated or dryland farming and the undeveloped land left for future settlers and the municipal *propios*.[6]

These views of the *ejido* have been complemented by many writers who have studied the subject since the appearance of the *Recopilación* in 1680. Mariano Galván y Rivera believed that the *ejido* was used primarily for grazing in Mexico during the mid-nineteenth century until com-

Scene of typical Hispanic village life in the summer. Many of the materials used in these activities are from the common lands. (Original painting by Glen Strock.)

munity expansion dictated others uses.[7] Manuel Fabila found a 1523 law requiring municipal authorities to locate the *ejidos* far enough from the center of population so that stock raising would not interfere with agriculture.[8] David Vassberg's studies of sixteenth-century Spain indicate that the word *ejido* derived from the Latin *exitus*, thus supporting Fabila's view of an *ejido* adjacent to a town. He also noted that Spanish *ejidos* were provided for the exclusive use of resident *vecinos* (townspeople) and those who were not citizens of the adjoining town would be fined for trespassing if they tried to use them without permission.[9] Clark Knowlton, a sociologist, has argued that the *ejidos* "belonged to the village as a social entity and not to any single group of first settlers. . . ."[10]

His belief is further developed in William DeBuys' description of the Las Trampas Grant in which the author identified the community *ejidos* beyond the narrow valley of the privately owned land. These lands "were open to all people of all villages on the grant to use as they saw fit." In order to make a living, grantees had to utilize all available resources, "and they had to cooperate with each other to do it." DeBuys further stated that the *ejido* had no marketable title under Spanish law and could be alienated only by royal decree "from the descendants of the grantees for whom it had been reserved."[11]

Mexicans of the twentieth century have preserved some of the same attitudes regarding *ejido* property while implementing changes brought about by a bloody revolution against *latifundismo* (large landed estates). The Agrarian Code establishing Mexico's modern *ejido* system, enacted in 1933 and revised in 1934, states in Article 139 that cultivatable land in the *ejidos* can be owned individually, but the "woodland, pastures, water and other natural resources on the land's surface, shall be held by the community." Article 140 says that the grantee "shall exercise domain over his *ejido* parcel" with the only limitation that it should not be alienated, encumbered, leased, or inherited except by certain designated people. Article 147 underscores the equal right of all *ejidatarios* to the common lands, and Article 150 expands this to include the "right to waters and their utilization for irrigation of *ejidos* which right "shall be vested in the *ejidatarios* in their corporate capacity." In the 1934 revision of the code, it was decreed that any land subject to division which is left over after each *ejidatario* receives his tract will be established as a "reserve zone" in which the "sons of *ejidatarios* upon coming of age, or people from neighboring villages having insufficient lands, may receive parcels."[12]

Clearly, the essence of the *ejido* idea has survived centuries of turbulent history. It was just as important a part of the land tenure system in the Rio Grande Valley as in other parts of New Spain and Mexico. The inhabitants of New Mexico, however, modified their understanding of the *ejido* to meet their needs, and they confused later generations by a lack of precision in their designation and administration of these lands. Still, their intent can be readily gleaned from the documents.

Ejidos: Legal Status and Measurement

The legal status of *ejidos* in New Mexico was not precisely defined in local laws nor clarified in pronouncements from Mexico City. But there was a general understanding on the part of property owners and territorial officials that a common area for grazing, watering livestock, and population increase was part of the land tenure system. In some documents, *ejidos* were supposed to be "*ejidos de común*" or

Scene of typical Hispanic village life in the autumn. Many of the materials used in these activities are from the common lands. (Original painting by Glen Strock.)

"ejidos realengos," meaning land that was technically under control of the sovereign but available for the use of some settlement. In contrast, community grants which included *ejidos* expected to receive title to their *ejidos*, thus removing them from use and settlement by others.[13] Bona fide members of the community enjoyed use rights in their *ejidos*, and if they sold the farming lands to which they had title, they lost their *ejido* rights. The new owners obtained the same usufructory title to the common areas.[14] When a community grant was made, grantees were given title to their house and farm lots as individuals and to their common land as a collective group (*de mancomún*).

Collective ownership of use rights was clearly distinct from the rights which citizens possessed in their ownership of *suertes, solares,* or *sitios* of land. It meant, as Manuel Martinez pointed out in his protest to the *ayuntamiento's* report objecting to his petition for the Tierra Amarilla lands, that what belongs to everyone in common belongs to no one in particular.[15] *De mancomún*, the phrase most frequently repeated, meant that settlers held joint responsibility of ownership and obligation in the use of their common property. What was important to the alcaldes, and other local officials, who placed grantees in legal possession of community grants was that they acknowledge their understanding of these rights and responsibilities by swearing *de mancomún*, or *de mancomunidad*, that they would work together for the benefit of the community and jointly maintain their common property.[16]

A blurring of lines between common lands of the public domain under total control of the sovereign, and *ejido* lands pertaining to a specific community, resulted in part because both Spaniards and Mexicans often referred to the public domain as *"común realengo,"* (Crown lands) or *"ejidos y comederos realengos,"* (Crown pasture lands). In other words, the right to use the public domain for wood, water, and pasture was confused with the more specific rights and responsibilities apurtenant to legitimate *ejidos*. The problem was also caused by referring to the public domain *(realengas, tierras realengas, baldías, tierra baldía)* as *ejidos* in an effort to distinguish between plowed, cultivated land, which was supposed to be fenced, and the grazing lands open to all on the public domain.[17] This confusion can be seen when Governor Vélez de Cachupín awarded a private grant to Juan Pablo Martin in 1766 with the warning that it not prejudice the Indians of Abiquiú in their *"sementeras* (sown lands) *y ejidos."*[18] The governor was probably referring to a specific *ejido* assigned to the Indians of Abiquiú, but one might misinterpret his orders as suggesting that the new grantee take care not to disturb the right, which all citizens held, to use the *tierra realenga* for water, pasture, wood, etc.[19] Governor Pedro Fermín de Mendinueta's 1765 Las Huertas Grant also contributed to future difficulties. When the alcalde put the grantees in possession, he pointed out that all the lands in their grant, with the exception of those specifically assigned as *tierra de pan llevar* (irrigated farm land), were *"ejidos del común de aquella población,"* whose pastures, woods and waters were common to *all*.[20] One supposes that he meant "common to all the grantees," but some *ejidos* were *not* exclusive to a single community. Furthermore, although Governor Mendinueta conceived of a community grant in which lands were either privately owned or *ejidos*, this pattern was not absolute in New Mexico.

Some communities had *no* ejidos. A good example is La Cañada. When Governor Vélez de Cachupín granted land to Francisco Montes Vigil, he noted that nearby La Cañada did not have legitimate *ejidos (ejidos utiles)*.[21] Still, the governor pointed out, the grant to Vigil should prejudice neither the expansion of *vecinos* from the town and jurisdiction of Cañada, nor their right to pasture cattle on the public lands. In other words, even without a specific *ejido*, a community was expected to have rights to water, pasture, wood, and grazing on the land surrounding its grant. This use right was central to New Mexican land tenure in the greater Rio Grande Valley. Land could be granted in a number of different ways, but underlying the use of that land was a certain right to enjoy the earth's resources, including its water, either through a specifically marked off *ejido* or a sphere of interest near the surrounding community which was understood to be that community's territorial prerogative.

The 1850 Mesilla Civil Colony Grant shows that the Mexicans were quite capable of specifying *ejido* conditions and uses. At Mesilla, Guadalupe Miranda, Commissioner General for the Removal of Families to Mexican Territory and the Settlement of Colonies, awarded two leagues of farming land *(tierra de labor)* to a group of colonists who had decided they preferred to live under Mexican sovereignty. He declared that this grant also included *ejidos*, so that Mesillans could enjoy the use of pastures, woods, waters, hunting and fishing, gravel quarries, fruit trees, and other products of the land. It was stipulated that these benefits of nature were for the use of the original grantees of Mesilla as well as those who would join the colony in future years. Additionally, Miranda noted, the Mesilla colonists would have a right to enjoy the pastures, woods and other products *(aprovechamientos)* of the *tierras baldías* (public domain or unclaimed and uncultivated land in the Mexican period) located outside the *ejidos*.[22] What Guadalupe Miranda had created was a community surrounded by its *own ejidos* which were in turn enveloped by public domain belonging to the Mexican nation. His view of these two levels of common lands, one belonging to the community for their exclusive use, the other belonging to the nation for all to share, represents an ideal New Mexican land pattern which was only rarely described so well.

Expressing this exclusivity in another way, authorities in the town of Mora made it clear that their *ejidos* were theirs alone to administer. They complained bitterly when Governor Manuel Armijo consented to a grazing grant for his friend Gervacio Nolan that would have encroached on their lands.[23] Both the Mesilla and Mora grants clearly distinguished between *ejidos* attached to the community and public domain lands available to all citizens for grazing, watering, wood collecting and other uses. Unfortunately, some *mercedes* (land grants) that specified *ejidos* were vague in regard to the location and size of these lands, thus making it very difficult to resolve disputes over boundaries.

Some community grants just mentioned a *paraje prefijado* (designated area or aforesaid place) which *ha de ser común no solo a ellos* [the grantees] *sino a todos los vecinos que se pueden ir congregando en el sucesivo.* This phrase, often attached as a condition to a grant, warned the original grantees that they must provide a common area for themselves as well as for newcomers who would attach themselves to the community in the future.[24] Setting aside this area, whether or not it was specifically called an *ejido,* was as much a responsibility of the community organizer *(principal capitulante, principal solicitante, poblador principal, apoderado de los mercenados)* as overseeing the building of a plaza, arming the citizens for defense, constructing an *acequia* madre, and commencing cultivation of the land. It was assumed by Spaniards, Mexicans, and Indians alike that each community would have common land for water, pasture, and wood. How large this area would be, where it would be located, and what it would be called varied with the circumstances of each grant.

In 1754, Governor Vélez de Cachupín awarded a grant of land to *los indios genízaros* of Abiquiú. Citing Book VI, Title Three of the *Recopilación,* the governor included an *ejido* one league in length so that the Indians could graze their animals without interfering with nearby Spaniards.[25] This view of the *ejido* as land removed from the public domain for communities to use as pasturage is typical of the *ejido* concept throughout the Spanish and Mexican periods. In 1766, the same governor underscored his point further by telling the settlers of San Fernando y San Blas that no one could use their *ejidos* without their permission, and that anyone caught doing so would be subject to a 30-peso fine.[26] The governor firmly believed that *ejidos* were the private property of the community to which they were assigned.

In 1844, as a result of the need to revalidate the San Pedro Grant of 1820, a chart was prepared to demonstrate the location of farming and *ejido* lands.[27] This is a revealing document. It shows that the settlers were granted 2,400 varas of farming land *(tierra de labor)* around which were located the *criaderos* or breeding grounds for livestock. The entire grant measured one league on each side while *tierras y pastos* were designated for the surrounding area. Each settler in the San Pedro Grant held *acciones* in the entire property, meaning that he shared equally *(de mancomún)* in the common area (probably the *criaderos)* while owning his own *labor* outright. If he sold his *labor,* he sold his use rights in the *criaderos (ejidos?).* Mention of *tierras y pastos* is either a reference to the common land (public domain) surrounding the grant, or to *ejidos.*

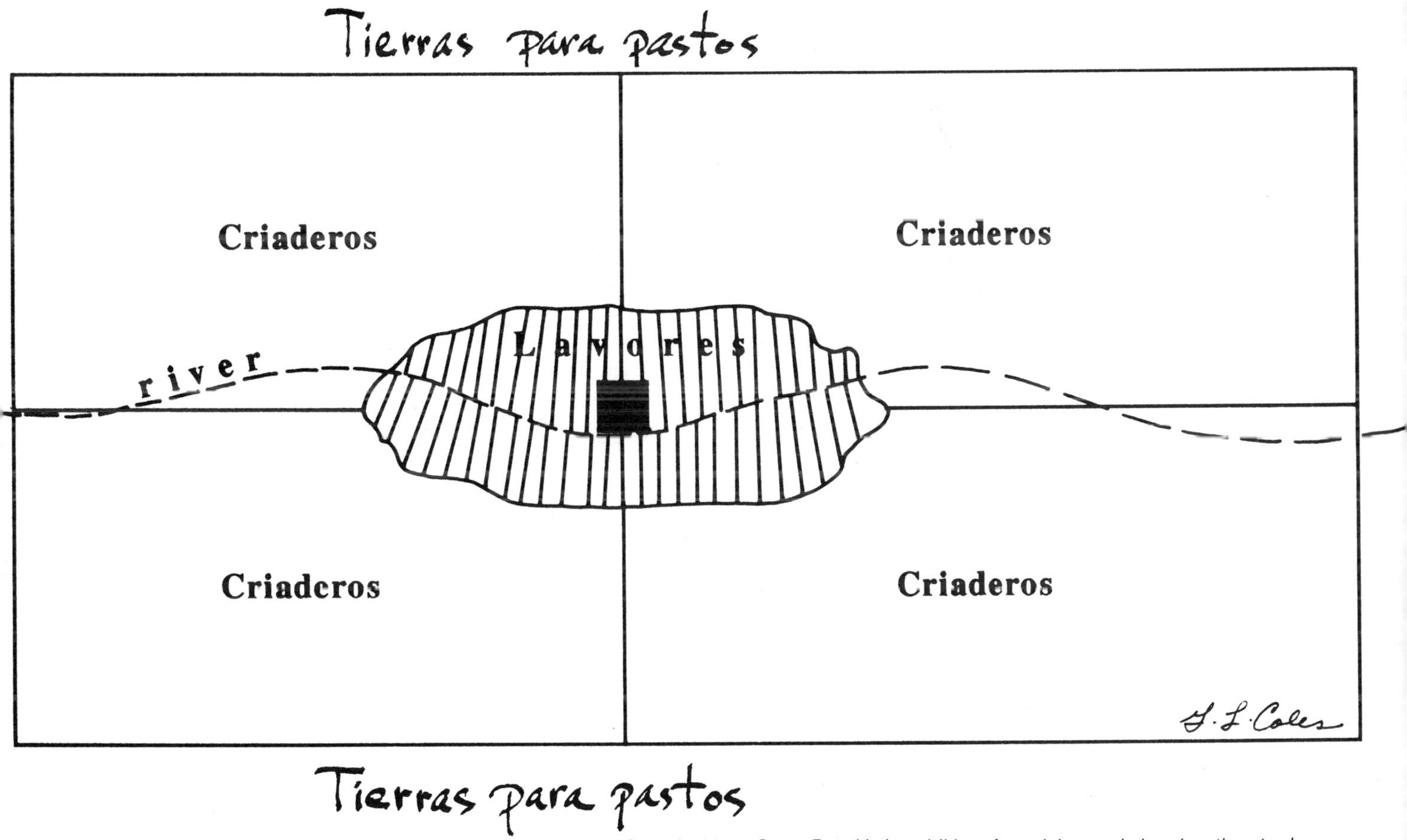

Schematic drawing based on diagram of the San Pedro grant in the State Archives, Santa Fe, with the addition of usual river and plaza locations to show typical land-holding pattern. Note the two kinds of common lands, the **tierras para pastos** *(public domain), and the* **criaderos** *(common lands within the grant), as well as the* **labores** *(irrigated strips of privately owned farmland).*

Even more specific were the settlement conditions for a community grant at Doña Ana in 1840.[28] Article 3 of the grant said that the *ejidos* would measure 2,500 varas long by 1,250 varas wide (⅛ of a *sitio de ganado mayor),* and within this area the population was expected to locate its *solares* (house lots). When the land was actually staked out for the settlers, however, the prefect of El Paso measured 2,500 varas south and north from the plaza, and 1,500 varas east and west of the plaza. The *ejidos* within this area were also measured from the plaza in accordance with the above Article 3. The effect was to have more than one-half of the community grant designated as *ejido* land within which new settlers were expected to build their homes with a guarantee (Article 20) of sufficient water for their *labores.*

In 1846, the departmental assembly of New Mexico made a similar grant creating the town of Chaperito. Lands were awarded to the grantees for farming plus one-half league for *ejidos.* In specifying the location of the *ejidos,* the assembly noted that they should be "*en contorno*" (around) the farming lands in the same manner as designated above in the San Pedro Grant.[29] The same idea was articulated in 1833 by alcalde Francisco Baca Ortiz when he placed petitioners in possession of the Ortiz Mine Grant. The *ejidos* granted in this case were for the "movement of machines and pasturing of animals." One *ejido* was located east of the mine; the others were described as "two leagues on each of the four sides of the mine."[30]

Sometimes the boundaries were marked by *mojoneras* (earth and stone mounds), sometimes with rocks or charcoal buried in the center as well as into the ground. Governor Juan Bautista de Anza insisted on the erection of *mojoneras* when he made a grant to the Town of San Isidro in 1786, and he warned that if they were not placed correctly, grantees would lose their land.[31] The governor was concerned that the grant might encroach on lands used by Indians of Zía and Jemez pueblos. Likewise, in the Mexican period, governors frequently ordered the placement of *mojoneras* to show a grant's geographical limitation and to lessen the confusion resulting between granted *ejido* lands within the *merced* and the *terreno baldío,* or uncultivated public domain surrounding it.[32]

A more frequently mentioned condition associated with land grants was to demand fencing of the cultivated land, leaving the perimeter boundaries with little more than vague references to terrain features. This practice reflected the concern of both Spaniards and Mexicans that livestock would do great damage to crops and water sources unless they were under proper physical restraint. Furthermore, since the task of placing grantees in possession of their granted lands fell to the *ayuntamientos, alcaldes,* justices of the peace, and prefects, these local officials hoped to reduce the incidence of expensive litigation resulting from property damaged by loose animals. If conflict had to come, citizens who fenced their property would have a much better case. Consequently, these officials frequently insisted, as a condition of possession, that new settlers fence their irrigated land so that animals grazing in adjacent *ejidos* would not be able to destroy crops or irrigation ditches.[33] When Governor Pedro Fermín de Mendinueta made the San Joaquín del Nacimiento grant to Joaquín de Luna and 35 others in 1769, he specified that each settler would own his farm land within the grant, and that all the rest of the land granted would be the property of the grantees for their use only, to pasture their animals and other uses to which they agreed. He instructed the alcalde to select the best spot for a town, and to choose farming lands as close together as possible "so that it may be more convenient for them to fence the land."[34]

Ejidos vs. Public Domain: A Source of Great Confusion

Governor Alberto Maynez approved a land grant in 1815 to several Santa Fe citizens who requested land near the Pecos Pueblo. He limited their *merced* to only the land they could reasonably plow and sow, explaining that the land petitioned for was probably *ejidos y comederos realengos* of the Pecos Indians. To avoid trouble with the Pueblo, he insisted that the grantees fence their land.[35] Maynez revealed both a concern for the rights of Indians as well as a generally accepted belief that land ownership included use rights to the public domain for grazing, wood, and water. He was also implying, although the documents are not entirely clear on the matter, that each community had a special area in the public domain that was theirs to enjoy by custom and tradition. His use of the words *ejidos* and *comederos realengos,* in the same sentence, indicates that he wasn't sure whether these lands were really *ejidos* of the Pueblo or public domain, the use of which the Indians had enjoyed for hundreds of years.

In a similar situation during the same year, Governor Maynez awarded a grant to 43 Taos citizens who wanted to establish a community at Arroyo Hondo. Here again, he directed that the petitioners be put in possession of only the land they could plow and cultivate, the rest remaining *ejidos realengos* for pasturing animals. If the *ejidos* were to belong to Arroyo Hondo, the dimensions were not made clear, but when the alcalde put the grantees in possession, he referred to the *paraje prefijado* (presumably what the governor had called *ejidos realengos*) and noted that this land would have to remain common to the existing grantees as well as to those who would join the community in the future.[36]

In both cases, the alcaldes had stated what was commonly believed: a grant of land allowed the grantees at least a *use right* to pasture, wood, and water in the surrounding area—a right which most probably extended to the grant boundaries. On some occasions, this right was specified as an *ejido*; at other times the grant documents only underscored citizens' rights to the use of resources on the public domain (*terreno realengo* or *terreno común*). Although the distinction between *ejido* rights and public domain use rights might have been academic for some Hispanos, *ejido* status represented a change in the public domain from land under unconditional control of the sovereign to a semi-privatized condition in which the community grantees enjoyed use rights, the local authorities (*alcaldes, ayuntamientos,* prefects, justices of the peace) preserved some control over who was granted *solares* and *suertes*, and the sovereign retained ultimate right to all the nation's land and waters.

Ejidos were located specifically or generally depending on the whims of granting authorities and the interpretations of their grant by the grantees. In the case of the Town of Mora, a grant of *pasteos* [*sic*] *cumunes* was designated for the new community at a point north of the Ocaté River in 1835. Ten years later, when Governor Armijo approved a grant to Gervacio Nolan, the *juez de paz* of Mora complained that Nolan's land encroached on *los exidos de esta Demarcación de lo Demora*.[37]. This was the first mention of Mora's *ejidos* and shows how often the words *ejidos* and "comunes" were interchanged, as well as how quickly a community arose to protect its commons. When Manuel Martínez requested the Tierra Amarilla grant in 1832, the citizens of Abiquiú complained that the land he sought would be located on their *pastos y habrevaderos comunes* (pasture and common watering places) even though, according to Martínez, his land would be situated seven leagues away from Abiquiú and its *ejidos*.[38]

Perhaps the best distinction between *ejidos* and common rights on the public domain appears in documents of the previously mentioned Mesilla Civil Colony Grant of 1850. Commissioner Guadalupe Miranda established the Mesilla colony with two leagues of farming land and with *ejidos* expressly laid out for the common enjoyment of the colony to be shared with outsiders only by permission. In addition, Miranda noted, the colonists would have rights to the pasture, woods, and other resources of the *tierras valdías* located *outside* the ejidos granted to the colony.[39] Here is a clear distinction between the assignment of *ejidos* to a community and the right enjoyed by Indians and Hispanos alike to the natural resources of the public domain, especially those resources adjacent to their lands.

Unfortunately, most petitioners for land, as well as most civil authorities, failed to make this distinction as clearly as did Commissioner Miranda. For example, when Governor Joaquín Real Alencaster approved the Cañon de Chama grant in 1806, he mentioned only the colonists' *derecho de pastos y abrevaderos* (grazing and stock watering rights) and their location.[40] Governor Fermín de Mendinueta had earlier approved the San Joaquín del Nacimiento grant, stipulating that after the irrigable land was assigned, the remainder of the grant should be common to all grantees for pasture grounds and other uses.[41] *Ejidos* were not specifically mentioned in either case, but in stark contrast, when Governor Armijo was petitioned for land, not necessarily by a group, he frequently replied that the grant should be made *en los limites y exidos que pide*, meaning that the petitioner, even though he did not specifically request or merit *ejido* rights, should be given what he asked for *including* the long established and accepted right to wood, water, and pasture on the public domain.[42] Armijo did not use the word *ejido* in its specific sense, and he may have been using pro forma language.

Legally, then, the *ejido* belonged to the community to which it was appurtenant. When the Las Huertas grant was made in 1765, the alcalde of Bernalillo put nine families in possession of land at the foot of the Sandía Mountains, and then informed them that all their lands were *ejidos del común* except for those deeded as farm land. He then noted that they would be given in common a *testimonio* to serve as *vastante título* (sufficient title) to the property.[43] If the entire community were sold, the *ejidos* remained attached to the land.[44] When the Refugio Colony grant was made in 1850, the colonists were promised a *título de mercenación y ejidos*, meaning a title to the deeded land (the *merced*) plus title to the *ejidos*. Because these same words are used repeatedly in making land grants of all kinds in the Rio Grande Valley, there can remain little doubt that community *ejidos* constituted a class of land separated from the public domain for the exclusive use of a select group.

Within the *ejido*, community members were allowed to raise, graze, and water their stock, cut wood, hunt, pick wild fruit, fish, and generally enjoy the fruits of nature. They were assured of being able to move their crops and stock in and out through *entradas y salidas* (entrances and exits), and they could move from one area to another, wherever the pasture was best, with rights of way (*servidumbres*) and freedom of movement (*trabecías*) guaranteed.[45] If one or more towns formed on a grant, they could not have greater rights as communities to the resources of the *ejido* than the individuals who owned house lots and farming lots in the pioneer settlement. Because every community was expected to grow, the *ejidos* also served as the area within which new settlers were located.

The *Recopilación* stated that common lands assigned to a community should be sufficient to accommodate increases in the settlers and their livestock.[46] These *ejidos*, according to Instruction No. 11 for the formation of the town of Pitic, Sonora, were to be designated on all four sides of the *Neuva Población* (new settlement), capable of providing recreation for the *pobladores* (settlers), room for their livestock, and land that could be granted to newcomers.[47] The same concept was carried forward in the founding documents of Doña Ana Colony, 1840, in which Article 3 specified an area to be designated *ejidos de la población*, and Article 15 noted that the municipal fund (*arbitrios y propios*) would receive the proceeds of sales from *solares* (house lots) situated within these *ejidos*.[48] Normally, *solares* were not sold.

In sum, the word *ejido* was often used incorrectly to stress the rights of Hispanic citizens to the use of grass, wood, water, and other resources of the public domain. Its real meaning, according to the laws of Spain and Mexico, as well as to the customary and accepted practices of New Mexico prior to United States occupation, was that a special portion of land was removed from the public domain, attached to a community which had legal title to and control of an area into which new settlers were expected to expand and in which they, too, had common use rights. Ownership, use, and control of water rights in these *ejidos* have defied a simple explanation due to the fact that the original *ejido* often went through many modifications as newcomers settled and small

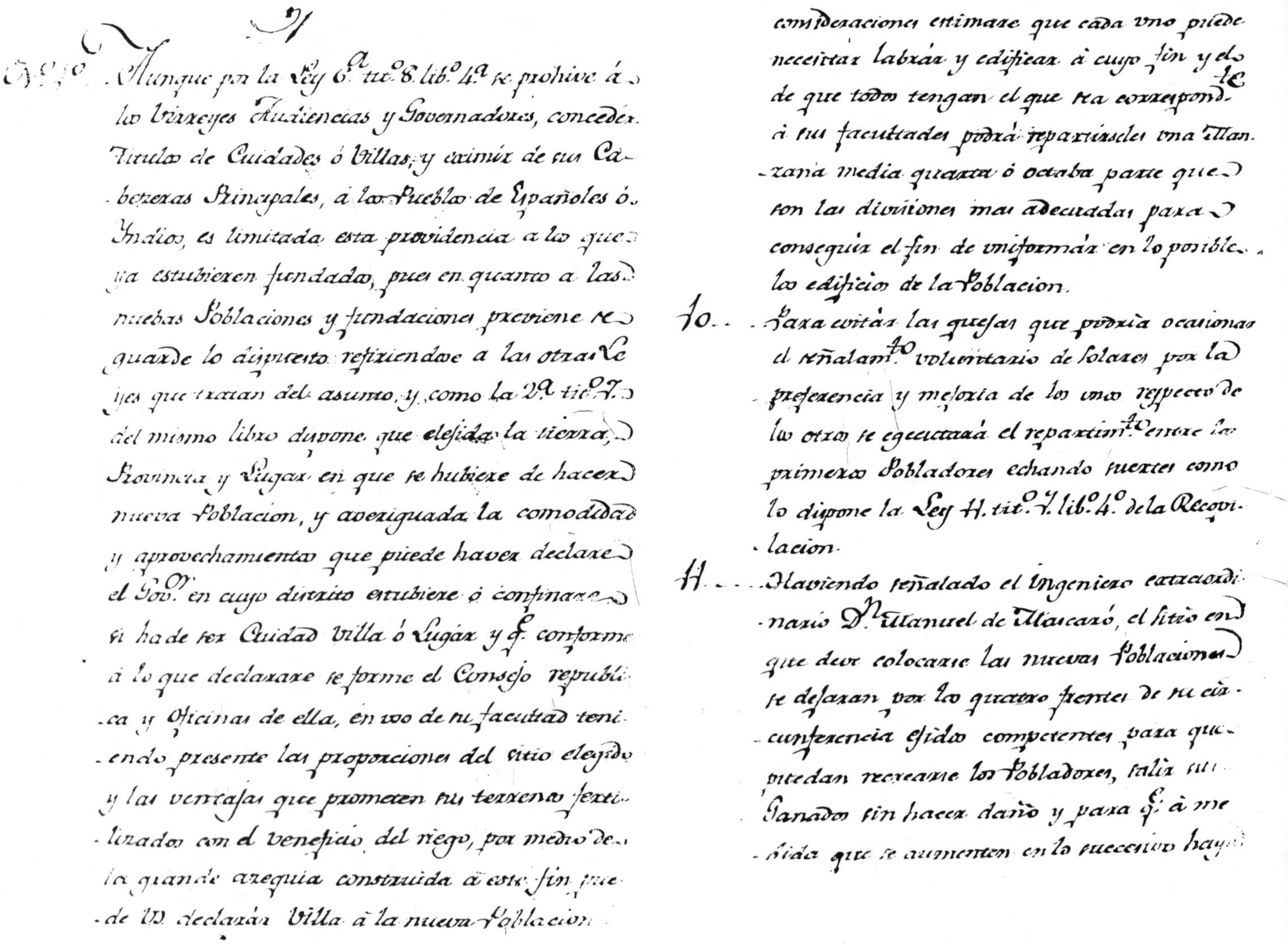

Aunque por la Ley 6.a tit.o 8. lib.o 4.a se prohive á los Virreyes Audiencias y Governadores, concedér Titulos de Ciudades ó Villas, y eximir de sus Cabezeras Principales, á los Pueblos de Españoles ó Indios, es limitada esta providencia a los que ya estubieren fundados, pues en quanto a las nuebas Poblaciones y fundaciones previene se guarde lo dispuesto refiriendose a las otras Leyes que tratan del asunto, y como la 2.a tit.o 7. del mismo libro dispone que elejida la tierra, Provincia y Lugar en que se hubiere de hacer nueva Poblacion, y averiguada la comodidad y aprovechamientos que puede haver declare el Gov.or en cuyo distrito estubiere ó confinare si ha de ser Ciudad Villa ó Lugar y &. conforme á lo que declarare se forme el Consejo republica y Oficinas de ella, en uso de su facultad teniendo presente las proporciones del sitio elejido y las ventajas que prometen sus terrenos fertilizados con el veneficio del riego, por medio de la grande arequia construida á este fin puede V.S. declarar Villa á la nueva Poblacion.

consideraciones estimare que cada uno puede necesitar labrar y edificar á cuyo fin y de que todos tengan el que sea correspondiente á sus facultades podrá repartirseles una Manzana media quarta ó octaba parte que son las diviciones mas adecuadas para conseguir el fin de uniformar en lo posible los edificios de la Poblacion.

10... Para evitar las quejas que podria ocasionar el señalam.to voluntario de solares por la preferencia y mejoria de los unos respecto de los otros se egecutará el repartim.to entre los primeros Pobladores echando suertes como lo dispone la Ley 11. tit.o 7. lib.o 4.o de la Recopilacion.

11.... Haviendo señalado el Ingeniero extraordinario D.n Manuel de Mascaró, el sitio en que deven colocarse las nuevas Poblaciones se dejaran por los quatro frentes de su circunferencia ejidos competentes para que puedan recrearse los Pobladores, salir sus Ganados sin hacer daño y para q.e á medida que se aumenten en lo succesivo hay...

Copy of the Plan of Pitic, with first page, instruction No. 11, and last page. (SANM I, No. 1265. State Records Center & Archives, Santa Fe.)

puestos (population centers) began to appear in what had once been an almost uninhabited tract.

Water Rights on the Commons

The Hispanic concept that water was public and available to all unless privatized by the sovereign in a specific water grant was applicable to *ejido* lands with the one exception that the "public" was usually restricted to the community to which the *ejido* was attached. *Las Siete Partidas* made it clear that the *ejidos* were granted for the common use of residents of each city or town.[49] The *Recopilación* further provided that all waters in the New World would be common, that their distribution by municipal councils should be directed at promoting the public welfare, and that each person should have access to the water he needed.[50]

Additional Spanish laws decreed that waters inside a town were to be held for the common benefit of the inhabitants, "but the source of supply was to be common to all persons."[51] Under Mexican law, rivers and streams belonged to the nation, but the use of the waters belonged to the inhabitants in common. So long as the rivers were flowing in their own channels, they were the common property of all inhabitants.[52] Water on the *ejidos,* therefore, was community water, subject to the control of the municipal authorities if used for agricultural purposes. It was primarily and equally available to all residents for domestic purposes and then for the needs of their livestock and farms. It was not supposed to be used for irrigation without permission, but in New Mexico, because farming lands were often located within the *ejidos,* all of the community's needs might be served by the same ditches.[53]

To assure new settlers that they would indeed have free and equal access to water, grants were almost always made with the admonition that pastures, woods, and watering places were common. Although *ejidos* were not always mentioned specifically, grantees were placed in "equal" possession of land, pasturage, woods, water, and watering places by an alcalde or prefect.[54] Because new settlers would also be occupying lands in the *ejidos,* it was incumbent upon local authorities to guarantee them adequate water for their domestic and agricultural needs. In the case of the Doña Ana Colony Grant of 1840, the prefect was instructed to provide

terreno que poder mercenarles para que edifiquen sus casas y havitaciones, seg.n lo disponen las Leyes 7.a 13. y 14. del citado tit.o 7.o lib.o 4.o de la Recopilacion.

12. — Asimismo se procederá á señalár y demarcar la dehesa ó prado vollal que se regule suficiente para que puedan pastar abundantem.te y con comodidad los ganados de Lavor y los que huviere para el abasto de la nueva Poblacion procurando elegir á este fin las tierras abundantes de Pasto que no sean de la mejor calidad para producir trigo ó otros efectos y legumbres utiles á el consumo y subsistencia de los Pobladores y sus familias como lo disponen las citadas Leyes 7.a y 14. tit.o 7. lib.o 4.o de la Recopilacion.

13. — Evacuado el señalam.to de los ejidos y de la dehesa ó prado vollál formará el comisionado un prudente calculo de todo el terreno util y fructifero, que por medio de la Asequia construida pueda regarse y del restante que sin tener este beneficio considere á proposito para siembras y cosechas de temporal y deviendo uno y otro en suertes iguales de 400 varas [illegible]

...nen, la q.e podrá imponerse y exigirse en los casos de contravencion, cuidando q.e sea mayor la que señalaren p.a los q.e causaren daño de noche por la mayor dificultad de ser aprehendidos, y castigados.

24. — Y por ultimo siendo propio y privativo de los Cabildos y Ayuntam.tos como mas instruidos de lo q.e conviene al Comun y Publico que representan acordar y proponer los arvitrios y providencias q.e consideren mas utiles y conducentes á su mejor regimen y govierno Economico y Politico, las q.e aprovadas por la superioridad, pasan a la clase de ordenanzas municipales, que deven observarse como Leyes particulares de cada Poblacion en quanto no se opongan á las generales establecidas por el Soberano, gozará esta misma facultad el Ayuntam.to de la Nueva Poblacion; y en uso de ella procediendo de acuerdo con el Comisionado á su establecimiento resolveran y estenderan los Capitulos y Ordenanzas Municipales, que estimaren mas utiles y conducentes de q.e daran cuenta á este superior govierno para que mediante su aprovacion, tengan vigor y observancia.

Es Copia Chihuahua 20 de En.o de 1800.

Taking water from the Rio Lucero at Taos Pueblo. (Department of Development Collection. Photo No. 2237. Courtesy State Records Center & Archives, Santa Fe.)

*Irrigation flume (**caroa**) at Córdova, transporting the village's **acequia** water across an annoyo. (Neg. No. 9051. Courtesy Museum of New Mexico.)*

new settlers with the "necessary" water for their *labores* and to inform the government (Chihuahua) how the water would be distributed and how irrigation would be developed.[55] The alcalde who distributed lands and waters to the settlers at Las Vegas five years earlier specifically advised them that pastures and waters would be held in common (*de mancomunidad*), and that they [the ditches] be built by everyone without compensation [as a community obligation].[56]

Ejido settlers in Mexico today are still guaranteed the right to use and profit from waters within their lands "in an *equitable* form [sharing] between private property owners and *ejidatarios*."[57] According to the 1933 Agrarian Code, land and water belonging to the modern Mexican *ejido* may only be expropriated by presidential decree after *compensation has been made* and proceedings instituted. Furthermore, the right to these waters is vested in the *ejidatarios* in their corporate capacity, and their use is subject to regulation by a committee representing users and the Department of Agriculture representing the Mexican government.

In New Mexico today, as well as in the past, the increase in population presents a potential water conflict between the municipality and the rights of the settlers on *ejido* lands who are using the same stream system. Prior to 1848, this potentially explosive issue did not fully materialize. Water supplies were generally adequate for the settlers and the communities to which they were attached. But testiness and minor disputes appear frequently enough in the documents of the 1840s to suggest that pressures on existing water supplies were being experienced within communities and between settlements on the same water course.

On only rare occasions did Hispanic authorities accede to requests to privatize the public waters in New Mexico's public domain. When Governor Facundo Melgares was petitioned for land in the vicinity of Valverde, he approved the request but insisted that watering places and pastures remain available to anyone passing through.[58] This respect

Grazing was, and still is, an important use of common lands. (Photo by T. Harmon Parkhurst. Neg. No. 68901. Courtesy Museum of New Mexico.)

for the public nature of water was also revealed in a heated battle over a reservoir built by a citizen on the public domain. A number of neighbors complained that a swamp was the unhappy and unhealthy result of imprisoning a small spring, but aside from the petty jealousies that emerged in the charges and counter charges, authorities focused on the need to preserve the right of access of *all* citizens to public water and concluded that the reservoir would have to be removed.[59] However, when José Ignacio Ortiz requested a water right to work a gold, silver, and copper mine in 1833, he was awarded the use of several springs out of the public domain in order to run his mill and mining machinery.[60] Local governments were especially favorable to this kind of economic development, and so long as previously established rights would not be jeopardized in making such a water grant, the greater good of the entire population could be enhanced by such a boon to the economy.

Conclusion

Throughout the Spanish and Mexican periods, the word *ejido* was used both generally to mean public water and pasturage, and specifically in reference to lands attached to community grants. When private citizens requested land with fixed boundaries plus *ejidos*, they were normally asking for deeded property plus a guarantee of land for expansion with primary use rights to the pastures, woods, and waters in

The village of San José, c. 1915, with surrounding lands including cornfields. Note horse-drawn wagon in foreground. (Neg. No. 13914. Courtesy Museum of New Mexico.)

The village of Questa in 1917, showing surrounding grazing lands and woodlands, with haystacks in the foreground. (Adella Collier Collection. Photo No. 32043. Courtesy State Records Center & Archives, Santa Fe.)

the surrounding area. Over a period of time, these usufructory rights became semi-privatized, not in the legal sense, but in custom and practice which succeeding generations came to see as a kind of territorial prerogative. In disputes regarding these areas, or when a new grant was considered in the same area, authorities and citizens tended to use the word *ejido* to connote the grazing and watering privileges appurtenant to extant privatized lands. Some private grants eventually became communities, and these communities believed they should also have specific *ejidos*. Since land and water were usually adequate, and because customs and tradition encouraged respect for wood, water and pasturage for everyone, most communities, including Indian pueblos, had the equivalent of *ejido* rights, even though, as this essay has made clear, the actual community *ejidos* enjoyed a unique, semi-privatized status separated from the common lands of the public domain.

One could accuse New Mexicans of sloppiness in describing and adjudicating important land matters. But in an area where the rule of law was sometimes absent or ineffective, it is understandable that the generic *ejido* concept (*baldíos* and *concegiles*) could be confused with the more specific *ejido* right attached to communities. New Mexicans who founded new communities believed that they were entitled to common lands for all the purposes specified by Spanish and Mexican laws over the centuries: recreation, grazing, cattle raising, cutting wood, watering animals, hunting, picking wild fruits and berries, etc. And they also knew, as it was so frequently documented, that their *ejido*, or *paraje prefijado,* was the area in which new settlers were expected to take up lands to farm. Granting authorities generally guaranteed them equal rights to water and other public resources, and indicated that their *ejidos* would remain detached from the public domain and under the control of the community. As expansion occurred, these resources were strained. No documentation shows a community asking for additional *ejido* lands, so one must assume that demographic pressures were not so great as to incapacitate the Hispanic methods of handling disputes through conciliation. In conflicts dealing with both land and water, it was understood that everyone benefited when disputes could be resolved with a compromise rather than through costly and time-consuming litigation.

With the arrival of more Anglo-Americans after 1848, the population increased, putting excessive pressure on the natural resources. Because United States authorities failed to understand the Hispanic system of land tenure in which *ejido* lands were an essential part of community grants, Mexicans who chose to stay in the United States lost property which they thought was protected under the Treaty of Guadalupe Hidalgo. It is now clear, and perhaps more significant than ever before, that they also lost a great deal of water when they lost their *ejidos*.

NOTES

1. Hunter Miller, *Treaties and Other International Acts of the United States of America* (Washington: GPO, 1957), 5:318.
2. See W.H. Timmons, "The El Paso Area in the Mexican Period, 1821-1848," *Southwestern Historical Quarterly*, 84 (July 1980): 27. One *real* was approximately ⅛ of a peso; a *fanega* approximated 2½ bushels.
3. In his article "The Tierras Baldias: Community Property and Public Lands in 16th Century Castile," *Agricultural History*, 48 (1974): 384, David E. Vassberg notes that the principle behind the public ownership of land in Castile was that "no individual had the right to appropriate for himself and monopolize a part of the resources of Nature that were produced without the intervention of man."
4. *Ibid.*, 391; and David E. Vassberg, *Land and Society in Golden Age Castile* (Cambridge and London: Cambridge University Press, 1984), 26-33. The author also mentions the *cotos* (a

cultivated *dehesa*) and *entrepanes* (common pasture between the cultivated fields), neither of which appear in New Mexico documents.

5. Vassberg, *Land and Society*, 19-21, 24; In New Mexico *Concegiles* are mentioned in the New Mexico Land Grants — Surveyor General records (NMLG-SG) as follows: Felipe Tafoya Grant, 1766, Reel 22, report 99, fr. 3 which mentions *pastos concegiles;* also Canōn de Carnue Grant, 1818, Reel 27, report 150, fr. 21 which discusses *comunes y concegiles para los Pobladores*.
6. *Recopilación de leyes de los reynos de las Indias*. Facsimile reprint of the 4th edition (Madrid: D. Joaquín Ibarra, 1971), 3 vols., Madrid: Consejo de la Hispanidad, 1943. I have also used Jane C. Sanchez' unpublished "Law of the Land Grant: The Land Laws of Spain and Mexico," 52 and 56. Her work is a translation of land laws found in the *Recopilación*.
7. Mariano Galván y Rivera, *Ordenanzas de Tierras y Aguas* (Mexico: 1842), 22.
8. See Manuel Fabila, *Cinco Siglos de Legislación Agraria en Mexico*. Mexico: Dpto. Agrario, 1941, 8.
9. See Vassberg, *Land and Society in Golden Age Castile*, 26-27.
10. Clark S. Knowlton, "The Town of Las Vegas Community Land Grant: An Anglo-American Coup D'Etat," in John R. and Christine M. Van Ness, eds., *Spanish and Mexican Land Grants in New Mexico and Colorado* (Manhattan, Kansas: Sunflower University Press, 1980), 13.
11. William DeBuys, "Fraction of Justice: A Legal and Social History of the Las Trampas Land Grant, New Mexico," *New Mexico Historical Review*, 56 (Jan. 1981), 74.
12. Eyler N. Simpson, *The Ejido — Mexico's Way Out* (Chapel Hill: The University of North Carolina Press, 1937), 13, 326, 795, 797, 799. See also *Ley Federal de Reforma Agraria* in *Leyes y Codigos de Mexico* (Mexico: Editorial Porrua, 1971), 32.
13. NMLG-SG microfilm, Las Huertas Grant, 1765, Reel 26, report 144, fr. 8; Arroyo Hondo Grant, 1815, Reel 29, report 159, fr. 4.
14. See for example *Ibid.*, The Town of El Rito Grant, 1808, Reel 27, report 151, fr. 39 in which a piece of land was sold with *entradas y salidas, ausiones y ejidos*.
15. ". . . *lo que es de todos en común no es de nadie en propiedad*." *Ibid.*, Tierra Amarilla Grant, 1832, Reel 12, report 3, fr. 17.
16. See *Ibid.*, Rancho de Rio Grande Grant, Reel 19, report 58, fr. 9; Alamitos Grant, Reel 20, report 69, fr. 3; Arroyo Hondo Grant, Reel 29, report 159, fr. 7; Las Vegas Grant, Reel 15, report 20, fr. 24.
17. *Ibid.*, Alexander Valle Grant, 1814, Reel 14, report 18, fr. 600.
18. *Ibid.*, Polvadera Grant, 1766, Reel 25, report 131. fr. 7.
19. *Recopilación*, Book IV, Title 17, Law 5.
20. NMLG-SG, Las Huertas Grant, 1765, Reel 26, report 144, fr. 8. Two years later in the San Joaquín del Nacimiento Grant (Reel 20, report 66, fr. 10), the governor directed that the common lands should be common to the grantees and to no one else.
21. *Ibid.*, Francisco Montes Vigil Grant, Reel 25, report 126, fr. 5.
22. *Ibid.*, Mesilla Civil Colony Grant, 1850, Reel 21, report 162, fr. 2. The phrase *tierra baldía* [valdia] and *terreno común* were the Mexican period equivalents of *tierra realenga* of the colonial period.
23. *Ibid.*, Gervacio Nolan Grant, 1845, Reel 16, report 39, fr. 11.
24. For examples see *Ibid.*, Town of Cieneguilla Grant, 1795, Reel 19, report 162, fr. 2; Town of San Miguel del Bado Grant, 1794, Reel 24, report 119, fr. 8; Arroyo Hondo Grant, 1815, Reel 29, report 159, fr. 7; Town of Anton Chico Grant, 1822, Reel 16, report 29, fr. 3.
25. *Ibid.*, Town of Abiquiú Grant, 1754, Reel 26, report 140, fr. 1.
26. SANM, I, Reel 1, fr. 815, citation brought to the author's attention courtesy of Malcolm Ebright in letter of August 13, 1985.
27. NMLG-SG, San Pedro Grant, 1820, Reel 14, report 14, fr. 19.
28. *Ibid.*, Doña Ana Colony, 1840, Reel 21, report 85, frs.12, 13, 35.
29. *Ibid.*, Town of Chaperito, 1846, Reel 30, file 7, frs.5, 6, 15.
30. *Ibid.*, Ortiz Mine, 1833, Reel 17, report 43, fr. 14.
31. *Ibid.*, Town of San Isidro Grant, 1786, Reel 16, report 24, fr. 3.
32. See *Ibid.*, Gervacio Nolan Grant, 1843, Reel 18, report 48, fr. 4; Santo Tomas de Iturbide Grant, 1853, Reel 26, report 139, fr. 2.
33. See *Ibid.*, Baca y Pino et al Grant, 1825, Reel 24, report 121, frs. 8-9; La Talaya Grant, 1825, Reel 31, file 86, fr. 3.; Jose F. Baca y Terrus et al, Cañada de San Francisco Grant, 1839, Reel 19, report 57, fr. 31; Apache Spring Tract Grant, 1842, Reel 20, report 72, fr. 1; Juan Ortiz, Mesita Blanca Grant, 1843, Reel 30, file 5, fr. 15; Cebolla, Juan Carlos Santiestevan Grant, 1845, Reel 19, report 61, fr. 3; El Cadillal Grant, 1846, Reel 31, file 90, fr. 3. The records also show that some citizens did *not* put up the required fences. See SANM, I, No. 1271.
34. *Ibid.*, San Joaquín de Nacimiento, 1769, Reel 20, report 66, fr. 10.
35. *Ibid.*, Alexander Valle Grant, 1814, Reel 14, report 18, fr. 600.
36. *Ibid.*, Arroyo Hondo Grant, Reel 29, report 159, fr. 4.
37. *Ibid.*, Town of Mora Grant, Reel 16, report 32, fr. 86.
38. *Ibid.*, Tierra Amarilla Grant, 1832, Reel 12, report 3, fr. 17.
39. *Ibid.*, Mesilla Civil colony Grant, 1850, Reel 21, report 71, fr. 1.
40. *Ibid.*, Cañon de Chama, 1806, Reel 20, report 71, fr. 2.
41. *Ibid.*, San Joaquín del Nacimiento, 1769, Reel 20, Report 66, fr. 10.
42. See *Ibid.*, Gervacio Nolan Grant, 1845, Reel 16, report 39, frs.2-3; Bosque del Apache Grant, 1845, Reel 16, report 35, frs.2:3; Antonio Sandoval Grant, 1845, Reel 20, report 70, fr. 10.
43. *Ibid.*, Las Huertas Grant, 1765, Reel 26, report 144, fr. 8.
44. *Ibid.*, Town of El Rito, 1808, Reel 27, report 151, fr. 39.
45. *Ibid.*, Town of Casa Colorado Grant, 1823, Reel 12, report 5, fr. 2.
46. *Recopilación*, Book IV, Title 7, Law 13.
47. Copy of the Instructions for the settlement of Pitic, certified by Manuel Merino, Chihuahua, Jan. 20, 1800, in SANM I, Reel 6, fr. 985.
48. NMLG-SG, Doña Ana Colony Grant, 1840, Reel 21, report 85, frs. 25, 27. Spanish and Mexican period records show few examples of *solares* being sold.
49. Partida 3, titulo 28, ley 9 in *Las Siete Partidas del sabio rey don Alfonso el IX, glosadas por el Lic. Gregorio Lopez*, 4 vols. (Madrid: Oficina de d.Leon Amarita, 1829-1831).
50. *Recopilación*,, Book IV, Title 17, Laws 5-14.
51. Iris W. Engstrand, "Land Grant Problems in the Southwest: The Spanish and Mexican Heritage" *New Mexico Historical Review*, 53, (October 1978), 323.
52. Clesson S. Kinney, *A Treatise on the Law of Irrigation and Water Rights and the Arid Region Doctrine of Appropriation of Waters*. 2nd edition, revised and enlarged to October 1, 1912 (San Francisco, CA: Bender-Moss Company, 1912), 989.
53. See Michael C. Meyer, *Water in the Hispanic Southwest: A Social and Legal History, 1550-1850* (Tucson: The University of Arizona Press, 1984), 122.
54. See for example, NMLG-SG, Bernabé Montoya et al, Grant 1753, Reel 18, report 49, frs.23-27.
55. See *Ibid.*, Article 20, Doña Ana Colony Grant, 1840, Reel 21, report, 85, frs.13, 35.
56. *Ibid.*, Las Vegas Grant, 1835, Reel 15, report 20, fr. 24.
57. See Article 57 on page 33 of the 1971 *Ley Federal de Reforma Agraria* (Mexico: Editorial Porrua, 1971); also articles 147, 150 of the Agrarian Code (1933) and the 1934 modifications as published in Simpson, *The Ejido*, 328, 329, 796, 799.
58. *NMLG-SG*, Pedro Armendaris Grant, 1819, Reel 16, fr. 21.
59. SANM, I, Reel 6, frs.1193-1226.
60. NMLG-SM, Elisha Whittlesey et al, Ortiz Mine, 1833, Reel 17, report 43, fr. 45.

Daniel Tyler is professor of history at Colorado State University. In addition to Hispanic land and water rights, he is working on a history of the Northern Colorado Water Conservancy District and the Colorado — Big Thompson project.

An Enduring Legacy: *California Ranchos in Historical Perspective*

Iris H.W. Engstrand

Old brass seal of Los Angeles County Court. (Courtesy Seaver Center for Western History Research, Los Angeles.)

IN California today, as new developments with such historic names as Rancho Peñasquitos, Rancho Jamul, Mission Viejo, and Laguna Niguel dot the landscape with homes and shopping centers, the heritage of the ranchos is a popular theme for residents and real estate promoters alike. Nevertheless, as the colorful aspects of rancho life continue to grace advertising brochures and "the days of the dons" provide nostalgia for barbecues and dances, the complicated and often difficult times faced by the earliest settlers recede further into obscurity. Newcomers to the state marvel at the abundance of Hispanic names along busy freeways but can only imagine the tranquil days when there were cattle instead of condominiums on a thousand hills.[1]

Those even slightly acquainted with California's past know that rancho life has always been an integral part of the state's history, but few can appreciate the tortuous paths through legal entanglements taken by those early "dons" and the subsequent clashes created as two distinct cultures came together in a rich frontier area. The purpose of this article is to trace the history of California's Spanish and Mexican land grants and to review the controversies surrounding their confirmation during the early American period.

In contrast to other areas of the Spanish Southwest, the granting of land for private ranchos in California came very near the end of Spain's colonizing effort in the New World. In fact, the first land grant was not made until 1775 when a retired soldier was encouraged to take a few acres of land near Mission San Carlos (Carmel).[2] Even then, the granting of additional ranchos proceeded slowly as soldiers who had accompanied the first expedition to Alta California in 1769 reached retirement age and Spain looked for ways to increase the productivity of its distant province. Because California lacked civilian settlers, was a long distance from central Mexico, and lacked apparent mineral wealth, no substantial land grants were made until the second decade of Spanish settlement, when Governor Pedro Fages approved three large concessions in the fall of 1784.[3]

At the time the first permanent ranchos were granted in 1784, nine Franciscan missions, four presidios, and two civilian pueblos had been established between San Diego and San Francisco in Alta California. The number of Spaniards was just a few hundred and the Indian population is estimated to have been somewhere between 150,000 and 250,000.[4] The missionaries, under the leadership of Fray Junípero Serra, father president until his death on 28 August 1784, had attracted approximately 8,000 natives into the missions to learn agriculture and Christian ways.[5] During the remainder of the Spanish period, 12 additional missions and one more civilian settlement were founded, leaving a significant expanse of territory available for grazing and cultivation. Much of the best land, however, was held by the Franciscans in trust for the Indians.[6]

The first major land grant petitions in 1784 came from Juan José Domínguez, José María Verdugo, and Manuel Nieto, three soldiers of the San Diego Presidio, who asked for tracts in the vicinity of the recently founded pueblo of Los Angeles.[7] Verdugo's original letter, written from his post at Mission San Gabriel, is typical:

> José María Verdugo, Corporal of the Royal Presidio of San Diego, at present stationed at the Mission of San

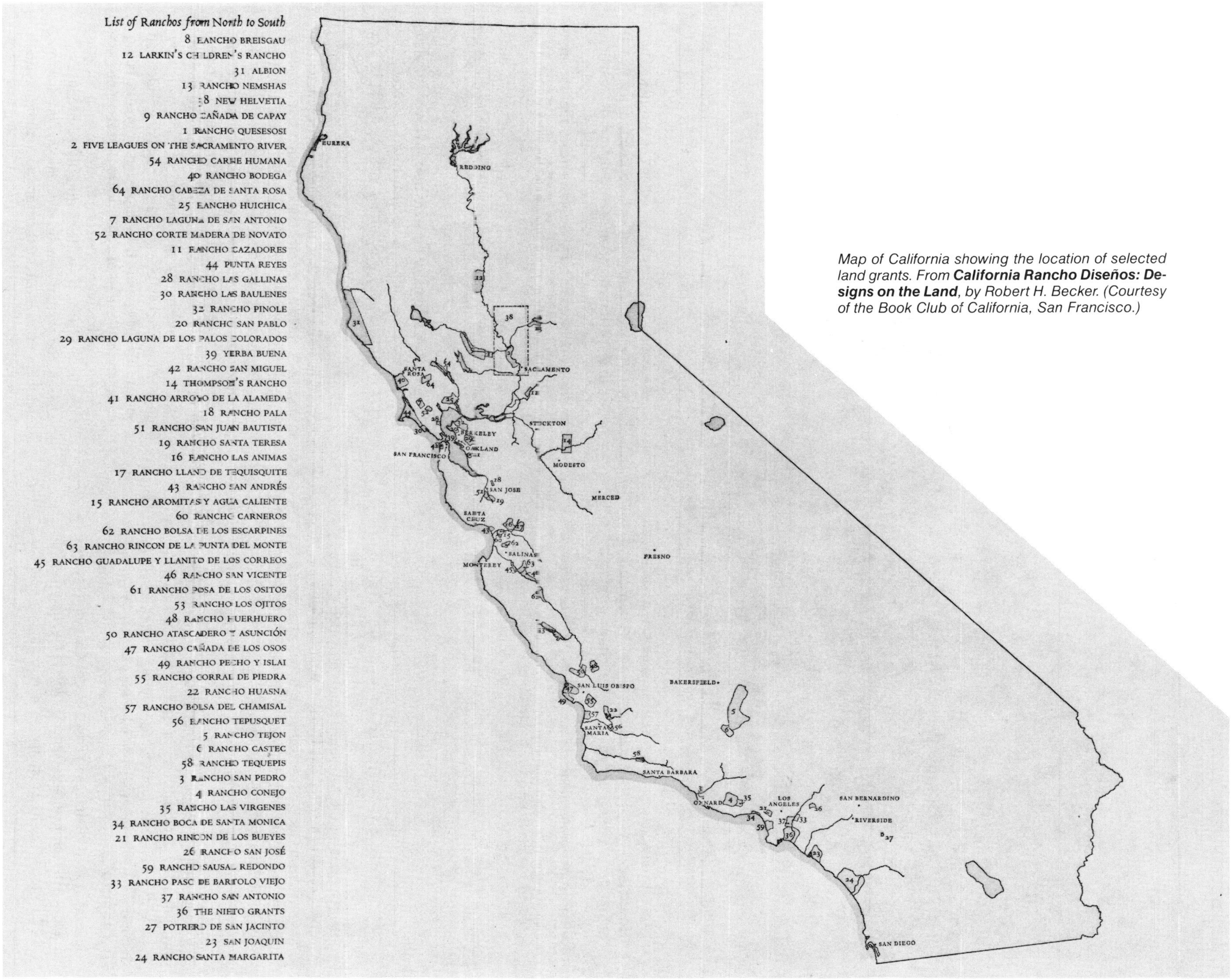

Map of California showing the location of selected land grants. From ***California Rancho Diseños: Designs on the Land****, by Robert H. Becker. (Courtesy of the Book Club of California, San Francisco.)*

Verdugo ranch house, Glendale. (Courtesy The Huntington Library, San Marino, California.)

> Gabriel, with proper severance, appears before your Honor and says, that in consideration of keeping my animals . . . at this mission . . . and not having a place where my above mentioned livestock may be pastured with proper convenience, I humbly ask for the very sincere charity of your Honor in order that you may be pleased to designate a tract . . . about a league and a half from this Mission at the "Arroyo Hondo. . . ."[8]

The governor's answer, dated at San Gabriel, 20 October 1784, simply stated:

> I concede to the petitioner the permission which he solicits to keep his cattle and horses at the "Arroyo Hondo" distant a league and a half from the Mission of San Gabriel on the Monterey Road; provided that he does not prejudice the said Mission, nor the inhabitants of the Reina de los Angeles, and has someone in charge, without being exposed to the Gentile Indians, or in any manner injuring them.
>
> Pedro Fages[9]

Although simple in nature, this early concession of land was based upon the legal heritage of Castile, as modified by the discovery of America and the opening up of new lands for colonization and settlement. In fact, the granting of lands in California was investigated and approved by the Attorney General of the Provincias Internas, Pedro Galindo Navarro, in a letter to Commandant General Jacobo Ugarte y Loyola on 27 October 1785. This opinion was careful to note that land concessions should respect all the safeguards provided by legislation concerning the Indies.[10] The key passages follow:

> The designation of sites for breeding cattle solicited by some settlers of California and proposed by the Governor in his official letter of 20 November 1784, cannot and must not be made within the boundaries assigned to each Pueblo. . . . By the laws from the 1st and continuing to the 13th, Title 12 of the same Book IV [Laws of the Indies] is permitted the distribution and designation of . . . sites for ranches of cattle and sheep, provided however that they be given far from the Indian pueblos and their cultivated fields. . . .[11]

The pueblo residents, who were also involved in raising cattle and growing crops, were also to be protected from injury. Governor Fages was further instructed that he grant lands

> at such a distance that no injury can result to the mission, pueblos and rancherias of Indians, nor to their planting ground, that he make grants and distribute sites for herding and breeding livestock, under the express condition that the residents and settlers, to whom such are granted, be obliged to furnish as many herdsmen and guards as may be sufficient to prevent injury and indemnify the amount of such which by chance may be caused, and further that no resident or settler shall have more than three sites or grants, being under the obligation of constructing a stone house on each one, of having at least two thousand head of cattle thereon, and that notwithstanding its grant and concession, the pastures remain to be enjoyed in common, and that in places where there are no herding grounds for stock, sites may be given for industry and other cultivation. . . .
>
> Chihuahua, 27 October 1785, Galindo Navarro[12]

Los Cerritos ranch house, Long Beach. (Courtesy The Huntington Library, San Marino, California.)

Rancho San Rafael of José María Verdugo included 36,403 acres adjacent to the northern border of the town of Los Angeles. It included a major portion of the present-day cities of Glendale, Eagle Rock, and Burbank.[13] The other two grants made in 1784 were Rancho San Pedro, over 75,000 acres in the area of San Pedro, Palos Verdes, Dominguez Hills, and Carson, assigned to Juan José Dominguez, and an immense 158,000-acre tract known as Rancho Los Nietos granted to Manuel Nieto. The latter rancho, some 33 square leagues extending over a large portion of today's Los Angeles and Orange Counties, was divided among Nieto's heirs in 1804. It was regranted in 1834 by the Mexican government as the five separate ranchos of Los Alamitos, Los Cerritos, Las Bolsas, Los Coyotes, and Santa Gertrudis. These included much valuable land in Long Beach and adjacent areas to the south along the coastal plain.[14]

One grant was recorded in 1785, and then no further concessions were made until 1795 when Governor Diego Borica rewarded a number of retiring soldiers with the granting of 10 ranchos during that year.[15] Among the best known were Rancho del Refugio, six leagues at Gaviota in Santa Barbara County granted to José Francisco Ortega, and Rancho Simi, 14 leagues in Ventura and Los Angeles Counties granted to Francisco Javier, Miguel, and Patricio Pico.[16]

Because the Franciscan missions controlled vast acres of choice agricultural land extending from San Diego to north of San Francisco Bay, there was considerable encouragement by the military governors for secularization of these establishments.[17] Even though the missions were, according to the Laws of the Indies, to become secular towns with parish churches in 10 years after their founding, the friars in Alta California did not believe the Indians would be sufficiently ready for an independent existence in that length of time. Not only did the Franciscans protect the land for the Indians, they opposed the granting of land to individuals.[18] Father José Señan, a future father president, reported to the Viceroy in 1796:

> I therefore believe that under no circumstances should retired soldiers or others with special credentials who wish to settle in the Province be permitted to establish themselves separately in remote areas or in villages outside the towns. . . . The consequences to be expected from scattered and isolated colonization are distressing to contemplate. Colonists thus openly exposed are likely to suffer mischief at the hands of gentiles [nomadic Indians]. . . . In short, they will live in these remote regions without King to rule or Pope to excommunicate them.[19]

Even though the Spanish governors wanted to move forward with secularization, they never succeeded in overcoming Franciscan objections. Additionally, applicants for grants were few and there remained an abundance of land; thus the matter was left unresolved for a time.[20]

During the remainder of the Spanish period (1796 through 1821), only 21 additional grants were made. These extended from present-day Orange County northward to the San Francisco Bay area and included such valuable parcels as Rancho los Feliz, bordering the pueblo of Los Angeles, granted to Vicente Feliz in 1802; Topanga Malibu Sequit, granted to José Bartolome Tapia in 1804; Rancho Santiago de Santa Ana, granted to Antonio Yorba in 1809; and Rancho San Antonio in Alameda County, granted in 1820 to Luis Peralta.[21]

After Mexico's successful bid for independence in 1821, local government officials proceeded in much the same fashion as their Spanish predecessors. Under native-born Luis Arguëllo, the first governor during the Mexican period, about 17 ranchos were granted, reaching as far south as San Diego and extending to the north of San Francisco Bay. With the adoption of a federal constitution in 1824, more liberal policies were designed to promote the settlement of frontier areas. Mexico's colonization law of 18 August 1824 provided in Article 2 that "The objects of this law are those national lands that are neither private property nor belonging to any corporation or pueblo and can therefore be col-

Los Feliz Ranch House, Griffith Park area, Los Angeles, c. 1900. (Courtesy Seaver Center for Western History Research, Los Angeles.)

Painting of Santa Margarita ranch house by James Walker. Now the Marine Corps' Camp Pendleton. (Courtesy Seaver Center for Western History Research, Los Angeles.)

onized.'' In order to attract colonists, this law not only made it possible, but encouraged foreigners to establish themselves in Mexican territory. The law also promised security of both person and property of landholders, as well as freedom from taxes for four years. Any Mexican of good character, or any foreigner willing to become a permanent resident of Mexico, could petition for up to one square league of irrigable land, four of non-irrigable land, and six of grazing land — a total of 11 square leagues.[22]

The next decree of 21 November 1828 authorized the governors to grant vacant lands to *empresarios*, families, or private persons, whether Mexican or foreign, who solicited them for habitation and cultivation. The conditions to be met were essentially the same as during the Spanish period and involved a petition, description, *diseño*, and proof of occupation.[23] Each new colonist, after having cultivated or occupied the land, was ordered to prove the same before the municipal authority so that the necessary record could be made and forwarded in a quarterly report to the supreme government.[24] Between 1825 and 1831, Governor José

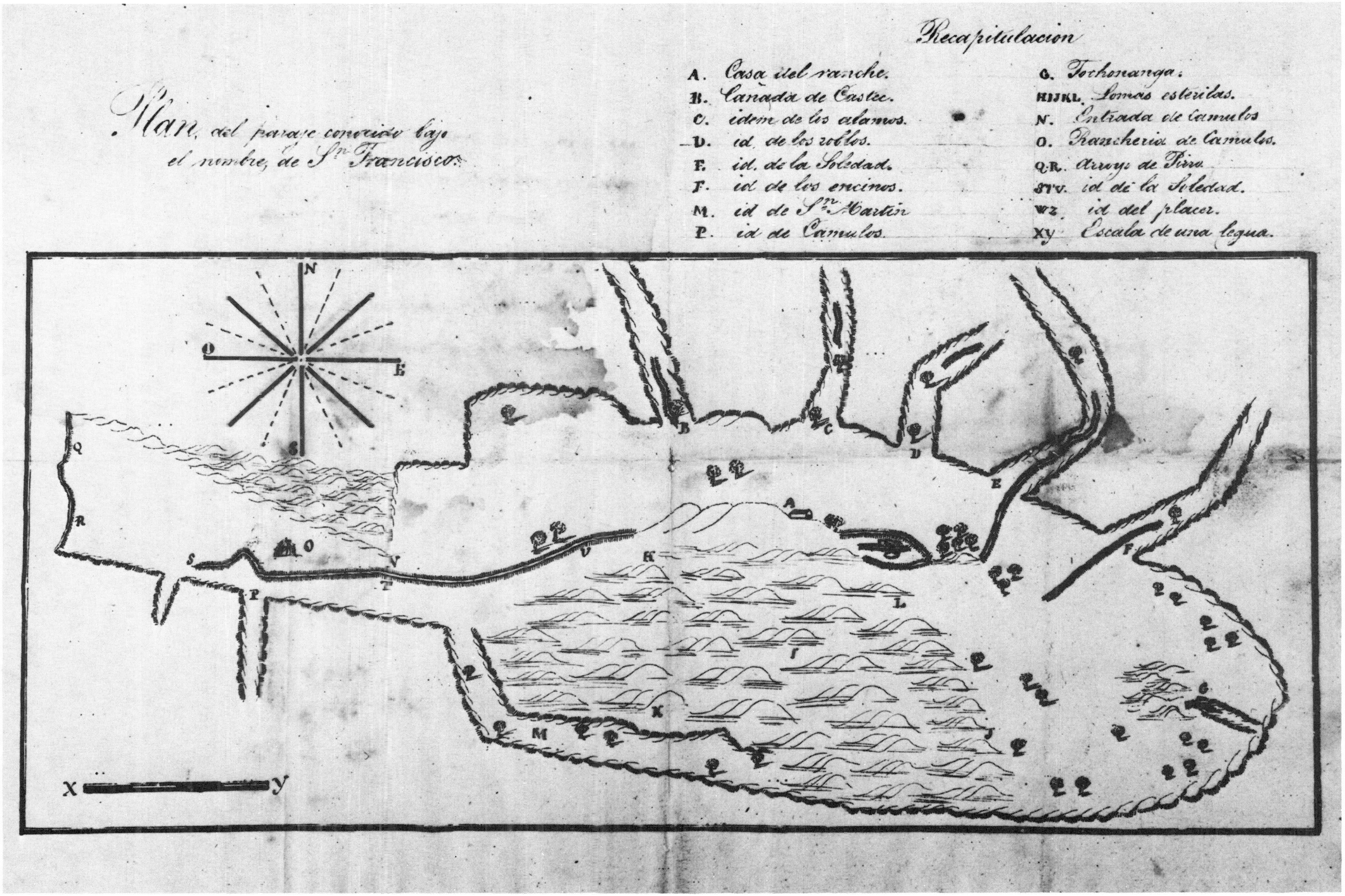

Map of Rancho San Francisco. (Courtesy Seaver Center for Western History Research, Los Angeles.)

María Encheandía granted only about 20 ranchos, including the historic tar pit area at La Brea to José Antonio Rocha in 1828.

From the beginning of the Mexican period, residents of California and other provinces newly freed from Spanish control looked towards the acquisition of good land suitable for cultivation and grazing. In its overall colonization program, the Mexican Junta envisioned partial Indian emancipation, secularization, and distribution of lands held by missionary orders.[25] Pursuant to these plans, and because of his personal opposition to the mission system, Governor Echeandía signed a decree in 1826 providing for freedom of Indians who had been Christians for 15 years, or since birth.[26] This decree achieved little success because many of the Indians, unprepared for a self-supporting independent existence, chose not to leave the mission. Echeandía's subsequent secularization plan of 6 January 1831 was suspended by his successor Manuel Victoria.[27]

In response to mounting pressure by residents, the Mexican Congress finally ordered secularization of the California missions on 17 August 1833. A year later, California Governor José Figueroa issued rules that forced the removal of the Franciscans from their missionary posts and indicated how the land was to be divided up. The missions were to be converted into civilian pueblos and the head of each Indian family was to receive land neither less than 100 varas nor more than 400 varas square together with livestock, tools, and seeds. The village thus created was also to receive sufficient common lands for pasture and other uses.[28] Even though Indians were to be granted up to one-half of the mission lands, and did in fact receive certain land grants, much of the land was parceled out to non-Indians. During the 10-year period from 1835 to 1845, nearly 700 land concessions, many of which included the most fertile ex-mission tracts, were made to private claimants. Often close friends or supporters of the governor received the choice areas. Former lands of Mission San Luis Rey in present-day northern San Diego County provide a typical example of land distribution during this period:

In 1836, the 17,634-acre Rancho Valle de San José, which later became a part of Warner's Ranch, was granted to Silvestre de la Portilla. In 1840, José Antonio Pico, brother of Pío Pico, received an adjacent 26,688 acres of former mission lands (Rancho San José del Valle) from Governor Juan Bautista Alvarado.[29] Also in 1840, Governor Alvarado further divided the mission lands and granted the 8,877-acre Los Vallecitos de San Marcos Rancho to José María Alvarado. By far the largest parcel carved from San Luis Rey was the 89,642-acre Rancho Santa Margarita granted by Alvarado to Pío and Andres Pico, and to which was added an additional grant of Las Flores in 1844. These two grants eventually totaled 133,440 acres and today contain the United States Marine Base of Camp Pendleton. In his last year as governor, Alvarado granted the 13,311-acre coastal tract of Agua Hedionda to Juan María Marrón; Governor Micheltorena in 1844 granted José Antonio Serrano the 13,309-acre Pauma Rancho and the Las Flores tract to the Picos.[30]

Pío Pico served as California's governor from February 1845 to August 1846 and made the last of the grants of San Luis Rey lands: 2,233 acres of Rancho Temecula to an Indian, Pablo Apis; 2,219 acres of Rancho Guajome to Indian brothers Andres and José Manuel; 1,184 acres of Buena Vista to an Indian, Felipe Subria; and the 13,322-acre Rancho Monserrate to Isidro María Alvarado. Some of the grantees, especially the former mission Indians, relinquished their titles within several years, although Pío Pico, Juan Marrón, and Isidro Alvarado managed to hold their ranchos well into the American period.[31]

The San Fernando Valley in Los Angeles County provides another example of granting activity after secularization. Altogether six ranchos, including the 116,858-acre ex-Mission de San Fernando patented to Eulogio de Celis, were granted to private owners between 1840 and 1845. The other

Rancho Guajome. Photo by H. F. Withay, November 13, 1936. (Courtesy Seaver Center for Western History Research, Los Angeles.)

five were Rancho Tujunga, 6,600 acres patented to David W. Alexander, Francis Mellus, Agustin Olvera, and the heirs of Francisco López; El Escorpion, 1,109 acres patented to Indians Urbano, Odon, and Manuel, and Joaquin Romero; El Encino, 4,460 acres patented to Vicente de la Osa, Aguila (widow) and Francisco (minor son), legal heirs of the Indian Roque, deceased, and Rita, minor daughter and only legal heir of the Indian Francisco; Rancho Providencia, 4,064 acres to David W. Alexander and Francis Mellus; and Rancho Cahuenga, 388.34 acres also to Alexander and Mellus. Several former mission Indians received land but did not hold on to it for long.[32]

The American conquest in 1846 and subsequent discovery of gold in 1848 forever altered the pattern of settlement in the once-isolated province of Alta California. Even before these two events, many Americans and other foreigners had found their way to Mexican California's peaceful shores and had carved out substantial land holdings. Because the tremendous herds of cattle provided hides for the leather industry and shoe manufacturers in New England and tallow for the soap makers in both Americas, petitioners could be found among settlers, traders, and adventurers of all countries. Those arriving between 1830 and 1840, for the most part, had been single men on board with the hide and tallow traders or mountain men following the overland trails in search of wealth and property. Many had married local Hispanic women and had participated in Mexico's generous colonization program. Those arriving after 1841 were generally family men with wives and children who made up the wagon trains of the mid-1840s. Some of these also obtained land grants, especially in northern California, and others were a part of the resistance known as the Bear Flag Revolt of June 1846.

With the American takeover and signing of the Treaty of Guadalupe Hidalgo on 2 February 1848, California's military governor, Richard B. Mason, felt bound to fulfill the obligations of the United States to Mexican landowners.[33] Governor Mason also believed it prudent to assign Captain Henry W. Halleck, Secretary of State for the territory of California, to investigate and "report on the [Mexican] laws and regulations which govern the granting or selling of public lands in California" and to consider those "respecting the lands and other property belonging to the missions. . . ." Halleck's report of 1 March 1849 concluded:

> a large number of land titles in California are very indefinite with respect to boundaries, the grants being for so many "sitios," creaderos, etc. lying between certain hills, streams, etc. as shown by rough sketches attached to the petitions. These sketches frequently contain double the amount of land included in the grants, and even now very few of these grants have been surveyed or their boundaries definitely fixed.

Halleck, custodian of the Mexican archives in Monterey, also expressed concern about the legality of many of the grants because the requirements of Spanish and Mexican law had not been followed.[34]

To assist the United States government in analyzing the land grant situation in California, President Zachary Taylor sent William Carey Jones, son-in-law of Senator Thomas Hart Benton, to investigate the condition of titles in California and make an independent recommendation. Jones had been a practicing lawyer in Louisiana and had gained a good knowledge of Spanish legal documents. As a result of his lengthy study, Jones concluded:

> The grants in California, I am bound to say are mostly *perfect titles,* that is, the holders possess their property by titles, that, under the law which created them, were equivalent to patents from our government; and those which are not perfect — that is, which lack some formality, or some evidence of completeness — have the same *equity* as those which are perfect, and were and would have been equally respected under the government which has passed away. . . . I think the state of land titles in that country will allow the public lands to be ascertained and the private lands set apart, by judicious measures, with little difficulty. Any measure calculated to discredit, or cause to be distrusted, the general character of the titles there . . . would, I believe, also retard the substantial improvement of the country: a title discredited is not destroyed, but every one is afraid to touch it, or at all events, to invest labor and money in improvements that rest on a suspected tenure. . . .[35]

Jones believed that the United States government and its people would be best served by a speedy confirmation of rancho grants and other land titles.

Halleck, also an able linguist familiar with both Spanish and French, had grave doubts about the legality of certain grants. Although several modern textbooks feel that Jones had the more "humane" position with regard to Mexican claimants, it is important to note that Jones' brother-in-law, John C. Fremont, was the beneficiary of a rich claim to Las Mariposas grant, one of the few on which gold had been discovered, and that Jones himself had acquired a claim to 12 leagues of San Luis Rey and Pala mission lands.[36] When Congress was not persuaded by his recommendation for speedy acceptance of land grant claims, Jones became a leading lawyer on behalf of claimants both in the San Francisco District Court and in the Supreme Court in Washington, D.C.[37] Henry Halleck and his law firm of Halleck, Peachy & Billings also became active in seeking confirmation of land claims.

Through the recommendation of Halleck and William Gwin, United States Senator from California (and rival of John Fremont), Congress passed the California Land Act of 1851. The Act placed full authority for adjudication of land claims in the courts and "marked a major step forward" by eliminating Congress from the procedure.[38] A Claims Commission of three members appointed by the President was to hear testimony and to study the documents presented by claimants. The Commission could either confirm or reject

Los Cerritos adobe house, c. 1900. (Courtesy Seaver Center for Western History Research, Los Angeles.)

the claims and either side could appeal to the District Court, but the process was fraught with delay.

Part of the delay in confirming land claims was the lack of documents in possession of the claimants, vaguely defined boundaries, a lack of improvements on the land to indicate compliance with Mexican law, and some fraudulent claims. The many newcomers to the state during the post-gold rush days were unsympathetic to large land holdings and often settled on portions of grants, claiming they did not know they were on private property. Squatters rights further confused the issue. Other problems stemmed from the necessity of hiring costly lawyers; the different laws, customs, and languages faced by Hispanic claimants; the cost of transportation to San Francisco; and the long time necessary to receive a final patent. Confirmation of the Simi grant, the first in Ventura County, took 14 years, or until 1865, to be patented.[39] Even though the Land Commission has been characterized as moving very slowly, it considered 813 claims in 5 years. Of these, 603 claims were confirmed, 190 rejected, and the rest withdrawn. Even though 209 claims were not appealed by either side, the appeals process for the others placed an additional burden of time and money on the claimants.[40]

Arguments for and against the process for confirming land claims in California abound. For an accurate appraisal of the work of the Claims Commission, one must look at the merits of each case. Several excellent books and numerous articles have been written about individual ranchos and their grantees in California. Many others with abundant manuscript sources await publication.[41] A typical example among recent contributions is the story of Rancho Jesús María in Santa Barbara County by Lois Roberts. A grant made to three members of the Olivera family in 1837 and sold to Lewis T. Burton, an American, is traced through the Claims Commission and brought up to modern times.[42]

An interesting sidelight to the usual discussion is Geoffrey Mawn's exception to a statement by William Carey Jones that there were no "regular surveys made of grants in California . . ." and that "[T]here was no public or authorized surveyor in the country."[43] Mawn's article on Jasper

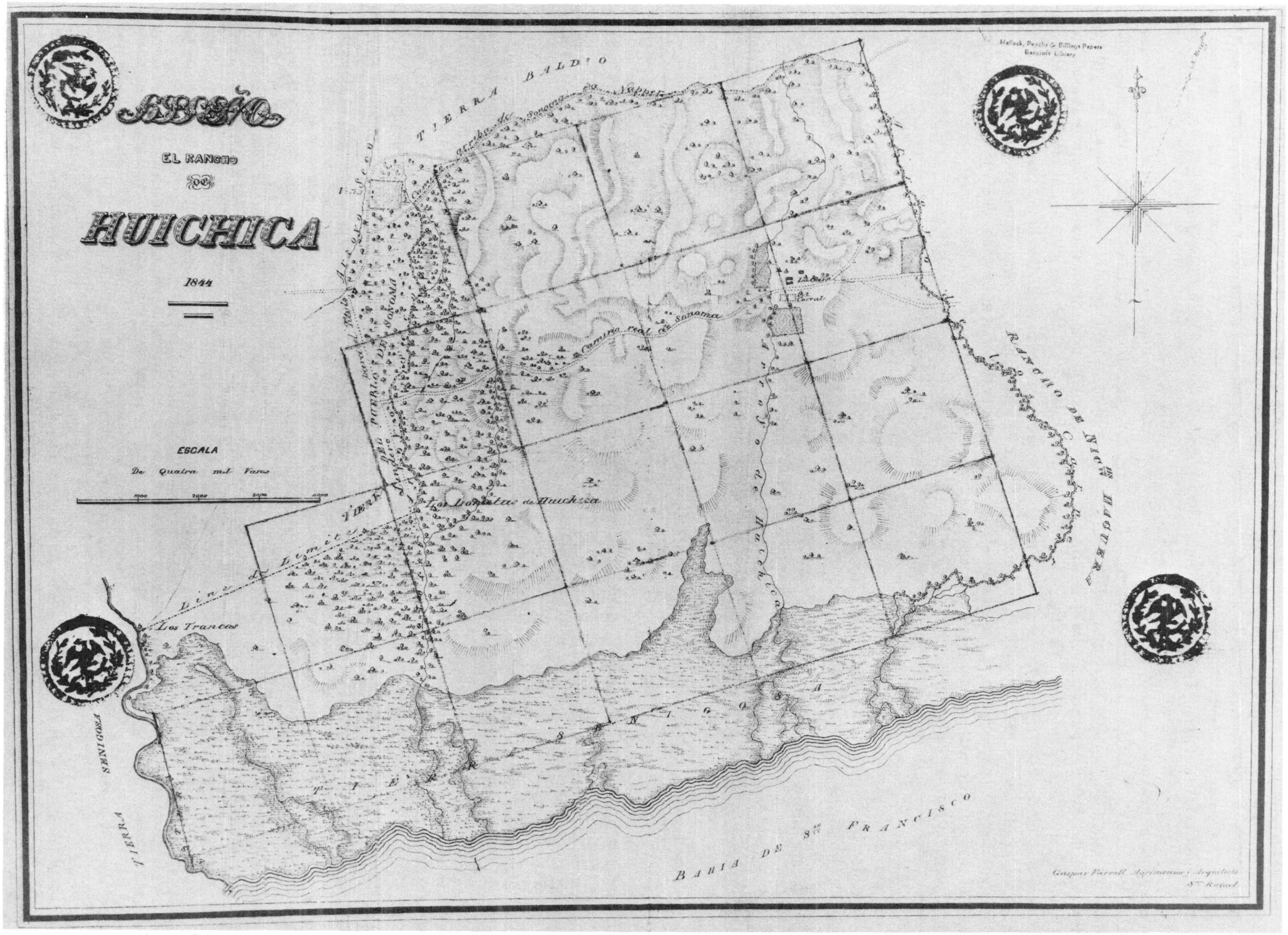

Jasper O'Farrell's diseño for Rancho Huichica, shown as grant no. 25 on the map of California This diseño was drawn for the grant's owner, Jacob P. Leese in 1844. Note the indication of common land (tierra baldio) on the north. (From ***California Ranco Diseños: Designs on the Land****, by Robert H. Becker. Courtesy the Book Club of California, San Francisco.)*

O'Farrell covers the career of this professional who surveyed and mapped at least 21 Mexican land grants in both southern and northern California between January 1844 and May 1846. O'Farrell's *diseños* of Timothy Murphy's Rancho Punta de San Pedro and Pío and Andres Pico's Rancho Santa Margarita y las Flores show that he was not only a competent surveyor, but also a skilled draftsman.[44]

If the 1850s were difficult for rancho claimants because of rigid land-title examinations, litigation costs, and interminable appeals, the 1860s brought new troubles in the form of grasshoppers, cattle disease, floods, and, finally, a severe drought. These, plus oppressive property taxes, made it difficult, if not impossible, for the California dons to maintain their large estates. Some of the more remote ranchos, and those of a few far-sighted families, remained intact through the years, but many of the original claimants sold out to new arrivals such as Lewellyn and Jotham Bixby and their partner James Irvine.[45] Even so, these large landholdings, one of the most enduring legacies inherited from Spain and Mexico, "remained the controlling factor in much of the state's settlement and agricultural development for nearly half a century."[46]

Although times have changed and California life seems to have given way to a frantic pace, the heritage of the ranchos lives on in memory. The romantic image of hard-riding vaqueros branding their calves on the unfenced range is a part of the state's history and allows many owners of ranch-style homes nestled in the Simi Valley or gracing the beachfront at Malibu to think in terms of this colorful past. As more individual stories are written, these, too, will enhance the understanding of California's earliest pioneers.

NOTES

1. Robert Glass Cleland, *The Cattle on a Thousand Hills: Southern California, 1850-1880* (San Marino, CA: The Huntington Library, 1941), remains popular as a standard work on the rancho period. Another is W.W. Robinson, *Land in California* (Berkeley, 1948).
2. *Merced de tierra de un soldado y sus descendientes.* California Archives 1, 177-180, Bancroft Library, Berkeley, CA. Butrón and his Indian wife abandoned their small plot three years later.
3. In comparison to New Mexico, where settlement began in 1598, and even to Texas, where the first settlers arrived in 1718, this is rather late. Ranchos begin in Baja California about 1730.
4. The natives were traditional hunters and gatherers with approximately 135 regional dialects. They lived in small villages called *rancherias* by the Spaniards within fairly well defined linguistic boundaries. See David Hornbeck, *California Patterns: A Geographical and Historical Atlas* (Palo Alto, CA: Mayfield Publishing Co., 1983), 32-37.
5. The first missionaries, accompanied by a contingent of soldiers, arrived in 1769 from Baja California where the Franciscans had replaced the Jesuits in 1768. Within a decade, the friars had established eight missions complete with church, cemetery, priest's house, schoolrooms, orchards, and vineyards.
6. The ranchos of the missions, called mission lands, did not seem to have any set limit and ultimately extended from one to the next. See Manuel P. Servín, "The Secularization of the California Missions," *Southern California Quarterly*, 47 (June 1965): 135-136.
7. El Pueblo de Nuestra Señora la Reina de los Angeles, second to San José (founded in 1777) was established by instructions from Gov. Felipe de Neve on 4 Sept. 1781, with 11 families.
8. Land Commission, Case No. 403, "Rancho San Rafael," 26.
9. *Ibid.* See also W.W. Robinson, *Ranchos Become Cities* (Pasadena, CA: San Pasqual Press, 1939), 33-39.
10. Basic legislation for the New World was gathered together under orders of Carlos II in 1690 as the *Recopilación de leyes de los reynos de las Indias* (*Laws of the Indies*). See Iris H.W. Engstrand, "California Ranchos: Their Hispanic Heritage," *Southern California Quarterly*, 67 (Fall 1985): 281-290.
11. Galindo Navarro to Ugarte y Loyola, 27 Oct. 1785; California Archives 52, 809-813, Bancroft Library, Berkeley, CA.
12. *Ibid.*
13. Robert G. Cowan, *Ranchos of California: A List of Spanish Concessions 1775-1822 and Mexican Grants 1822-1846* (Los Angeles, CA: Historical Society of Southern California, 1977), 87. See also Rose H. Aviña, *Spanish and Mexican Land Grants in California* (MA Thesis, University of California, Berkeley, 1932, repr. in San Francisco by R and E Associates, 1973).
14. Cowan, *Ranchos in California*, 52, 86.
15. During Borica's administration, from 1794 to 1800, five missions and a third civilian pueblo, Villa de Branciforte, were founded.
16. Formally called Rancho Nuestra Señora del Refugio and San José de Gracia de Simí. See Cowan, *Ranchos of California*, 67, 98.
17. Servin, "Secularization of the California Missions," 139.
18. Father Serra had opposed Governor Neve's founding of towns. See Serra to Bucareli, Monterey, 30 June 1778, in Antonine Tibesar, *Writings of Junípero Serra* (Washington, D.C,: American Academy of Franciscan History, 1955), vol. III, 99.
19. Servin, "Secularization of the California Missions," 137.
20. Secularization was first proposed by the exiled Spanish Cortes in a decree of 4 Sept. 1813, and again by the revolutionary regime of Rafael Riego in October 1820. See James M. Breedlove, "Effect of the Cortes, 1810-1822, on Church Reform in Spain and Mexico," in *Mexico and the Spanish Cortes*, Nettie Lee Benson, ed. (Austin, TX: University of Texas Press, 1966), 133.
21. Cowan, *Ranchos in California*, 36, 71, 90, 104.
22. Manuel Dublan and José María Lozano, *Legislación Mexicana* (2 vols., Mexico, 1876), 712; John W. Dwinelle, *The Colonial History of the City of San Francisco* (San Francisco, CA, 1863), add. XII, 23-24. One square league equals 2.6 miles square and contains 4,438 acres based on the 1837 Mexican measurement of 32.99206 inches to a *vara*.
23. Dwinelle, *Colonial History of San Francisco*, add. XII, 25-26; Avina, *Spanish and Mexican Land Grants*, 133-134. There were no empresario grants in California such as those given in Texas.
24. This record comprised the Jimeno and Hartnell Index of Land Concessions in California from 1830 to 1846. See also Robert H. Becker, *Diseños of California Ranchos. Maps of Thirty-seven Land Grants [1822-1846] from the Records of the U.S. District Court* (San Francisco, CA: The Book Club of California, 1964).
25. Gerald J. Geary, *The Secularization of the California Missions (1810-1846)* (Washington, D.C., 1934), 89-91.
26. Echeandía, Decreto de Emancipación a favor de Neófitos, 25 July 1826, MS quoted in Hubert Howe Bancroft, *History of California* (San Francisco, CA: The History Company, 1886), vol. III, 102-103.
27. Geary, *Secularization of the California Missions*, 108-113; Servin, "Secularization of the California Missions," 140-141.
28. Decree of José Figueroa, 9 Aug. 1834; Avina, *Spanish and Mexican Land Grants*, 32; Dwinelle, *Colonial History*, add. XV, 26-27.
29. Regranted with above in 1844 to the American Juan José (Jonathan Trumbull) Warner. The ranch, well known for its hot springs, later became a stop on the Butterfield Stage route.
30. Cecil C. Moyer, *Historic Ranchos of San Diego County* (San Diego, CA: Union-Tribune Publishing Co., 1969), 11-15, 22-30, 37-40, 61-63.
31. Eugene B. Drake, comp., *Jimeno's and Hartnell's Indexes of Land Concessions, from 1830-1846* (San Francisco, CA: Kenny & Alexander, 1861).
32. For a complete list of Los Angeles County ranchos, see Robinson, *Ranchos Become Cities*, 219-226.
33. Quoted in Chris Perez, *Grants of Land in California Made by Spanish or Mexican Authorities* (Sacramento, CA: State Lands Commission, 1982), 3.
34. Henry W. Halleck, "Report on the Laws and Regulations Relative to Grants or Sales of Public Lands in California" (Washington, D.C.: U.S. Congress, *House Executive Document No. 17*, 1850), 119-122.
35. William Carey Jones, *Report on the Subject of*

Land Titles in California (Washington, D.C., 9 Mar. 1850), 38-39.

36. Paul W. Gates, "The Fremont-Jones Scramble for California Land Claims," *Southern California Quarterly*, 56 (Spring 1974) 21.
37. Paul Gates, a leading authority on land in California, believes the land commission did as well as possible under the circumstances. See Gates, "The California Land Act of 1851," *California Historical Quarterly*, 50 (Dec. 1971): 395-430; "California's Embattled Settlers," *California Society Quarterly*, 41 (June 1962): 99-130.
38. Gates, "The California Land Act," 398.
39. Andrew Rolle, *California: A History*, 4th ed. (Arlington Heights, IL: Harlan Davidson, 1987), 237. Leonard Pitt, *The Decline of the Californios* (Berkeley, CA: University of California Press, 1966), presents a good summary of the rancheros' plight.
40. Ogden Hoffman, *Reports of Land Cases, Determined in the United States District Court for the Northern District of California, 1853-1858* (San Francisco, CA: Numa Hubert, 1862), app., table of land claims; Perez, *Grants of Land in California*, 4.
41. In 1961, the judges of the U.S. District Court in San Francisco gave the Bancroft Library more than 100,000 pages of testimony, legal documents, and exhibits regarding land grants. These included 1,500 maps with several hundred diseños. See Becker, *Diseños of California Ranchos*, intro.
42. Lois J. Roberts, "Rancho Jesús María, Santa Barbara County," *Southern California Quarterly*, 48 (Spring 1986): 1-35. Another good example is Richard Griswold del Castillo, "The del Valle Family and the Fantasy Heritage," *California History*, 59 (Spring 1980): 2-15.
43. Geoffrey P. Mawn, "'*Agrimenso y Arquitecto*': Jasper O'Farrell's Surveying in Mexican California," *Southern California Quarterly*, 56 (Spring 1974): 1-12.
44. *Ibid.*, 4.
45. The Bixby and Irvine families gained a vast amount of former rancho land in Los Angeles and Orange Counties.
46. Cleland, *Cattle on a Thousand Hills*, 4.

Iris H. W. Engstrand is currently professor and chair, Department of History, University of San Diego. She is the author of numerous books and articles on the Hispanic and American West and serves as a consultant on land and water rights for the states of California and New Mexico.

Land Litigation and The Idea of New Mexico Progress

G. Emlen Hall

SINCE the sixteenth century successive sovereigns have washed over the surface of New Mexico. With the waves of conquest, Spain, Mexico, and then the United States each brought their own legal system for arranging the underlying land. When the waves receded, each sovereign left the flotsam and jetsam of its land laws on the New Mexico beachheads. Even today, the New Mexico land is littered with important elements of Spanish and Mexican land law and Native-American practice.[1]

In addition, each successive wave of sovereignty encountered an established culture, or, in the case of the more recent conquerors, cultures, when they reached the new shores. Those established cultures saw the land, and its applicable laws, in distinct ways. Indians, Hispanos, and Anglos conceive differently the shared space to which the changing land laws applied. Native-American Pueblos relentlessly organized the natural world around them to reflect fundamentally religious values. Hispanos placed their conception of land on the hard rock of human use and, as a result, tied property directly to the life-giving rivers, largely disregarding the rest. Anglo-Americans returned to the Pueblo system, but this time reflected the peculiar American view of property as a marketable commodity.[2]

The combination of the changing land laws of each sovereign and their fundamentally different conceptions of real property guaranteed confusion. That confusion resulted in misunderstanding, suspicion and bitterness. But it also produced a society that could not agree on methods for solving differences of any kind, but especially those related to the land base. This fundamental disagreement meant that the legal systems of all New Mexico sovereignties had great difficulty resolving land disputes.

In the language of the law, *stare decisis* (the principle that once a decision is made, it is made forever) was hard to achieve. Common law systems for adjudicating disputes are based on the principle of *stare decisis*. American law has latched onto the doctrine with a vengeance, making it particularly applicable to disputes over land. United States courts have created a special, particularly hidebound form of *stare decisis* called "the rule of property."[3] According to this rule, once a property matter involving land is decided, whether right or wrong, it cannot be litigated again or altered in the courts.

This fundamental conservatism reflects a general antipathy toward change in the American legal system. It also embodies a unique legal contribution of United States law to property law in general — a contribution which made real property a fully marketable commodity, a basis for great American wealth, and the ground for investment-backed expectations of great return.[4] To make such investments sure, United States courts made property decisions particularly hard to relitigate, reconsider, or change.

The problem was that in New Mexico, this legal preference for permanent property decisions ran smack up against the fact that sovereigns and their laws kept changing while the local cultures never sufficiently integrated to achieve a single vision of what "property" was and how the rules of law should apportion it. As a result, the same property disputes surfaced again and again throughout New Mexico legal history, without becoming completely resolved. The cycles of New Mexico conquest produced endless rounds of the same litigation.[5]

This repetition of the same legal complaints is found throughout New Mexico history. Take the long view and it is pervasive.

New Mexico Pueblos have the longest history by virtue of their settling in the high desert first. From the Pueblos' perspective, the history of New Mexico land is the history of their endless effort to defend their holdings against the relentless pressure of newcomers and settlers to New Mexico, using whatever sovereign jurisdiction and laws were available at that particular time.[6] But there are more subtle and important threads in this tapestry of endless litigation which show more clearly the warp and woof of New Mexico land law over the centuries.

Take, for example, the 250-year Santa Clara Pueblo struggle, under Spanish, Mexican, and United States law, to work out the relationship of the Pueblo and the individual Indian tribes and the lands they occupied. The story does not involve brash attempts by outsiders to take Pueblo resources. Instead, it involves a Pueblo's efforts to define itself under essentially foreign laws.

The Santa Clara effort began in 1744 when Roque Conjuebes, a self-described "Indio-ladino" (by which I think he meant that he was a Spanish-speaking Pueblo Indian) filed a curious petition regarding land in the Santa Clara Pueblo of which he was a member.[7] Some background on the legal status of Pueblo land in 1744 helps explain the Conjuebes

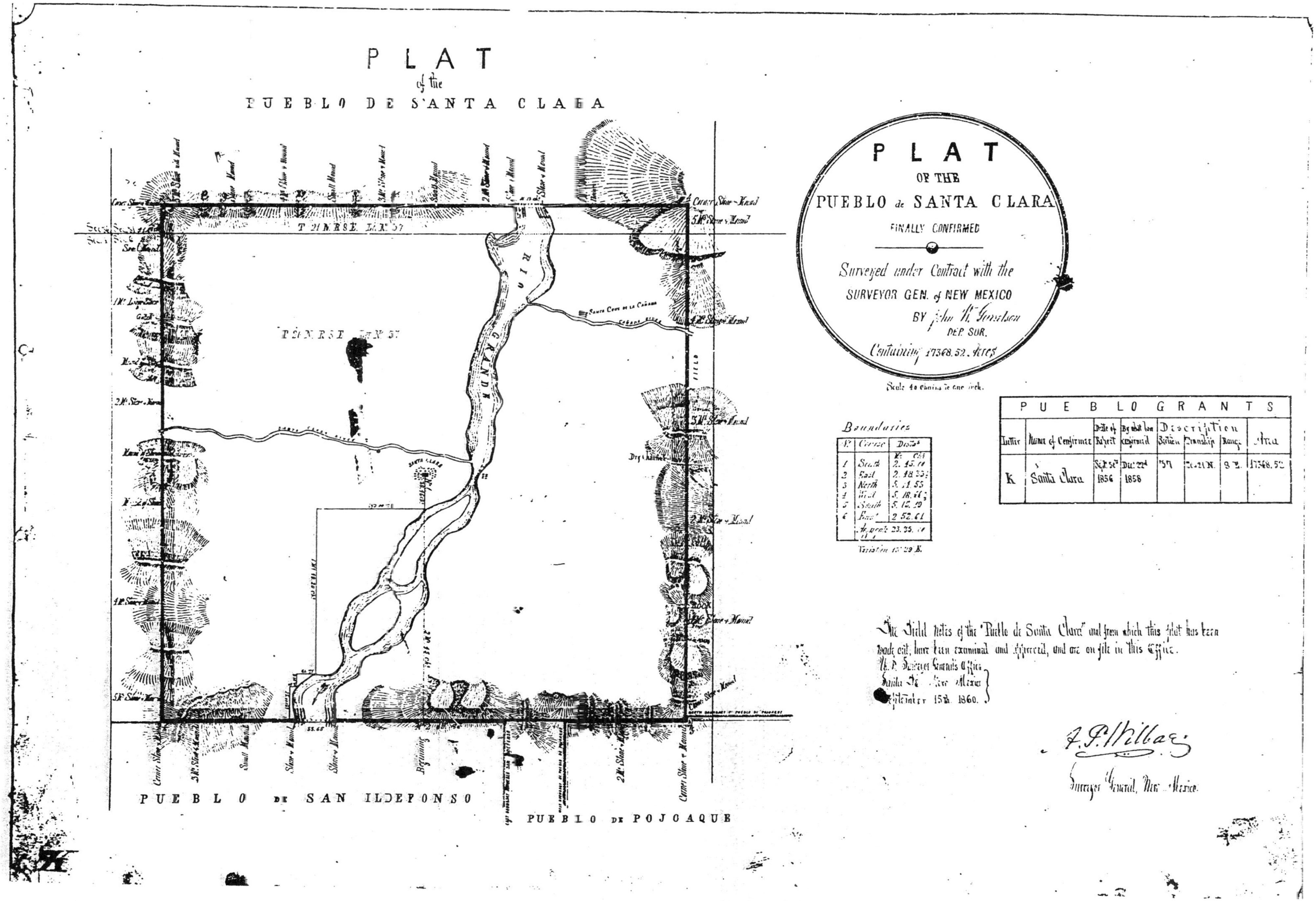

1860 survey plat for Santa Clara Pueblo. (Courtesy Bureau of Land Management, Santa Fe.)

This May 1951 aerial photograph shows the reach of the Rio Grande River between the Santa Clara Pueblo at the center on the north, just west of the river, and Black Mesa to the south, just east of the river. Roque Conjuebes's 1744 petition did not identify the particular land he sought, but it probably lay opposite the Pueblo and east of the river, in the vicinity of present day La Mesilla. (Photo part of the public records of the USGS.)

petition. Pueblo land use then, as today, resembled Hispanic land use. Both agreed that the relatively unproductive and jointly used uplands belonged to the community. Individual Indian families, like Hispanic ones, farmed particular irrigated tracts along the river bottoms and for the most part, kept what their tract produced. But Hispanos owned their particular tracts. Individual Pueblos generally understood that they held their farming plots not as private property but on temporary assignment from the Pueblo entity.[8]

The 1744 Conjuebes petition to New Mexico Governor Codallos y Roybal went to the heart of this ownership distinction. In it, Conjuebes described himself as the owner of more than 100 cattle, 80 mares and some other stock. As a member of the Santa Clara Pueblo, he worked land assigned to him. But the demands of the Pueblo on him were so great that he did not have time to care for his own farm operations. He petitioned the New Mexico civil governor to emancipate him from the Pueblo and grant him the lands that he worked as his own private property.[9]

Governor Codallos y Rabal treated Conjuebes' application as a petition for a land grant from the Spanish public domain despite the fact that the land lay well within the league of land traditionally viewed as belonging to each Pueblo. First, the Spanish governor sent a priest to Santa Clara to make sure that Conjuebes knew and accepted the Catholic faith. Not only did Conjuebes recite perfectly the prayers from the rosary, he also guaranteed that he would pay his tithe to the Church if the governor granted him the land.[10]

On 15 September 1744, the Governor sent a civil official, the alcalde from nearby Santa Cruz de la Cañada, to check out the Conjuebes application. Alcalde Francisco Ortiz reported that he went to Santa Clara and consulted with the Pueblo officials. They had, he said, no objections to Conjuebes' request. So Ortiz took Conjuebes by the hand and, following the ritual act of possession common to Spanish land grants of the public domain, put Conjuebes in private possession of a part of the aboriginal Santa Clara Pueblo lands and emancipated him from the Pueblo.[11] In the process, Conjuebes had gone from an "indio ladino" to a "latino" and the Santa Clara Pueblo had lost communal land to a private citizen.

The grant to Conjuebes went against the grain of existing Spanish treatment of Pueblo lands in two ways. In the Spanish view, Pueblo land belonged to the Pueblo as a corporate community, not to its individual members. In any case, no one could convey Pueblo land to non-Indians. New

Threshing with horses at Santa Clara Pueblo, c. 1915. (Photo by Carlos Vierra. Neg. no. 42732. Courtesy Museum of New Mexico.)

Mexico Governor Codallos y Rabal violated both principles in granting the Conjuebes request.[12]

But for more than 70 years no one formally complained about the grant. Roque Conjuebes and two succeeding generations used their ranch within the boundaries of the Santa Clara Pueblo grant as their own.

Then, in 1813 Alberto Maynez returned to New Mexico on his second stint as governor, and all hell broke loose among the Pueblos and their Hispanic neighbors in general and in particular at Santa Clara. Trouble began in 1815 when the Taos Pueblo complained to Governor Maynez about non-Indians living within the boundaries of the Taos Pueblo Grant. In fact, said the Taos Pueblo, the plaza of the Hispanic town of Taos sat on Indian land. The Taos Pueblo wanted all the non-Indians out. After much procedural finagling, Governor Maynez upheld the sanctity of the Taos Pueblo land and ordered Hispanos out.[13] In fact, they never left; in 1815 more Hispanics lived within the boundaries of Pueblo grants than did native Indians. Pueblos were bitter. Hispanos were jumpy. Word of Maynez's Taos Pueblo decision sent shock waves up and down the spine of New Mexico's nervous system, the Rio Grande.

The news soon reached Antonio Conjuebes, Roque's grandson, then working land, within the Santa Clara Pueblo, inherited from his grandfather. Pueblo officials heard of the Maynez decision at Taos Pueblo and started to grumble at the presence of non-Indians among them. Instead of waiting for Maynez to throw him out, using what Antonio Conjuebes called the Governor's "*raras ideas*" (crack pot theories), Conjuebes took the initiative. He went straight to Durango, Mexico, more than a thousand miles away, and asked military authorities there to confirm his family's private possession of land within the Santa Clara Pueblo granted by the Spanish government 70 years before in 1744.

On two separate trips in 1815 and 1816, Antonio Conjuebes argued his case to the Durango commander general. He intimated that the Maynez decision at Taos had so "agitated" the Rio Grande Pueblos that violence might break out. He begged for government protection of his individual property rights. He insisted that, if nothing else, more than 70 years of actual adverse possession by his family had to confer some property rights no matter what the Santa Clara's legal title might be.[14]

For the next 150 years Hispanos would repeat each of Antonio Conjuebes' arguments to justify their possession of Pueblo land. In particular, the claim that long-standing adverse possession justified non-Indian trespassers on either legal or equitable grounds would return again and again. Seventy years seemed sufficient to Conjuebes. Two hundred years would seem even more compelling when the same issue returned in the 1920s.[15] But in 1816 neither Conjuebes nor his threats worked in Durango.

On Conjuebes' second trip to Durango in 1816, several Santa Clara Pueblo officials accompanied (or followed) him. The Indian leaders told the Durango officials that they did indeed object to the Conjuebes landholdings. The Santa Clara Pueblo grant, they argued, belonged to the Pueblo as an entity. No individual Indian owned a particular part of it. To make matters worse, the Conjuebes weren't even Pueblo anymore. Seventy years could not change the fact that the non-Indians did not belong.[16]

The Durango officials finally agreed. The last 1816 order in the archive directs the Conjuebes to rejoin the Pueblo, acknowledge its superior title, and submit to the obligations of Pueblo membership if they wanted to stay on their land. Otherwise Antonio Conjuebes and his family would have to get out.[17]

At this point, Spanish law had resolved Santa Clara Pueblo's internal land problems by affirming the exclusively Indian and communal nature of the Pueblo claim to land. It is not clear from the surviving record what election, if any, the Conjuebes made. But it is clear that the debate within the Santa Clara Pueblo about the relative rights of the Pueblo continued into the period of Mexican sovereignty after 1821.

The change from Spanish to Mexican sovereignty affected Pueblo landholdings in a particularly controversial manner. Among other things, the Mexican government instituted legal changes in property ownership. These changes favored the individualization of communally held property and eliminated any racial distinctions between Indians and non-Indians in New Mexico. After 1821, New Mexico officials brought these new rules to bear on local Pueblos with a vengeance. The Pueblos suffered great land loss as a result, particularly at the Pecos Pueblo.[18]

At the Santa Clara Pueblo, the new Mexico land policy favoring individual over communal property fell right into the legal abyss that had divided the Santa Clara Pueblo since 1744. The Mexican version of Pueblo status and land ownership clearly favored the Conjuebes faction of the Pueblo and its belief in private, non-Indian land within Pueblos. While no formal Santa Clara Pueblo suit galvanized the Pueblo factions concerning the new Mexican law, debate did surface quietly through the marked increase in sales by individual Pueblo Indians to non-Indians after 1821. The principles that the Conjuebes faction had fought for and lost under Spanish rule in Durango in 1816, prevailed under Mexican rule. The deeds of sale from Pueblo farmers to Hispanos between 1821 and 1846 represented the victory of individual over communal ownership and of racial homogeneity over distinct — and preferred — racial class.[19]

Under Spain the Santa Clara Pueblo had triumphed, at least in principle. Under Mexico, it had lost. However, the battle did not end with the arrival of the United States in 1846. It just shifted laws — from Mexican to United States' — and forums — from private deeds of sale to the office of the United States Superintendent for Indian Affairs in New Mexico.

Apparently, New Mexico Pueblos welcomed United States' rule or at least the change from Mexican sovereignty that it offered. Almost as soon as the Americans opened shop in Santa Fe in 1848, emissaries from the Pueblo came into town, welcoming the new government, complaining about the terrible land losses they had suffered under Mexican rule and asking for relief from the new United States government. For the most part, federal officials had no idea what the Pueblos were talking about.[20]

Among other things, a new slot had opened for the old Santa Clara debate. On 16 October 1852, Indian agent John Ward recorded the following entry in the agency day book:

> The Governor of Santa Clara with another Indian from the same Pueblo came in to see the Superintendent today about some land belonging to the Santa Clara Pueblo, [whose owner] sometime ago left the said Pueblo in consequence of his disobedience to the authorities thereof and now it appears that he wants to sell the land which he lived on previous to his leaving the Pueblo. [The Superintendent] told them that they must have a council composed of three Pueblo governors and to lay the case before them, and whatever they decide on, the parties must abide by in order to put an end to the question.[21]

An end to the question, indeed. Here in 1852, a brand new United States official viewed a problem that had popped up in 1744, 1816 and the 1830s with no sense of the historical depth of the problem he confronted.

Existing federal law, brought to New Mexico in 1848 by the United States, might have settled (and eventually did settle) the ancient Santa Clara issue brought to Indian Agent Ward in 1852. But for the moment, he referred the problem

*Harvest and corrals with **horno** (outdoor oven) in foreground. Santa Clara. (Photo no. 33250 taken in 1920s or 1930s. Virginia Johnson Collection. Courtesy State Records Center & Archives, Santa Fe.)*

to the Pueblos themselves for application, presumably, of their own law. A week later, a Santa Clara Pueblo leader brought back the Pueblo answer:

> The council which Mr. Grenier ordered to take place on Thursday last had come off . . . and that the Indians of San Juan, San Ildefonso, and Santa Clara were the principals of the council and that they had decided that the Pueblo lands are a general gift to the people of said Pueblo by the Spanish government, and that if any individual thinks proper to disobey the orders of the authorities of said Pueblo and leaves in consequence thereof, in such cases the individual so doing has no right to sell any of the land which he might have had in his charge, or neither has a right to sell the improvements thereon, and if he or they insist on leaving the Pueblo, as in this case, they may leave and suffer the consequences.[22]

Indian Agent Ward did not know it in 1852, but in Durango, Mexico, exactly the same decision was written in 1816. The problem was that the 1816 decision had not ended the internal Pueblo debate nor did the one in 1852.

United States rule between 1846 and 1912 left the Pueblos to their own devices just as Ward's 1852 "solution" to the Santa Clara Pueblo problem had. With no permanent solution, the old Santa Clara debate went right on. Individual Pueblos continued to sell to non-Indians, property that they considered their own and not the Pueblos'. In one of the most egregious instances, individual Santa Clarans got together in the 1890s and sold a huge tract on the east side of the Rio Grande and within the Pueblo grant to the Surveyor General of New Mexico, the primary federal land official in New Mexico.[23]

By then, of course, no new sovereigns would arrive to provide a new bottle into which the Santa Clara Pueblo could pour its old troubles. As it turned out, however, shifts in United States jurisdictional arrangements for New Mexico provided enough new and different forums to keep the endless Pueblo debate alive.

For one, in 1912 New Mexico went from territorial status to that of a full-fledged state. Ironically, the increase in status for New Mexico also deprived the new state of any control over Pueblo affairs. As the price for statehood, the United States required New Mexico to disclaim any interest in Pueblo lands. In a case involving Santa Clara Pueblo land, the new State of New Mexico immediately challenged that restriction on state sovereignty and lost.

That decision left only federal law as the means for working out this ongoing Pueblo land debate: whether individual Indians, and, possibly, those non-Indians who might have purchased from them, had any right to lands within the boundaries of land grants confirmed to a corporate Pueblo community? Antonio Conjuebes had raised the issue in Durango in 1816. The Santa Clara Pueblo itself had presented it again in 1852 to the Indian agent. Now in 1913, the United States Supreme Court told the Santa Clara Pueblo that only federal Indian law could decide that question.[24]

Clara True, sometime missionary and Bureau of Indian Affairs employee, arrived in New Mexico c. 1910, as a school teacher at Glorieta, near the defunct Pecos Pueblo. From there she moved to the area of the Pueblos in the Northern Rio Grande basin. From ***Willie Boy: A Desert Manhunt****, by Harry Lawton. (Photo courtesy the Tome's Rivera Library, University of California, Riverside.)*

Despite the new context, the Santa Clara Pueblo divided bitterly once again over the same old problem. This time United States Indian law defined this issue: did Federal prohibitions against non-Indian acquisition of Indian property apply to Pueblos, so that people like Roque Conjuebes and his heirs could not legally own Pueblo land? And this time, a nosey intermeddler named Clara True, the sometimes representative of a Philadelphia-based Quaker group interested in Indian business, the Indian Rights Association (IRA), fanned the old Santa Clara Pueblo fires.[25]

Beginning in 1910 and continuing for years thereafter, Clara True reported to her Eastern employers about the split between the so-called "Santa Clara Conservatives," that group of traditional Santa Clarans who favored Pueblo corporate ownership and opposed all individual claimants to Pueblo land no matter how long they resided there, and the so-called "Santa Clara Progressives," a local Pueblo group who supported the individual holdings of families like the Conjuebes and their sometimes non-Indian successors. Tales of intra-Pueblo mayhem went regularly to IRA headquarters in Philadelphia.[26] True did not know it but this was an ancient Santa Clara Pueblo war.

She picked sides by favoring the Progressives' willingness to recognize individual possessions and railed against what she considered to be the Conservatives' slavish devotion to ancient ways. Clara True thus further divided the Santa Clara Pueblo against itself. More than political philosophy informed her choice of sides. In the federal investigations that followed the enactment of the Pueblo Lands Act of 1924, Clara True turned out to be a principal private claimant of Pueblo land.[27]

By any measure, the "Progressive" position at Santa Clara Pueblo won out in the 1924 legislation that prompted those investigations. In the Pueblo Lands Act, Congress recognized individual land claims against the Pueblo entities based on adverse individual possession for specified time periods.[28] As a result, all the Pueblos, including Santa Clara, lost much of their most valuable land.[29] But advocates of the position taken by the Santa Clara Conservatives did rescue some victories from the adjudication process established by the act. Among other things, John Collier, the chief architect of the losing Conservative position, which insisted on clearing the Pueblo grants of all individual claimants, still became Commissioner of Indian Affairs in 1933.[30]

Under Collier's direction, Congress enacted in 1934 the Indian Re-Organization Act (IRA). This comprehensive, and at the time radical, piece of Federal legislation was intended to revive and protect the right of tribal entities to communal self-government.[31] The Progressives at Santa Clara and others of like persuasion may have bested Collier with the 1924 Pueblo Lands Act and its recognition of private property within the Pueblos. But Collier had wrested a victory for the Conservative position in the 1934 Act's strengthening of Indian tribes' sovereign right of self-governance. This power was akin to the power that the Indian agent had recognized in the Pueblos in general and Santa Clara Pueblo in particular in 1852 when he had allowed the Pueblos themselves to determine the nature of individual and communal claims to Pueblo land. Then the Pueblos had acquired that power by default; now, in 1934, Congress explicitly confirmed it.

The Santa Clara Pueblo seized these new corporate powers and began to define formally, as the 1934 Indian Re-Organization Act said it could, membership in the Pueblo and the rights of individual access to the Pueblo's natural resources. By 1937 the Santa Clara Pueblo, as a formal body, had decided that the children of Santa Claran males who married outside the Pueblo could become members of the Pueblo community but that the children of Santa Clara females who married outside the Pueblo could not.[32] Much later, when required to explain this regulation first implemented in 1937 under the IRA, Santa Clarans and their representatives offered several justifications. Traditionally, they said, Santa Clara Pueblo was patriarchal; that tradition justified the preference for men embodied in the regulation. Furthermore, they suggested, internal growth had so strained Santa Clara's remaining resources that the Pueblo had to impose some restrictions on land use. The "male only" Santa Clara rule accomplished that.[33] It remained true to the Pueblo's own internal preferences. Even if individual Pueblos, particularly the heirs of Santa Clara women who had married non-Santa Clarans, chafed under the rule, the 1934 Indian Re-Organization Act authorized this blatantly gender-based discrimination against individuals in the name of the

Shucking corn at harvest time. Santa Clara Pueblo. (Neg. no. 42773. Courtesy Museum of New Mexico.)

corporate Pueblo authority to manage its own internal affairs.

Had the matter ended there under United States federal rule, individual Pueblos might have reached the end of the vein that Roque and Antonio Conjuebes and Clara True, among others, had mined since 1744 at the Santa Clara Pueblo. But in 1968 Congress intervened again in Indian affairs and enacted the Indian Civil Rights Act (ICRA). The 1968 law was designed to protect the rights of individual Indians against the perceived excesses of the tribal governments under which they lived. Nothing in the act's legislative history indicates that the situation in New Mexico Pueblos in general or, at Santa Clara in particular, prompted the new law.[34] But the fact remains that the 1934 Indian Re-Organization Act and the 1968 Indian Civil Rights Acts together staked out the boundaries of the same debate that had torn Santa Clara apart since 1744. If the 1934 act defined the rights claimed by the Pueblo since it first went to Durango in 1815, then the 1968 act re-affirmed those contradictory individualistic principles claimed by Roque Conjuebes when he first petitioned the Spanish government in 1744.

Of course, in the second half of the twentieth century, the new federal laws simply provided some new hooks on which the Pueblo could hang its old problems. With the contradictory 1934 and 1968 laws in place, it didn't take long for the old Santa Clara problem to re-appear.

In the fall of 1971, Julia Martinez, a full-blood Santa Clara Pueblo Indian, went to see a legal services attorney. For ten years she and her Navajo husband had tried to enroll the couple's eight children as members of the Santa Clara Pueblo. The children had all been born and resided in the Pueblo. They spoke the Santa Clara language and practiced the Santa Claran religion. However, Pueblo authorities refused to admit the Martinez children to formal membership because their father was not Santa Claran, even though their mother was, and the 1937 Pueblo rule, adopted under the 1934 IRA, still prohibited participation by the children of such mixed marriages. The rule seemed unfair to Mrs. Martinez, especially since it allowed full membership to the children of Santa Claran men who married outside the Pueblo while denying it to Santa Claran women in exactly the same circumstances.[35]

The legal aide lawyer to whom Mrs. Martinez brought her complaint immediately recognized the gender-based discrimination as a possible violation of the 1968 Indian Civil Rights Act and wrote the Santa Clara Pueblo governor telling him so.[36] That September 1971 letter began the litigation process that became the 1978 United States Supreme Court decision *Pueblo of Santa Clara v. Martinez*.[37] From the start, the issue posed by the litigation pitted the individual rights of Pueblo members, now embodied in the ICRA, against the communal rights of the corporate Pueblo entity to arrange its own affairs, now embodied in the IRA.

For a United States court in the twentieth century, the problem involved steering between two contradictory federal acts. But even in that esoteric world, the Martinez-Santa

Aerial view of Santa Clara Pueblo, c. 1931. (Photo by George Law. Neg. no. 48784. Courtesy Museum of New Mexico.)

THE LONG, SAD LIFE OF SANTA CLARA PUEBLO'S EFFORT TO DEFINE ITSELF

1540: Spain "discovers" New Mexico including the ancestral homelands of the Santa Clara Pueblo.

1744: Santa Clara Pueblo member Roque Conjuebes petitions the Spanish government for permission to leave the Pueblo but remain on the Pueblo land he traditionally had used. The Spanish government grants the request.

1815: Santa Clara Pueblo protests the continued occupancy by the heirs of Roque Conjuebes of land within the Pueblo granted by the Spanish civil authorities to Roque Conjuebes. Durango, Mexico authorities side with the Pueblo and order the heirs of Roque Conjuebes either to re-join the Pueblo or get out.

1821: Mexico takes over control of New Mexico from Spain. Individual non-Indians purchase Pueblo land either from individual or from Pueblos.

1848: United States takes over control of New Mexico from Mexico.

1852: Santa Clara Pueblo protests presence of non-Pueblo members on their lands. The United States government ducks the issue.

1851-1912: Pueblo Indians not allowed full federal protection of United States law. The Territory of New Mexico treats their lands a private lands and much land is lost to non-Indians.

1912-1924: New Mexico enters the union as a State but loses control over Pueblo Indian lands. Clara True and other Pueblo advocates resurrect the question of whether individual landholders who are not members of the Pueblos, like the heirs of Roque Conjuebes, have any rights to land within the Pueblos.

1924: Congress settles the Santa Clara debate by passing legislation approving non-Indian ownership of Pueblo land under certain circumstances.

1934: Congress enacts the Indian Re-Organization Act and reaffirms the communal power of Indian tribes, including Pueblos, to direct their own internal affairs.

1968: Congress enacts the Indian Civil Rights Act and affirms the rights of individual Tribal (and Santa Clara Pueblo) members against the Tribes (and Pueblos).

1971: Julia Martinez, like Roque Conjuebes a member of the Santa Clara Pueblo, protests the fact that the Pueblo will not allow her children to become members of the Pueblo because their father is not a member of the Pueblo. If their father had been a member of the Pueblo, but their mother had not, Pueblo rules would have allowed the children membership. Julia Martinez's protest begins six years of litigation.

1977: The United States Supreme Court decides on technical grounds in favor of the Santa Clara Pueblo's communal rights and against the rights of the individual members.

Clara Pueblo debate must have raised the specter of battles past. True enough, the demands of Julia Martinez and Roque Conjuebes differed. Mrs. Martinez's children wanted into the Santa Clara Pueblo and Roque Conjuebes and his children wanted out. The Martinez's were using the individual rights guaranteed by federal law to gain admission to the community while the Conjuebes asserted their rights under Spanish and Mexican law to gain their freedom from it. But in spite of these different alignments, the issue in both the earliest and in the most recent cases involved how the law would apply to the individual and the community.

Basically, the courts followed an unsure course in reaching an ultimate resolution of the Santa Clara problem. The Federal District Court, where Mrs. Martinez's case was first heard, sputtered along for almost three years in arcane legal maneuvering and finally chose the tribal sovereignty guaranteed by the Indian Re-Organization Act over the individual Constitutional guarantees afforded by the Indian Civil Rights Act. "Much has been written," concluded District Judge Edwin Mechem in his 1975 opinion, "about tribal sovereignty. If those words have any meaning at all, they must mean that a tribe can make and enforce its decisions without regard to whether an external authority considers those decisions wise."[38] On that basis, the Federal District Court denied the claim of Mrs. Martinez's children to full participation in the Pueblo. Chalk up a twentieth-century win for the Pueblo as a community.

The Tenth Circuit Court of Appeals then erased it. The appellate court began its review by noting that the gender-based discrimination against Mrs. Martinez and her children clearly violated the equal protection clause of the U.S. Constitution, whose protection the ICRA had guaranteed to individual Tribal members. From that point of departure, the court considered whether the interests guaranteed the Pueblo by the IRA outweighed the protections offered by the ICRA. Circuit Court Judge Doyle found they did not. The Tenth Circuit Court of Appeals reversed the balance struck by District Judge Mechem.[39] Both courts found themselves caught in the same dilemma that had plagued Santa Clara Pueblo since Roque Conjuebes had first appeared on the scene in 1744. These were old problems and hard choices in New Mexico, and none of the authorities felt either comfortable or very sure in picking between them.

Of course, that left the final choice to the United States Supreme Court. It chose not to choose. Justice Thurgood Marshall, speaking for a badly divided Supreme Court, ruled that Congress, in enacting the ICRA, had not intended to allow individual Indians like Mrs. Martinez to sue their own

Aerial view of Santa Clara Pueblo, c. 1931. (Photo by George Law. Neg. no. 48785. Courtesy Museum of New Mexico.)

tribes. No matter the injustice of the Santa Clara Pueblo in discriminating against the children of women, Congress had not authorized this suit.[40]

In a way, the Supreme Court decision favored the sovereignty of the Santa Clara polity over the claims of its individual members. To that extent, the court had come down on the side of the Pueblo against the claims of the likes of Roque Conjuebes. But, at a more fundamental level, the Supreme Court had simply found a new and equally arcane legal peg on which to hang the age-old Santa Clara problem.

In *Santa Clara v. Martinez,* the 1977 Supreme Court talked the language of sovereign immunity. In the Pueblo Lands Board Act of 1924, Congress had talked the language of adverse possession. In 1852, the Office of the Surveyor General talked self-determination. In the 1830s, Mexico talked privitization of corporate property. In 1816, Durango military officials talked the sanctity of the Pueblo community. In 1744, Spanish officials talked the sanctity of individual Catholic-conforming Pueblo members.

In all those two centuries of legal talk, no legal system had been able to lay the Santa Clara Pueblo problem to rest. The legacy of Roque Conjuebes survived while the laws and governments changed. In the relative scale of things, the problem posed by the likes of Roque Conjuebes was relatively minor, restricted as it was to an internal problem of the small group of Pueblos on the northern rim of the Hispanic southwest. But much bigger problems burst out in the same area over the same two hundred years, problems that involved the common use of shared waters by Indians and non-Indians, the development and ownership of aboriginally occupied lands, and the intricate relationship between undeveloped common land and unappropriated common water.[41] The courts and congresses of Spain, Mexico, and the United States were no more successful at putting these intractable problems to rest.

As a result the terrain of legal history in New Mexico and the Southwest is littered with the ancient detritus of old, incomplete lawsuits. Viewed in the long run, the mosaic of repetition has its own beauty. As the heirs of Roque Conjuebes and the Santa Clara Pueblo will tell you, the beauty has had its costs. But those costs are at least equalled by the terrifying prospect of laws that don't work and problems that won't go away.

NOTES

1. Myra Ellen Jenkins and Albert H. Schroeder, *A Brief History of New Mexico* (Albuquerque, NM: University of New Mexico Press, 1974).
2. Alfonso Ortiz, *The Tewa World: Space, Time, Being and Becoming in a Pueblo Society* (Chicago, IL: University of Chicago Press, 1969); Victor Westphall, *Merecedes Reales: Hispanic Land Grants of the Upper Rio Grande Region* (Albuquerque, NM: University of New Mexico Press, 1983); Victor Westphall, *The Public Domain in New Mexico, 1854-1891* (Albuquerque, NM: University of New Mexico Press, 1965). As usual, Walt Whitman expressed the Anglo drive best when in "Song of the Redwood Tree" (1874) he described ". . . the New arriving, assuming, taking possession. A swarming and busy race settling and organizing everywhere."
3. See most recently *Nevada v. United States*, 463 US 110, 129 and FN 10 (1982).
4. Milton J. Horwitz, *The Transformation of American Law, 1780-1860* (Cambridge, MA: Harvard University Press, 1977), 31 ff.
5. Edward Spicer, *Cycles of Conquest: The Impact of Spain, Mexico and the United States on the Indians of the Southwest* (Tucson, AZ: University of Arizona Press, 1962).
6. G. Emlen Hall, *The Four Leagues of Pecos: A Legal History of the Pecos Grant, 1800-1933* (Albuquerque, NM: University of New Mexico Press, 1984).

7. Undated 1744 petition of Roque Conjuebes to Governor Codallos y Rabal, Spanish Archives of New Mexico, SANM, I:213.
8. For example, United States v. Sandoval, 13 US 28 (1913); Leo Crane, *Desert Drums: The Pueblo Indians of New Mexico, 1540-1928* (Boston, MA: Little, Brown and Co., 1928).
9. 1744 petition of Conjuebes to Governor, SANM, I:213.
10. 24 Aug. 1744 certificate by Vic. Santiago de Roybal, SANM, I:213.
11. 1 Sept. 1744 order of Governor Codallos y Rabal and 15 Sept. 1744 report of alcalde Francisco Ortiz in SANM, I:213. For a description of the ritual act of granting possession of land see generally Ebright, *The Tierra Amarilla Grant: A History of Chicanery* (Santa Fe, NM: Center for Land Grant Studies, 1980), and Myra Ellen Jenkins, "The Baltasar Baca Grant: History of an Encroachment," *El Palacio*, 68 (Spring 1961): 47-64; (Summer 1961): 87-105.
12. *U.S. v. Candelaria*, 271 US 432 (1926); Recopilación de las Leyes los Reinos de las Indias, book IV, title 12, law 9 and VI-3-20.
13. Dispute concerning Taos Pueblo Land 1815-1816; SANM, I:1134; Myra Ellen Jenkins, "Taos Pueblo and Its Neighbors, 1540-1847," *NMHR*, 41, No. 2 (1966): 85-114.
14. Undated (August 1815) petition by Antonio Conjuebes to the Honorable Commander General of Durango, and second petition 15 Oct. 1815, SANM, I:213.
15. Hall, *Four Leagues of Pecos*, 234-237; G. Emlen Hall, "Pueblo Grant Labyrinth" in Briggs and VanNess, eds., *Land, Water and Culture* (Albuquerque, NM: University of New Mexico Press, 1987).
16. Undated (Summer 1816), The Republic of Santa Clara to the Honorable Commander General, SANM, I:213.
17. 8 Aug. 1816 Decree, SANM, I:213.
18. G. Emlen Hall and David J. Weber, "Mexican Liberals and the Pueblo Indians, 1821-1829" *NMHR*, 59:1 (January 1984): 1-32.
19. Hall and Weber, "Mexican Liberals," and Hall, "Pueblo Grant Labyrinth."
20. Hall, *Four Leagues of Pecos*, 66-90.
21. Ward entry, 16 Oct. 1852 in Annie H. Abel, *The Official Correspondence of James C. Calhoun* (Washington, D.C.: U.S. Government Printing Office, 1915) 217-218.
22. Ward entry, 23 Oct. 1852 in Abel, *Correspondance*, 220.
23. Richard H. Frost, "Relations Between the Pueblo Indians and the Federal Government, with Particular Reference to Water Rights" (Unpub. ms., Chicago, IL: Center for the History of the American Indian, 1980), 117-124.
24. *United States v. Sandoval*, 13, US 28 (1913).
25. See, e.g. Hagerman to Wilbur, 22 July 1929 in NARG (National Archives, Record Group) 75, 013, pt. 3-A.
26. For example, statement of Father Ketcham, including letter from True on split at Santa Clara Pueblo, before Senate Committee on Indian Affairs on Senate Bill 6085, Feb. 1913 (Washington, D.C.: Government Printing Office).
27. Hagerman to Wilbur, 22 July 1929; Hagerman to Charles J. Rhodes, 2 Oct. 1929, in NARG 75, 013, pt. 11; True is listed as a defendant in *U.S. v. Rupert Archuleta*, one of the first twentieth century suits asserting the Pueblo right to land.
28. Act of 7 June 1924, 43 Stat. 636; Hall, *Four Legends of Pecos*, 221-245.
29. Summary of Reports and Court Actions by the Pueblo Lands Board, Sept. 1933, in Misc. General, Pueblo Lands Board, Southern Pueblo Agency, Albuquerque, NM. Hall, *Four Leagues of Pecos*, 265-268.
30. Lawrence C. Kelly, "John Collier and the Pueblo Lands Board Act," NMHR, 58:1 (Jan. 1983): 5-34.
31. Act of 18 June 1934, 48 Stat. 984 as amended by Act of 15 June 1935, 49 Stat. 378. See generally, Kenneth Philp, *John Collier's Crusade for Indian Reform 1920-1954* (Tucson, AZ: University of Arizona Press, 1977).
32. Article II ("Membership") of the Constitution and By Laws of the Pueblo of Santa Clara, New Mexico, Approved Dec. 20, 1935 (Washington, D.C.: Government Printing Office, 1957). See *Santa Clara Pueblo v. Martinez*, 436, US 49, 52 (1977).
33. *Martinez v. Santa Clara Pueblo*, 402, F. Supp. 5 (1975).
34. Canby, "The Status of Indian Tribes in American Law Today," *Washington Law Review*, 62:1 (1987), 1-22.
35. Affidavits of Audrey Martinez and Julia Martinez, 2 Oct. 1972, in *Julia Martinez v. George Romney et. al.*, No. 9717, United States District Court for New Mexico.
36. Alan Taradash to Santa Clara Pueblo Governor Paul Tafoya, 14 Sept. 1971 in *Martinez v. Romney*.
37. *Santa Clara Pueblo v. Martinez*.
38. *Martinez v. Romney*, 402, F. Supp. 5 (1975).
39. *Santa Clara Pueblo v. Martinez*, 540, F.2 1039 (1976).
40. *Santa Clara Pueblo v. Martinez*, 436, US 49 (1977).
41. Hall, "The Pueblo Grant Labyrinth."

G. Emlen Hall teaches at the University of New Mexico Law School where he specializes in natural resources and legal history. In 1984 the UNM Press published his *Four Leagues of Pecos, A Legal History of the Pecos Grant*. He writes extensively in the area of New Mexico land and water history and is a director of the Center for Land Grant Studies. He graduated from Princeton University and the Harvard Law School.

The Mora Land Grant: *A New Mexican Tragedy*

Clark S. Knowlton

THE social history of Spanish and Mexican community land grants in New Mexico is largely unexplored and is complex and difficult to untangle. At bottom it seems to be a multifaceted conflict between Anglo-American and Spanish-American systems of land tenure: the first highly legalistic, expensive, adversarial, dependent upon written titles recorded in government agencies/offices; the second simple, inexpensive, vague, and nonlegalistic based upon community recognition of land titles. The first system is highly individualistic and the second more corporate and communal in nature. Lack of accommodation between the systems has created a chaotic land title situation in northern New Mexico in which few titles have a perfect chain. Most titles there can be challenged, and such titles cannot be perfected without considerable litigation.

The complicated legal and political struggle over Mexican land grant titles in the region was fundamentally an effort by Anglo-American lawyers, judges, businessmen, political leaders, and ranchers not only to secure desirable sections of land but to force upon the recalcitrant Spanish-Americans the Anglo-American legal and political systems of land tenure. In spite of these efforts, large numbers of Spanish-Americans buy and sell land without recording title changes in county offices, ignoring the requirements of Anglo-American laws. The result is a legal tangle of awesome proportions in northern New Mexico.

Thus, land grant research often resembles the assembling of a giant, complicated jigsaw puzzle in which some of the pieces are missing. It is very difficult for any land-grant researcher to avoid becoming sympathetic toward the Spanish-Americans, victims of so much land-grant litigation. Few social scientists working intimately with Spanish-Americans can remain aloof from their efforts to protect or to recover their lands. But such sympathy toward

Santa Gertrudis church. Mora, October 22, 1938. (Photo by Paul A. Wilson. Neg. no. 86693. Courtesy Museum of New Mexico.)

the Spanish-Americans does not preclude the possibility of rigorous objective research into the social history of New Mexican land grants. Social history warped by bias is poor social history, but sympathy for the Spanish-American people can infuse a warmth that brings life to an otherwise cold recital of facts.

The town of Mora Community Land Grant is located in Mora County with intrusions into neighboring Colfax and San Miguel Counties. The eastern part of the grant is over 6,000 feet in altitude and is characterized by high rolling plains, mesas, and plateaus dissected by river valleys. The land in the central section of the grant, with numerous foothills, broad valleys, buttes, and mesas, rises toward the high mountain peaks in the western part of the grant, some over 12,000 feet. High mountains separated by narrow canyons, mountain valleys, and plateaus dominate the western sector of the grant. The mountain passes between Mora and Taos Counties, its western neighbor, are few and far between.[1]

Considerable climatic variability exists within the grant. As the winters are long, though not excessively cold, the growing season is apt to be short. Summers are cool and pleasant with few days higher than 86 degrees. Precipitation is highly localized and fluctuates dramatically from year to year. In the eastern portion of the grant, where the growing season may reach 120 days, precipitation averages around 16 inches. As one moves toward the western mountains precipitation increases. Most of the precipitation falls during the growing season. The differences in mean annual temperature between the eastern and western portions of the grant may, according to Hunt, "be as great as the difference between the mean annual temperature of the plains and that of Alaska."[2] Hunt also points out that the growing season in the higher mountain valleys is about half that of the Yukon Valley in Alaska.[3] The grant is fairly well watered with a small network of streams flowing into the Mora River, a tributary of the Canadian River, and provides good grazing throughout the late spring, summer, and early fall.

The first European to visit the Mora land grant region may have been Coronado on his way back from the plains to the Rio Grande Valley in 1541.[4] As early as the eighteenth century Spanish-American buffalo hunters and Indian traders traversed the region. But as the area was utilized by Indian tribes such as the Jicarilla Apache, Comanche, Kiowas, and Utes, few Spanish-Americans cared to settle in the area until the nineteenth century, although shepherds from the Pecos River villages may have grazed their flocks of sheep and cattle in the Mora region toward the end of the eighteenth century.[5] Anglo-American and French-Canadian and French-Missourian trappers had penetrated the Mora area by the 1820s. Among them were Ceran St. Vrain, Joseph Rouelle, Antonio Ledoux, Juan Bautista Brichal, and Santiago Bone. Many of them settled in the Mora country, married Spanish-American women, and founded families. Their descendants, now Spanish-Americans, still live in the region.[6]

It is uncertain when the first permanent Spanish-American settlements appeared on the Mora grant. According to Gonzalez, Mora Valley was first settled in 1835 when settlers requested and received a community land grant.[7] However, Chavez and Vigil, utilizing data from Catholic Parish records, found settlers in Mora in the very early years of the nineteenth century.[8] Although the original title papers of the grant vanished during an attack by American troops on the Community of Mora in 1847, a report of the justice of peace and *alcalde* of San Jose de Las Trampas to the territorial governor did survive. He reports that in 1835 he traveled to the Mora grant to formally allot land to 76 family heads in the neighboring valleys of Mora and San Antonio. The majority of these settlers came from Rio Arriba and Taos counties just over the mountains to the west.[9]

Within a few years, Spanish-American rural farm villages or *placitas* sprang up wherever good arable land and water could be found in the broad low foothill valleys. Later settlers occupied the higher mountain valleys to the west and the drier valleys in the lower eastern plains. Within a few years almost every stream flowing through the grant was beaded with communities. Later settlers coming onto the grant requested permission from the local *alcalde,* a local Mexican political position combining the powers of a mayor, county commission, and justice of the peace. During the first years of the American period, land seekers obtained permission of the county commission before entering the grant. According to Spanish-American customs, people could not settle on a community land grant without requesting permission of the local public officials. As long as arable land was available new settlers were welcomed, as they increased the military strength of a population faced with hostile Indian attacks.[10]

During the last decades of the nineteenth century, the local grant inhabitants developed a semi-subsistence economy based upon intensive farming of small agricultural plots and the grazing of livestock, primarily sheep, upon the common lands of the grant. Cut off from the major centers of Spanish-American society in the Rio Grande Valley, the Taos regions, and the Pecos River Valley by high mountains, they turned to the Great Plains. Each fall when the crops were harvested, young men known as *Ciboleros* (buffalo hunters) went off to hunt on the plains. Other village men gathered the surplus products of the village economy and set off in cart caravans to trade with the Comanche and other southern plain tribes. Known as the *Comancheros,* they later became a thorn in the side of federal officials in Santa Fe and to the State Government of Texas as they were not adverse to buying cattle and horses taken from the Texans.[11]

The opening of the Santa Fe Trail from Independence, Missouri, to Santa Fe, New Mexico, not only integrated New Mexico into the economic system of the United States but also ended the semi-isolation of the inhabitants of the Mora grant. As the Mora villages were located close to the trail, their inhabitants prospered from the sale of grain, flour, hay, vegetables, and livestock to travelers. Many young men from the villages found employment as teamsters, guides, and hunters diversifying the local occupational structure.[12]

Celebration of the centennial of the Mora land grant. Mora, October 1935. (Neg. no. 132443. Courtesy Museum of New Mexico.)

But the location of the Mora communities on the trail had its disadvantages as well. Texan bandits marauding on the trail found the unfortified villages attractive targets. Thus in the spring of 1843, a gang of Texan bandits attacked the community of Mora, running off livestock and killing five people. A village posse caught up with the Texans, recovering the village livestock, leaving the attackers on foot in Indian country. From that time on, the inhabitants of the Mora grant communities have had a very negative attitude toward Texans.[13]

Three years later in 1846, New Mexico was occupied by American troops and its Spanish-speaking inhabitants became American citizens. Although Connor and Skaggs argue that the Spanish-Americans welcomed their Anglo conquerors,[14] Ruxton, an English traveler passing through New Mexico shortly after the American occupation, found an almost universal hostility toward the Americans throughout the territory.[15]

This hostility erupted in the well-organized (but poorly studied) Taos Revolt of 1847, which spread rapidly throughout Northern New Mexico. The poorly armed rural village population in the region rose against the American Army of Occupation, fighting pitched battles with American troops. Unfortunately, very little is known about the well coordinated revolt, about its leaders, or its possible connection with Mexico. In Mora itself, seven American Santa Fe traders passing through the community were killed. In putting down the revolt, an American military unit unsuccessfully attacked the community of Mora on 24 January 1847, losing its commanding officer in the battle. Repulsed, the unit returned on 1 February and destroyed the village, whose inhabitants had fled to the mountains.[16]

To strengthen its hold on New Mexico, the American Army of Occupation established a major military post at Fort Union, on the Mora land grant. The troops stationed at the fort not only provided moderate protection against Indian raids but were also an important market for the hay, grain, flour, fruits, vegetables and livestock produced by the local Spanish-American population. Many Spanish-Americans found employment on the post, others made money providing illicit services to the troops.[17]

Many Anglo-American and European-immigrant males settled close to the fort on the Mora land grant. A few purchased land from Spanish-American residents, but others "squatted on choice land along the streams" defying the Mexicans to put them off.[18] Irish immigrants farmed and worked at numerous skilled trades such as carpentry and masonry. German Jews opened retail stores in the town of Mora and in the larger villages on the grant. Many of the settlers married local Spanish-American girls, and their children were assimilated into Spanish-American communities. Representing a second wave of foreign immigration, they joined earlier French-speaking immigrants from French speaking Canada, Louisiana, and Missouri. The ability of Spanish-American society to absorb and assimilate foreign immigrants is evidenced by the large number of local Spanish-Americans with French, German, Irish, and English last names.[19]

Commerce along the Santa Fe Trail between Missouri and New Mexico not only integrated New Mexico firmly into the American economy, it also opened channels of socioeconomic mobility to enterprising Spanish-American entrepreneurs who shifted capital from agriculture to commerce and freighting. Unfortunately, the rise of a Spanish-

American commercial and professional class and its relationship with the dominant Spanish-American landowning elite has been largely ignored by historians and social scientists. Perrigo and Sandoval are among the very few scholars to comment on the development of Spanish-American freighters, businessmen, and professionals in the early American period.[20]

Although the United States promised, in the Treaty of Guadalupe Hidalgo (which ended the state of war with Mexico) to protect the property and civil rights of former Mexican citizens residing in the United States, the national government did little to honor the provisions of the treaty in New Mexico until 1854. In that year Congress established the position of Surveyor General of New Mexico to investigate the validity of all land claims growing out of Spanish and Mexican land grants and to recommend their acceptance or rejection by Congress. To discharge his responsibilities, the Surveyor General was authorized to gather evidence, hold hearings, take testimony under oath, and collect and translate documents.[21]

Heeding the call of the newly appointed Surveyor General of New Mexico to the inhabitants of New Mexico to submit their land claims and evidence of titles to his office for adjudication, Jose Maria Valdez and Vicente Romero, residents on the Mora community land grant, submitted a petition on 20 June 1851, "On behalf of Themselves and other Inhabitants, Settlers of Mora." Through their attorneys, Ashurst and Jackson, they requested confirmation of the Mora community land grant to them and to other settlers on the grant. Assigning the file number 32 to the Mora Land Grant Case, the Surveyor General held a hearing on the case on 1 July 1859. Even though the original land grant documents had been lost, the Surveyor General found that a valid community land grant had been made by the Mexican government to the settlers on the Mora land grant. He, therefore, recommended that Congress confirm the grant to its inhabitants. Congress, acting with unusual celerity, confirmed the grant on 21 June 1860 to its residents. The confirmed boundaries of the grant were: on the north, the Rio de Ocate; on the east, the Aguaje de la Yegua; on the south, the mouth of the Sapello stream where it empties into the Mora River; and on the west, the Estillero. Although these boundary calls were well known to the local inhabitants, they had to be surveyed and marked on the ground, and the grant's acreage ascertained precisely before the patent could issue.[22]

Thus, on 4 July 1861, Alexander D. Wilbar, the current Surveyor General of New Mexico, signed a contract with Thomas Means to survey and mark the outboundaries of the grant, establish well-marked corner posts, locate and mark the boundary calls, and ascertain the grant acreage. Hiring a crew of two chainmen, one corner maker, one compassman, and one flagman, Means spent July and August in the field. He began his survey at the southeastern boundary call, the Aguaje de la Yegua, a series of springs on the joint boundary of the Las Vegas grant (just to the south of the Mora grant) and the Mora grant. The springs were a well-known watering place on the trail between the communities on the Mora grant and the Llano Estacado, or Staked Plains, traversed by the Ciboleros, and Comancheros. Running north from the Aguaje de la Yegua he established the eastern boundary of the grant up to the Ocate River. Turning left he ran the boundary along the river. Unable to trace a western boundary line through the high mountains, he ran a traverse or estimated line as best he could. Upon his return on 16 August 1861, Means reported to the Surveyor General that the grant contained 827,621 acres, turned in his maps and survey books, and awaited payment for his labors.[23]

John A. Clarke, the new Surveyor General, astonished at the reported size of the grant, unhappy at the western boundary line, and the uncertain eastern boundary, sent special agent John M. Clark to the community of Mora to take sworn testimony on the location of the Aguaje de la Yegua. While six sworn witnesses testified that the Aquaje de la Yegua was accurately located by Means, a dissident stated that the Aguaje de la Yegua was the name of a pond a few miles from Mora. Without approving the survey, the Surveyor General submitted it along with the report of his agent to his superior, the Commissioner of the General Land Office, a bureau of the Department of the Interior, in Washington, D.C.[24]

On 4 January 1862, Commissioner of the General Land Office, J.M. Edmunds, rejected Means' survey on the grounds that the acreage was larger than Mexican law allowed at the time the grant was made. He was quite dissatisfied with the boundary lines run by Means. He felt that Means had not properly located the Aguaje de la Yegua and that his survey did not close on the northern boundary of the Las Vegas Community Land Grant, which was also the southern boundary of the Mora Community Land Grant. He was also disturbed by the discrepancy in the testimony of the witnesses taken by special agent John M. Clark as to the location of the Aguaje de la Yegua. The Surveyor General, therefore, went to the community of Mora, probably in February of 1862, and took the sworn testimony of seven leading citizens of Mora, all of whom placed the Aguaje de la Yegua where Means had surveyed it.[25]

Still not satisfied, the Commissioner ordered the Surveyor General on 10 May 1862 to personally go to the Mora grant and locate the mysterious Aguaje de la Yegua. The Surveyor General replied that owing to the presence of hostile Indians in the region, it would be impossible for him to take to the field without a strong military escort. In view of this, the Commissioner suspended the trip and requested that Clarke submit the written testimony that he had taken earlier.[26] The Surveyor General, on 12 December 1862, directed Means to return to the field and rerun his lines on the eastern and southern boundaries to close properly with the northern boundary of the Las Vegas community land grant. Means did so in the spring of the next year. Upon receiving the corrected survey, the Surveyor General approved it and transmitted it to the General Land Office with recommendations that it be accepted by the Commissioner. Willis Drummond, a new commissioner of the General Land Office, accepted the Means Survey.[27] But Means had still not been paid as late as 18 May 1863. On that date he wrote to the Surveyor General:

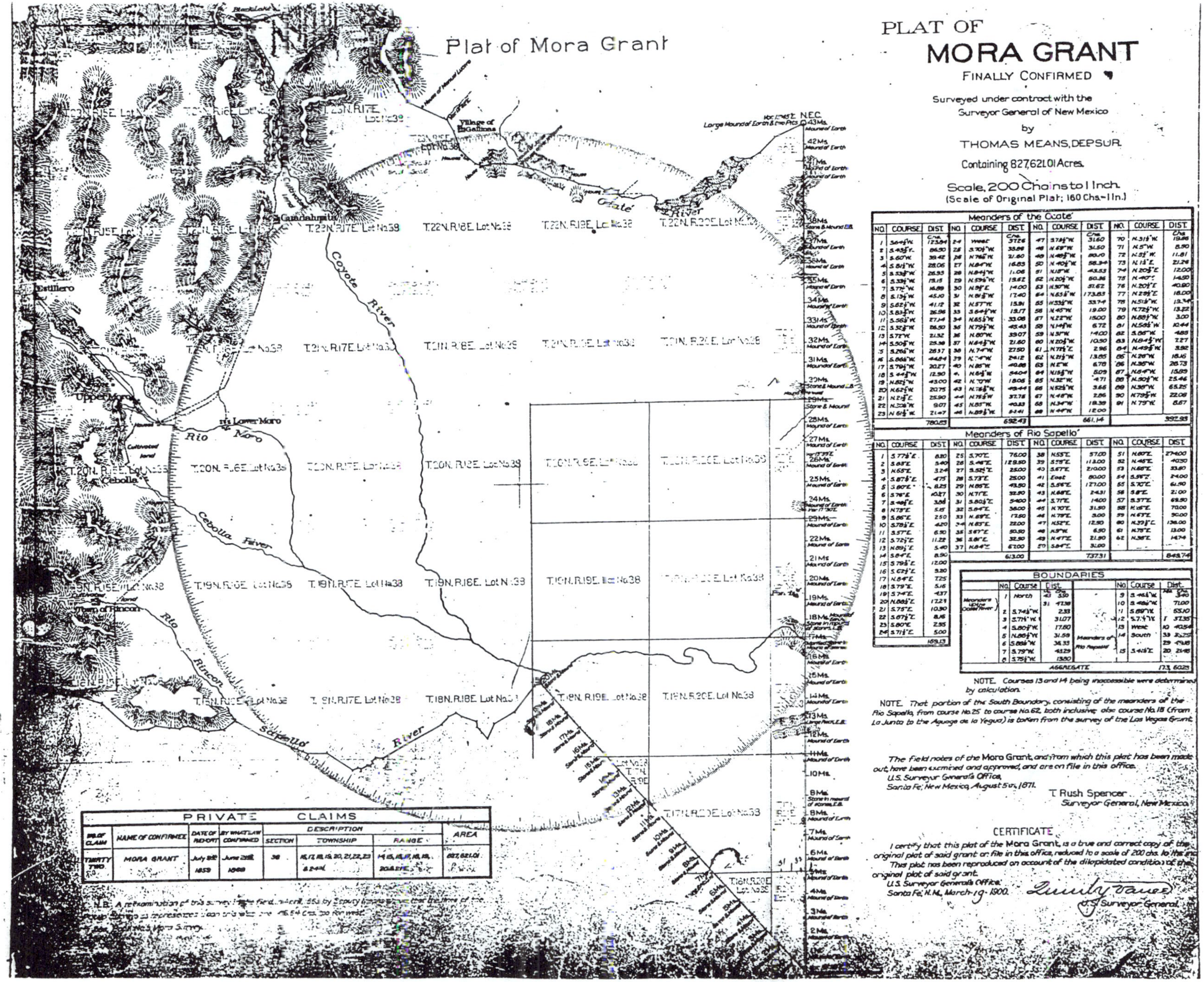

Survey plat for the 1861 survey of the Mora grant by Thomas Means, showing the Estillero along the northern part of the eastern boundary. (Courtesy Bureau of Land Management, Santa Fe.)

Street scene in Mora, c. 1900. (Photo by Royal A. Prentice. Neg. no. 110763. Courtesy Museum of New Mexico.)

> My Dear Sir: You know and see my situation now nearly two years delayed out of my hard and honest labor, in debt, and having no means of sustaining myself, but what little is allowed to be paid. When the work is prepared, be so kind and at your earliest convenience to pay my account.[28]

The General Land Office paid little attention to the Mora land grant during the last years of the Civil War and its immediate aftermath. Undoubtedly it had more pressing affairs on its agenda. In spite of, or perhaps because of, this neglect, the Spanish-American population on the grant prospered. By the time of the Civil War, the population of the grant numbered around 1,000 people. But their future welfare was threatened by a horde of Anglo-American lawyers, land speculators, merchants, politicians, ranchers, and fortune hunters who crossed the plains to New Mexico in the 1860s and 1870s. The Comanches, the traditional protectors of the eastern approaches to New Mexico, had lost much of their efficiency as border guards by the 1870s. Among these immigrants were two Missourians, life-long friends, Stephen B. Elkins and Thomas C. Catron.[29]

Elkins and Catron became friends and roommates at the University of Missouri before the Civil War. Elkins came to New Mexico in 1863 after a brief stint in the Union Army. Catron served throughout the Civil War in the Confederate Army and entered New Mexico with Elkins in 1866, Elkins having previously returned to Missouri to marry a local girl. Both learned Spanish, joined the New Mexico Bar, and began their New Mexican careers in Mesilla, in southern New Mexico. Elected to the territorial legislature in 1866, Elkins moved to Santa Fe, followed by Catron two years later, who was also elected to the territorial legislature from Mesilla. After serving a term in the territorial legislature, Elkins was appointed U.S. District Attorney in 1868, again followed by Catron who secured the same appointment in 1872.[30]

But then their political paths began to diverge. Elkins was elected New Mexico's territorial delegate in 1873, and moved to Washington, D.C., never to return to New Mexico. A widower, he married the daughter of influential and wealthy senator from West Virginia, Henry C. Davis, in 1877. Under the tutelage of powerful Republican chieftans in Washington he became an important national Republican leader. While maintaining an avid interest in New Mexican land grants, he developed major business interests in New York City, West Virginia and elsewhere. Appointed Secretary of War in President Benjamin Harrison's cabinet, he was later elected the Republican senator from West Virginia in 1891. As one of the more powerful Republican leaders in Washington during a long period of Republican ascendancy in government, Elkins was in an effective political position to exert pressure on government agencies, such as the General Land Office and the Surveyor General of New Mexico.[31]

Catron and Elkins played important roles in the organization and management of the Santa Fe Ring, an informal organization which controlled much of the economic and political life of New Mexico during the territorial period. Lamar pointed out that the Santa Fe Ring was:

> . . . essentially a set of lawyers, politicians and businessmen who united to run the territory and to make money out of this particular region. Although located on the frontier, the ring reflected the corporative, monopolistic, and multiple enterprise tendencies of all American business after the Civil War. Its uniqueness lay in the fact that rather than dealing in some manufactured item, they regarded land as their first medium of currency.[32]

Lamar further comments that the Santa Fe Ring "was a

logical and sometimes brilliant combination of able men''[33] of both political parties. Lamar goes on to say that the Ring was extremely successful because it would accept into its circles cooperative businessmen, lawyers, or governmental officials. As a result it included leading lawyers, politicians, wealthy merchants, surveyors general and other federal and state officials, including governors and judges. Ring members had excellent personal and business connections in the East and enjoyed substantial benefits from the long Republican dominance of national affairs from 1865 to 1885. Through these Eastern economic and political contacts the Ring could interest Eastern U.S. and European investors in the Spanish and Mexican land grants of New Mexico. One of the first land grants to attract the attention of Catron and Elkins was the Mora community land grant.[34]

In the 1860s, Elkins received an undivided share of the common lands of the Mora grant as payment for defending an impecunious resident charged with a crime. The notion adopted by some Anglo-American lawyers and courts that the common lands of a community land grant belonged to the first settlers and their heirs, could have started here.[35]

Impressed by the natural resources of the Mora land grant, Catron and Elkins quietly bought up as many presumed rights in the common lands of the grant as they could, registering their purchases in Elkins' name in the Mora County courthouse. By 1870, they had acquired 16 such rights. Perhaps to secure more capital and to improve the opportunities of selling their land purchases, they formed an investment pool with Col. Samuel S. Smoot, a land speculator; Cap. E.N. Darling, a government surveyor; and T. Rush Spencer, the current Surveyor General of New Mexico. Each member of the pool received a one-fifth interest in all lands purchased.[36]

On 5 December 1871, Col. Smoot sold, without knowledge of his partners, his presumed one-fifth share in Western lands to an avid English investor, William Blackmore, for $5,000. He represented falsely that his one-fifth share would be close to 138,000 acres. At the time, Smoot owned none of the land in his own name; all purchases were still registered in Elkins' name. All the land held by the pool fell far below the 138,000 acres. Blackmore killed himself in 1878, and his heirs were never able to obtain the land or the return of the money advanced.[37]

T. Rush Spencer, the Surveyor General of New Mexico, approved the Means survey of the Mora land grant on 1 July 1871. He sent to the Commissioner of the General Land Office a survey and a petition for a patent of the Mora Community Land Grant for Catron and Elkins rather than for the inhabitants of the grant even though Catron and Elkins owned only a small portion of land rights there. Willis Drummond, commissioner of the General Land Office, bowing to the political pressures exerted by Elkins and his friends, issued the patent to them in spite of serious protests from the inhabitants of the grant.[38]

But the uncertain location of the western boundary and of the boundary calls mentioned in the title papers prevented prompt issuance of a patent to the Mora grant. The Commissioner of the General Land Office rejected the Means survey with its estimated western boundary. The problem of the western boundary location became more immediate with the survey of public lands to the west of the grant. In 1862 the Surveyor General of New Mexico signed a contract with two

Stacking hay on the Mora grant. (Bureau of Immigration Collection. Courtesy State Records Center & Archives, Santa Fe.)

Hispanic farming family photographed in the Mora Valley, September 1895. (Neg. no. 22468. Courtesy Museum of New Mexico.)

surveyors, Baylor and Holland, to survey the townships bordering the west boundary of the grant. In their report they claimed, without evidence in their field notes, that they had closed their survey upon a mythical west boundary of the Mora land grant. At the time no one protested the survey, and it was accepted as accurate by the Surveyor General and the Commissioner of the General Land Office.[39]

In spite of its acknowledged imperfections the General Land Office finally accepted Means' Survey. Over the stiff opposition of both Anglo-American and Spanish-American residents on the grant, the commissioner of the General Land Office issued a patent to the Mora land grant on 20 June 1876, to Catron and Elkins. But since the description of the grant in the patent included the military reservation of Fort Union, the Secretary of War protested the issuance of the patent. The patent was then withdrawn and amended to exclude Fort Union, over the protests of Catron and Elkins. The amended patent was finally issued to them on 15 August 1876.[40]

With the patent in their possession, Catron, Elkins, and their allies petitioned the court of New Mexico's First Judicial District in March 1877 to partition the common lands of the grant. The court appointed special masters to determine the names of the first settlers, trace their descendants who might have valid claims, and determine how the land should be partitioned among them. If the numbers of claimants were extremely large, the court might order the common lands of the grant sold and the proceeds distributed to the claimants, as it did in this case. Often the land in partition suits was sold by the sheriff at the courthouse door for a fraction of their real value.[41]

As news of the issuance of the patent and the pending partition suit spread among the Anglo-American and Spanish-American settlers on the grant, each group sent in a petition to the General Land Office denouncing the issuance of the patent to the Catron and Elkins interests. The representatives of the Anglo-American protesters stated their case as follows:

> The Undersigned . . . residents of the County of Mora, having learned that the Interior Department of the United States is about to issue a patent for said land grant to certain representative claimants, respectfully represent: That said claimants consist principally of speculators who derived their claims from the few remaining original grantees, with the undisguised view of ejecting from the grant, the settlers who have preempted, homesteaded, or purchased their lands from the United States government.[42]

The following quote is taken from the protest of 1,073 Spanish-American residents against the issuance of the patent to Catron and Elkins. One senses both the outrage of the local people and their misplaced faith in the integrity of the Commissioner of the General Land Office:

> The title to possibly one fifth or less of the grant (the common lands of the grant) has passed into the hands of the original grantees and is now vested in two or three speculators who were particularly careful to conceal from the sellers the extent of the land they were buying, many having disposed of their claims for the inconsiderable sum of five or ten dollars and more than one or two deny all knowledge of any conveyance whatever of their claims, so that chicanery and fraud have obtained in various of the alleged purchases.
>
> The grant includes within its limits, a population of about ten thousand souls, many of whom have at the risk of their lives, settled and improved the lands they occupy, and many lives have been lost through the hostile Indians surrounding them on all sides at the time of their settling the said land.

> Quite a number of the original grantees have never resided upon the grant or taken any other steps, as required by the Mexican laws, to secure or make good their titles.
>
> Many persons were invited and solicited to go upon, settle, and cultivate land within the grant, by the original grantees as a protection to themselves from the hostile Indians, with the understanding that they would enjoy equal rights and privileges with the grantees; and many did so.
>
> In fine, it is seriously believed that the vesting of this territory in those who are now so unjustly soliciting it, will cause a quasi-revolution here, for many of the present settlers are determined to defend what they consider their just rights, at all hazards, and will not consent to any circumscription of those rights, and it would, evidently be a very bad policy to disturb such a large body of people and deprive them of what they consider their justly acquired homes, to satisfy the greed of a few hungry sharks.[43]

Having acquired title to the common lands of the Mora Community Land Grant, the land sharks of the pool were anxious to profitably dispose of their land claims. But the partition suit bogged down with the unresolved problem of the western boundary line. As Catron was not reimbursed by his partners for the land purchased in the name of the pool, he registered new purchases in his own name.[44] Furthermore, the pool discovered that T. Rush Spencer, who in exchange for one-fifth share in the purchased land had agreed to market the land to Eastern capitalists, had not even signed the contract with other parties in the pool until two days before he died. Victor Westphall claims that Spencer's failure to sign the contract or to try to market the grant lands resulted in serious and lengthy litigation.[45] Because of these and other factors the pool disintegrated during the 1870s and early 1880s. Smoot and Darling, unable to agree on a selling price for their holdings in the grant with other members of the pool, sold their interests in 1885, for a small amount down, to Gen. Benjamin F. Butler, a Massachusetts politician and Civil War general of tarnished reputation. Smoot and Darling were forced to sue Butler to get the rest of their money. Elkins also bailed out of the pool by selling his holdings to Adelbart Ames, a Massachusetts businessman.[45] Thus, the number of interested parties in the grant common lands, apart from the residents, was reduced primarily to Catron, Butler, and Ames.

In 1888 Butler tried to get full title to the lands purchased in the name of the pool in order to control the stalled partition suit. As most of the claims of the pool were registered in Elkins' name, Butler secured power of attorney from Elkins to dispose of the lands. Catron protested strongly to Elkins claiming that Butler had not paid for these interests, nor had he paid Catron for his legal services in the partition suit. Butler died in 1893 having benefited little from his land holdings in the Mora land grant. His heirs resolved their problems with Catron by paying him $2,000 for his legal services and rehiring him as the Butler attorney for litigation involving the grant.[46]

The Butler heirs, Adelbart Ames, and Catron found it extremely difficult to cooperate in the business affairs of the grant. The three parties could not agree on either the selling price or terms of sale and as a result possible sales fell through. Westphall refers to "a series of complicated negotiations in which the Butler heirs could not agree and Adelbart Ames proved to be hard-headed beyond belief."[47] Finally, the common lands of the grant legally held by the group were divided. Catron received 250,000 acres in the section of the grant north of the 36th parallel; Ames and the Butler heirs received 350,000 acres south of the 36th parallel. From this point on the two sets of claimants went their own ways. In 1909 Thomas B. Catron deeded his interest in the Mora land grant to his son Charles C. Catron, who spent many weary, unprofitable, and at times, dangerous years trying to force the local inhabitants to recognize his title.[48]

During this period of complicated and devious infighting among members of the disintegrating pool, the General Land Office and the Surveyor General continued to struggle with the proper location of the western boundary line of the grant. In July 1896 the Surveyor General signed a contract with Russell B. Rice to complete the survey of sections 13 and 14 to the west of the land grant. Rice replicated the earlier unsuccessful survey of Baylor and Holland. Rice was given specific instructions to close on the western boundary of the grant. Then, on 3 April 1902, the Surveyor General signed a contract with John R. Walker to survey Townships 20, 21, and 22 to the west of the grant. He was instructed to close on the western boundary of the grant, and was also directed to locate on the ground the western boundary call of the Mora grant. The Walker survey was examined in 1905 by Frank Warner, Examiner of Surveys of the General Land Office, who recommended its rejection because of inaccuracies. To be acceptable, Warner stated, it would be necessary for Walker to "thoroughly overhaul his work from beginning to end and submit same for re-examination." Walker's survey was definitely rejected on 10 October 1907.[49]

On 6 June 1906, George D. Kirkpatrick, Examiner of Surveys of the Public Land Office, was instructed to travel to one of the geographic features mentioned in the Means Survey, Black Lake, and trace Means' estimated line along the base of the western mountains, to locate his south corner of Black Lake, and definitely locate the Estillero, the western boundary call. In his report Kirkpatrick states that he could not totally retrace Means' lines because of "impassable cliffs and ledges," nor could he locate the Estillero, the western boundary call. He claims that Means' description of the Estillero could fit any number of points in the region. As a result, the Land Registrar and Receiver in Santa Fe, New Mexico, was ordered not to dispose of any more public lands in the disputed area.[50]

Finally on 31 August 1906, William Strover, a clerk of the General Land Office, was sent to Mora with instructions to definitely locate the Estillero, establish and mark the definitive western boundary of the Mora land grant, and establish corners and set up firm corner posts. With the establishment of Pecos National Forest just to the west of the grant, the

Main Street in Mora, 1906. (Bureau of Immigration Collection. Photo no. 12063. Courtesy State Records Center & Archives, Santa Fe.)

matter of an accurate western boundary had become pressing.[51]

Strover discussed in his report the impact upon the local settlers of the failure of Means and subsequent surveyors to establish an accurate, recognized west boundary. He comments as follows:

> Some years after the Means survey, settlers began to locate in the formerly called inaccessible mountain valleys and canyons, sawmills made their appearance and started operations in the vicinity of the west boundary of the Mora grant and from that time on there has been trouble for the government and for the grant owners. Nothing was known of the true location of the grant boundary and timber trespassers when called to account by the government claimed to have cut timber on the grant and when prosecuted by the grant owners, they claimed to be on public land.[52]

Strover was aghast at the condition of public and private surveys in the western section of the grant. In discussing the situation he observed:

> The public lines (survey lines) in T. 19 N., R. 14 E., are in a fearful mess, most of the patented claims have been surveyed privately by local surveyors, who have set corners wherever it suits their convenience and who have replaced public corners with their own at any old place, destroying the former because their location did not agree with their own work, I did not find a single corner on subdivisional lines in this township which I could identify as an original corner and the lines are in an awful condition.
>
> In this neighborhood I expected to obtain some testimony in regard to the location of the Mora grant boundary, but after innumerable interviews with old native settlers I find that it is useless to try any further to get any information which would be of any value. Owners of patented lands seem all willing to testify to anything I may choose to write down, providing it tends to keep the Mora grant away from their lands, while those whose interests are with the Mora grant would cheerfully swear to any number of miles west of its present location.[53]

Strover was successful in locating the western boundary call, the Estillero, and in running an accurate western boundary line. It should be observed that by the early 1900s considerable improvement had taken place in survey instruments and methodology. Strover observed that the current accepted boundary line between the National Forest and the Mora land grant was the product of an erroneous survey in 1882 that put the boundary line several miles to the east of the correct boundary. He further observed that the erroneous survey of 1882:

> . . . caused at that time great hardship among many people living on lands adjoining the west boundary of the Mora grant, especially among the poor natives (Spanish-Americans). Most of the settlers had obtained title from the Mora grant owners and the survey of 1882 which placed the lands upon public domain compelled the settlers to again get title from the government. Many natives and a few others, through ignorance of the land laws, lost their homes by reason of others filing thereon at the land office. Now my

Old Mora County Courthouse. Built in 1889, it was abandoned c. 1939 after a newer courthouse was built next to it. The building burned in 1960 and was demolished the next year. (Bureau of Immigration Collection. Photo no. 22692. Courtesy State Records Center & Archives, Santa Fe.)

> location of the true boundary line will again throw many patented lands within the Mora grant and probably some others not yet patented. Much litigation will probably be the result of this investigation, and while it cannot affect the owners of patented lands, there will be much trouble between others who are not so fortunate and the grant owners. The survey of 1882 was a very unfortunate affair that would not have been approved and accepted had the authorities insisted upon some reasonable proof for the proper location of the west boundary of the Mora grant, based upon the boundary call, the "Estillero."[54]

Strover recommended that the 1902 Walker survey of the western boundary be rejected. He pointed out that it did not conform to the western boundary call, the Estillero. As the Strover boundary line would take around 20 to 30 square miles of good timber land from the Pecos National Forest and add them to the Mora land grant, the Commissioner of the General Land Office, in a letter to the Secretary of the Interior dated 28 October 1907, recommended that the boundary line established between the grant and the National Forest be accepted and that further attempts to establish the true western boundary of the Mora land grant be abandoned. His suggestion was not accepted. Surveyor Alonzo E. Compton was sent out by the General Land Office in 1911, to once again resurvey the western and part of the northern boundaries of the Mora land grant. The General Land Office, in protecting the accepted eastern boundary of the Pecos National Forest, officially adopted the Compton survey in 1911. After many surveys and considerable expense, a western boundary of the Mora land grant was finally formalized.[55]

As the Compton Survey of the Western Boundary line of the Mora Land Grant was not acceptable to the State Investment Company, who had acquired the Catron interests, the General Land Office brought suit in the U.S. District Court of New Mexico to quit title to a tract of land about three miles wide and 33 miles long lying between the Mean and Compton Surveys. The case was finally decided by the U.S. Supreme Court in 1923 that found against the government. Thus, the much maligned Means Survey of the western boundary line by court action became the official western boundary of the Mora land grant.

While the Surveyor General and the Commissioner of the Public Land Office sent one survey crew after another in an effort to locate the Estillero and the correct western boundary line of the grant, local Spanish-American and many Anglo-Americans on the grant ignored the legal claims of the Catrons, the Butlers, and the Ameses and continued to utilize the natural resources of the common lands. They refused to pay royalties to the Catrons and others and fought off attempts to put them off their lands.[56] The continued efforts of Charles Catron to collect royalties and to force the inhabitants to recognize his legal title led to the murder in 1911 of his land grant agent and representative, Robert Sammon. Virtually every penny Charles Catron collected from the grant went into the impossible job of trying to establish a clear title to the lands claimed so that they could be sold. It was an impossible task. Catron's struggle ended on 27 February 1913, when, because of non-payment of the property taxes in Mora County, the Catron interests were sold at the Mora County Courthouse door to Frank Roy, a resident of Las Vegas.[57]

The Elkins-Catron suit to partition the common lands of the grant was initially filed in 1876. Between 1876 and 1915 several generations of judges, lawyers, claimants, and land grant inhabitants had come and gone. Catron and other Anglo-American land speculators had failed to force the local people to recognize their titles. Probably very few of the Spanish-American inhabitants of the grant remembered that a partition suit had been filed. Now that the Catron interests had collapsed, the partition suit was suddenly recalled to life in the local district court. Mainly to avoid violence and tumult, this partition suit was secretly called back to life. As a former governor of New Mexico, L. Bradford Prince, pointed out:

> The determination of the Grant suit, therefore, virtually affects the whole population. The great majority of them do not speak or read English, and are ignorant of matters of law, by which their property can be taken from them, without their receiving any actual notice. In this suit, few were personally notified originally, and that was almost a generation ago. Those interested at present had no knowledge that anything was being done which affected them; and have no such knowledge today. In such a peculiar case, including the rights of a whole population, and in which the suit had slumbered for so many years, it would seem just that a general notice should be given, that the action is renewed, and that it is to be pushed to a conclusion; so that all may have a chance to assert and protect their rights. . . . Without some such notification and allowance of opportunity to appear, great injustices will be done to hundreds and probably thousands of people, to almost an entire county. There is no other way in which they can be notified of their danger and the jeopardy of their property. The court would thereby become the fountain of justice instead of the instrument of depriving these people of their property and rights; and the Judge would be recognized as the friend of the people, and their protector against oppression, and against secret proceedings, which though they may comply with the letter of the law, yet work rankest injustice.[58]

Unfortunately, the court chose to be the instrument of "rankest injustice" and ordered the unallocated common lands of the grant, so essential to the welfare of hundreds of poor Spanish-American village families, sold at the courthouse door in Mora, 22 February 1916.[59] As one contemplates the sale of the grant, one wonders how many Spanish-speaking families in Mora County were aware that the lands they and their families had used for many generations were being sold from under them. One is also curious why the partition suit was so quietly and furtively revived at this time after being quiescent for generations. Finally, one suspects a quiet arrangement between the court and speculative Anglo-American land interests. The common lands in the Butler section of the grant, also sold at this time, were purchased by Leonard B. Wheeler for a mere $6,000. The former Catron interests were bought by a newly organized Las Vegas, New Mexico, company, the State Investment Company.[60]

The almost 100 years of chronic litigation over the common lands of the Mora community land grant seem not to have enriched the nineteenth-century Anglo-American land speculators who fought hard and long to secure title to the common lands of the grant. Nor did the complex prolonged litigation ever settle the question of titles on the grant. Margaret Meaders points out that:

> The land-title situation in Mora as in many other New Mexican counties . . . is baffling and frustrating and costly. Records are inadequate or missing altogether; adequate mapping is badly needed; surveying is incomplete. Some inhabitants avoid efforts to acquire clear titles either because of a fear of losing their land or because of the cost of the necessary procedures. Many persons remain traditionally reluctant to record land transactions.[61]

Many of those who deplore the chaotic land title system in Mora and other counties of northern New Mexico fail to comprehend that the chaos is one of the best defenses the rural Spanish-American population have against continued land loss to Anglo-American intruders who desire a clear title. Spanish-Americans continue to buy and sell land among themselves often boycotting the whole county recording system. Their boycott is a form of protest against the expensive lawyer-dominated land title system imposed upon them by the Anglo-American occupation of their region.

The loss of access to the natural resources of the common lands of the Mora community land grant severely damaged the rural village economic system, structured on the base of semi-subsistance agriculture, the grazing of large herds of livestock, the cutting of timber, and some migratory labor. The first response of the village people was the gradual drifting of men into migrant farm labor and sheepherding in nearby Western states. Some entered nearby mines or worked on the railroads, and a few migrated to Western cities in search of employment. The wives and children of the married migrants carried on agricultural activities to the best of their ability. But the depression and drought of the 1930s and the coming of World War II brought drastic changes to Mora County. Unable to find employment in migrant farm labor, and laid off by the railroads, mines and urban corporations, the population sharply increased in the rural villages. The drought of the 1930s destroyed farming activities and almost brought the village population to destitution. They were rescued to a significant degree by government employment programs in the 1930s such as the Works Progress Administration and Public Works Administration. Many migrated with their families to the cities to participate in other New Deal programs. During World War II, the federal government developed throughout New Mexico a network of vocational training centers for defense workers. Once partially trained, the workers were sent to defense plants throughout the West, setting into motion currents of migration from Mora County to the larger cities of the West that still persist.[62]

Although the loss of access to the natural resources of the common lands of the Mora community land grant was not the only factor responsible for the heavy migration from the county or the impoverishment of its population, it was a major factor. From 1940 to 1980 Mora's population (86.8 percent Spanish-American in 1980) fell from 10,981 to 4,205. No other county in New Mexico had such heavy population losses during this period. Neighboring counties also lost heavily in population.[63]

Mora County is still the poorest county in New Mexico. In 1980 the median family income for the State of New Mexico was $16,928, several times larger than the median family income of the County of Mora of $6,819. Mora has become a severely depressed area, characterized by heavy population losses, poverty, and all the social pathology of poverty, such as high unemployment, high rates of welfare payments, and impoverished county institutions.[64] Many of the Anglo-American business and professional men dependent upon local Spanish-American clientele and patronage have had to leave with their customers.

The tragedy of Mora County is the tragedy of northern New Mexico. If the Spanish-American rural population had managed to retain ownership of the common lands of their community land grants, the region might have maintained a large rural Spanish-American population supported by communal and individual development of the natural resources.

NOTES

1. Warren A. Beck and Ynez D. Haase, *Historical Atlas of New Mexico* (Norman, OK: University of Oklahoma Press, 1969), 2-7; Charles B. Hunt, *Natural Regions of the United States and Canada* (San Francisco, CA: W.H. Freeman and Co., 1974), 377-391.
2. Hunt, *Natural Regions*, 291.
3. *Ibid.*
4. Erna Ferguson, *Our Southeast* (New York, NY: Alfred Knopf, 1940), 330.
5. *Ibid.*
6. Eugene J. Hannosh, *A History of Mora, 1835 to 1887*, M.A. Thesis, New Mexico Highland University, 27.
7. Nancie Gonzalez, *The Spanish Americans of New Mexico* (Albuquerque, NM: The University of New Mexico Press, 1967), 6.
8. Fray Angelico Chavez, "Early Settlement in the Mora Valley, *El Palacio*, 62 (November), 315-323, Julian Josue Vigil, Personal Communication, 1982.
9. House Executive Document No. 14, 36th Congress, 1st Session, 1860.
10. Alice Bullock, *Mountain Villages* (Santa Fe, NM: Sunstone Press, 1972), 53-58. See also Hilario Rubio, *La Gente Del Otro Lado, A Historical, Economic and Genealogical Survey of Rociada, New Mexico* (Santa Fe, NM: Yucca Speedway Printers, 1980).
11. Ernest Wallace and E. Adamson Hoebel, *The Commanches: Lords of the Southern Plains* (Norman, OK: University of Oklahoma Press, 1952), 289. The attitude of Anglo-American officialdom in New Mexico toward the Comancheros is well expressed in the following quotation from Asheurfelter, U.S. attorney for New Mexico to Atkinson, Surveyor General, New Mexico dated October 9, 1871: (Catron Collection, Coronado Room, Zimmerman Library, University of New Mexico).

    It has come to my knowledge that the main incentive to the thieving raids of the Commanches of Northwestern Texas lies in the fact that certain citizens of this Territory find it profitable to trade with those Indians for the plunder secured in such raids. Large numbers of cattle stolen in this manner from the herders and settlers on the Texas frontier are constantly being driven into New Mexico by Mexican traders who purchase them from the Commanches for very slight considerations. A regular system of traffic has grown up, and it is now estimated that fully five hundred traders are engaged in making regular trips from the Valley of the Rio Pecos in this Territory to the Staked Plains of Northwestern Texas for the purpose of bartering with the Commanches for stolen cattle . . . for these petty traders who are for the most part men without property and who seem to operate under the direction of merchants and small dealers within the Territory who receive stolen stock.
12. Warren A. Beck, *New Mexico: A History of Four Centries* (Norman, OK: University of Oklahoma Press, 1962), 109-118. See also Ray A. Billington, *Far Western Frontier, 1836-1860* (New York, NY: Harper, 1956), 26-36. Josiah Gregg, *Commerce of the Prairies*, Max Moorhead, ed. (Norman, OK: University of Oklahoma Press, 1954). Victor Westphall, *Thomas Benton Catron and His Era* (Tucson, AZ: The University of Arizona Press, 1973), 39-40.
13. Beck, *New Mexico*, 128.
14. Seymour V. Connor and Jimmy M. Skaggs, *Broadcloth and Britches* (College Station, TX: Texas A. and M. Press, 1977), 125.
15. Leroy R. Hafen, *Ruxton of the Rockies* (Norman, OK: University of Oklahoma Press, 1950), 188.
16. Hubert H. Bancroft, *Arizona and New Mexico, 1639-1888* (San Francisco, CA: A.L. Bancroft and Co., 1888). Republished by Horn & Wallace Publishers, Albuquerque, NM, 1962, 428-435. See also James W. Goodrich, "Revolt at Mora, *New Mexico Historical Review*, 47 (January 1971) 49-60. Ralph Emerson Twitchell, *The History of the Military Occupation of New Mexico from 1846 to 1851* (Chicago, IL: The Rio Grande Press, Inc., 1963), 124-138.
17. Chris Emmett, *Fort Union and the Winning of the West* (Norman, OK: University of Oklahoma Press, 1965). See also Herbert O. Brayer, *William Blackmore: The Spanish American Land Grants of New Mexico and Colorado, 1863-1878* (Denver, CO: Bradford Robinson, 1949), 165-166.
18. Brayer, *William Blackmore*, 166.
19. A perusal of the census schedules for Mora County in 1860 reveals the presence of many French names in the population such as Leroux, Brichal, Bone, Blanchard, Lefevere, and St. Vrain. Most of them were born in Taos County and migrated to Mora County. With few exceptions they were married to Spanish-Americans. Even as early as 1860 there were forty-one Anglo-American men and twelve Anglo-American woman living in Mora County. Among the men, nineteen were married and eleven were single. Nine men had married Anglo-American women and eight men married Spanish-American women. One man had married a woman born in New Mexico of a French-Canadian father. Among the women, two were single, two had married Spanish-American men, and the rest married Anglo-American men. Thirteen of the men were born in Missouri, seven in Kentucky, six in New York, two in Pennsylvania, and one each in Vermont and Massachusetts. The birth places of the two men were unknown. Twelve of the men were farmers, eight form laborers, two carpenters, two masons, and one man in each of the following occupations: printer, blacksmith, distiller, innkeeper, clerk, and merchant. The occupations of two men were not listed. Immigrants from seven different nations lived in Mora County in 1860. A slightly larger number of immigrants came from Mexico — twenty-four, followed by twenty from Germany, twelve from Ireland, nine from England, eight from Canada, six from France, three from Spain, and one from Italy. It should be noted that although some competition with Spanish-Americans for land was beginning, the foreigners as well as the Anglo-Americans frequently provided craft skills that may have been lacking in the local population.

    The Mexicans blended into the native Spanish-American population. Of the twenty-one men, seventeen were married and four were not. All seventeen had married Spanish-American women. Of the three Mexican women, one was single — a servant — and two were married to Spanish-Americans. Eight of the men came from Sonora and eight men and three women from Chihuahua. Four were born in Durango, and two each in Monterey and Nuevo Leon. And, finally, one immigrant came from Matamoros, one was a cook, and one a carpenter. Among the Germans, seventeen were single men, and seven were married. Among those married, three had married girls from Germany, and two Spanish-American girls. Six Germans were merchants, five were laborers, one a blacksmith, and one a carpenter. There were no Irish women immigrants in Mora at that time. Of the twelve Irish men living in Mora, seven were single and five had married Spanish-American women. Three were farmers, five laborers, and one Irishman was found listed in each of the following occupations: mason, carpenter, teamster, and clerk. 1860 Census Schedules, Mora County, New Mexico. For a discussion of Spanish American/Anglo-American intermarriage during a period slightly earlier than this, see Craver, Rebecca M., *The Impact of Intimacy: Mexican-Anglo Intermarriage in New Mexico, 1821-1846* (El Paso, TX: Texas Western Press, 1982).
20. Lynn Perrigo, *Gateway to Glorieta* (Boulder, CO: Pruett Publishing Co., 1982), 7; 157-161. David A. Sandoval, "Trade and Manito Society in New Mexico, 1821-1846," Ph.D. Thesis, University of Utah, 1978.
21. Olen E. Leonard, *The Role of the Land Grant* (Albuquerque, NM: Calvin Horn Publisher, Inc., 1970), 101-103.
22. J.J. Bowden, "Private Land Claims in the Southwest," 6 vols. (LLM thesis, SMU, 1969), 4:813-815. Petition of the representatives of the Spanish American inhabitants of the Mora Community Land Grant for approval of their grant by the Surveyor General of New Mexico, M. Ashurst and J. Jackson for claimants to the Surveyor General of New Mexico. (no date) NA Record Group, No. 49, Mora Land Grant, New

Mexico.

23. Thomas Means to A.P. Wilbur, Surveyor General of New Mexico, August 4, 1861, NA Record Group, No. 49, Mora Land Grant, New Mexico.

    The survey of Mora Grant is so extensive that I cannot submit it then with any justice to myself without laborious calculations and protraction. There are at least 118 miles on the three boundaries which I exceed in 10 days. A great amount of physical labor and no small share of scientific ability were required in the survey of the Mora Grant.

24. John M. Clark to Surveyor General of New Mexico, 27 Nov. 1861, NA Record Group, No. 29, Mora Land Grant, New Mexico.

    Special agent Clark wrote:

    Immediately upon receipt of your letter of instructions, I proceeded by stage to Fort Union, where I remained one day making inquiries among the Mexican volunteers stationed at that Fort but obtained no reliable information. I then proceeded to the town of Mora where several of the original grantees reside. By several of the most prominent citizens of the place to whom I had disclosed the object of my mission, I was referred to Don Miguel Mascarenas as being a man of intelligence and integrity and also as one of the oldest inhabitants of the valley.

    I called upon him at his home and examined him under oath relative to the subject in question, and his answers to the question prescribed in your letter of instructions were as follows. . . . I am one of the persons to whom the Mexican government granted this grant. I know the boundaries of the grant. . . . The Aguage de la Yegua is a spring or holes of water, these holes never go dry, and from this fact the place was used as a camping place by the inhabitants of this valley while out on their buffalo hunts and trading expeditions to the Commanches. It was so used at the time the grant was made and also before that time. The Aguage de la Yegua is situated in a small valley or canyon of a mesa. There is not now and never has been to my knowledge any other place in this vicinity called by that name.

    See also Willis Drummond, Commissioner of the General Land Office to T. Rush Spencer, Surveyor General of New Mexico, 24 July 1871, and Commissioner of the General Land Office to John A. Clark, Surveyor General of New Mexico, 18 Mar. 1862, NA Record Group, No. 49, Mora Land Grant, New Mexico.

25. For a brief historical summary of the Means Survey controversy see Willis Drummond, to T. Rush Spencer, 24 July 1871.
26. J.M. Edmunds, Commissioner of the General Land Office to John A. Clark, Surveyor General of New Mexico, 6 Oct. 1861. NA Record Group, No. 49, Mora Land Grant, New Mexico.
27. Drummond to Spencer, 24 July 1871.
28. Thomas Means to John A. Clark, Surveyor General of New Mexico, 18 May 1863. NA Group Record, No. 49, Mora Land Grant, New Mexico.
29. Westphall, *Thomas Benton Catron*, 39-40.
30. Westphall, *Thomas Benton Catron*, 5-32. See also William A. Keleher, *The Maxwell Land Grant* (New York, NY: Argosy-Antiquarian, 1964), 147-151. Oscar D. Lambert, *Stephen Benton Elkins* (Pittsburgh, PA: University of Pittsburgh Press, 1955), 1-34.
31. John A. Williams, "New York's First Senator from West Virginia: How Stephen B. Elkins Found a New Political Home," *West Virginia History*, 31 (January 1970): 73-87. See also Lambert, *Elkins*, 1-34; Keleher, *Maxwell*, 147-151.
32. Howard R. Lamar, *The Far Southwest, 1846-1912: A Territorial History* (New Haven, CT: Yale University Press, 1966), 136-170.
33. *Ibid.*
34. Westphall, *Thomas Benton Catron*, 40-41.
35. *Ibid.* See also Brayer, *William Blackmore*, 166-170.
36. Westphall, *Thomas Benton Catron*; Brayer, *William Blackmore*, 166-170.
37. *Ibid.*
38. Victor Westphall, *Mercedes Reales: Hispanic Land Grants of the Upper Rio Grande Region* (Albuquerque, NM: University of New Mexico Press, 1983), 158.
39. R.A. Ballinger, Commissioner of the General Land Office to the Secretary of the Interior, 28 Oct. 1907, NA Record Group, No. 49, Mora Land Grant, New Mexico.
40. Westphall, *Mercedes Reales*, 158.
41. *Abstract of the Mora Land Grant*, A.A. Jones Papers, Mora Grant, State Records Center, Santa Fe.
42. Protest against Issuance of Patent of Ownership in the Mora Land Grant from 18 Anglo-American Landholders on the Mora Grant to the Secretary of the Department of Interior, 22 June 1876, NA Record Group, No. 49, Mora Land Grant, New Mexico.
43. Petition to the Secretary of the Department of the Interior from a Committee Appointed in a Convention of the Residents of the Mora Grant held on 15 June 1875 in the Community of Mora, NA Record Group, No. 59, Mora Land Grant, New Mexico.
44. Westphall, *Thomas Benton Catron*, 43.
45. *Ibid.*, 40.
46. *Ibid.*, 43-44.
47. *Ibid.*, 44-45. Adalbert Ames was Butler's son-in-law having married his daughter Blanche in 1847. See Howard P. Nash, Jr., *Stormy Petrel: The Life and Times of General Benjamin F. Butler, 1818-1893* (Rutherford, WV: Farleigh Dickinson University Press, 1969).
48. *Ibid.*, 44; Ralph C. Ely to Thomas B. Catron, 27 July 1910. Catron Papers, Mora Land Grant. Coronado Room, Zimmerman Library, University of New Mexico.
49. R.A. Ballinger, Commissioner of the General Land Office to the Secretary of the Interior, 28 Oct. 1907, NA Record Group, No. 49, Mora Land Grant, New Mexico.
50. *Ibid.*
51. William Strover, Report of the Investigation of the True Location of the West Boundary of the Mora Grant in New Mexico, 19 July 1907, NA Record Group, No. 49, Mora Land Grant, New Mexico.
52. *Ibid.*
53. *Ibid.*
54. *Ibid.*

    In his discussion of the location of the Estillero, the long sought-after western boundary call, Strover writes:

    The word Estillero is probably derived from *estilla* (stick or splinter), meaning a place with many splinters or sticks. . . . Some of the Mexicans claim that Estillero means a place where the winds blow very strong, breaking and throwing down the trees; other natives assert that Estillero means a place where it is very cold and where the water seeps out of the ground — a marshy place. The latter contention is supported in one of the old grant papers where the boundary call is referred to as "La Cienega de Estillero" (marshy meadow of the Estillero). I have not been able to obtain a definition of the word from any of the Spanish dictionaries which I consulted.

    At the time [of the Means Survey] the country at the Estillero and in the vicinity of the southwest corner (of the Mora Grant) and for some distance east of said points was wild and almost inaccessible, there being no nearer settlers than those in the Mora Valley. An Indian trail led through the Estillero Valley to the Indian Pueblos of Taos and Picuris, which trail was also used by native hunters going from the valleys to the mountains and the hunters probably first applied the name Estillero to the mountain covered all over with fallen timber blown over by the strong winds which prevail at that place.

55. Commissioner of the General Land Office to the Honorable T.B. Catron, 13 Aug. 1912, Catron Papers, Mora Land Grant, Coronado Room, Zimmerman Library, University of New Mexico.
56. *United States of America vs. State Investment Company and Edward B. Wheeler*, vol. 264, U.S., 206, 1924.
57. *Abstract of the Mora Land Grant*, A.A. Jones Papers, State Records Center, Santa Fe, New Mexico:

    Thomas B. Catron reported that his life was in danger in the Mora Land Grant. He writes as follows: Petition of Thomas B. Catron, 24 Apr. 1889, District Court Records, State Records Center and Archives, Santa Fe, New Mexico:

    Your petitioner further represents that many times when he attended the said court in the County of Mora to attend to said cause on behalf of said complainant (Stephen B. Elkins), he did so at great risk and peril to himself, and danger of his life, caused by the excitement of the people originating out of the fact that the said complainant had commenced the above entitled suit . . . the said people in their excitement having many times met and congregated together and made divers and sundry threats that they would do personal injury and harm to your petitioner. . . . Your petitioner was therefore compelled, in order to quiet the said people and disabuse their minds, to employ various persons who were influential with the said people, to go among them, explain the situation, and quiet them, and cause them to abandon their threats and purposes; that in doing so, he was compelled to lay out a large sum of money to . . . of twenty five hundred dollars, which said sum of money however, was supplied and furnished to him by one, Blackmore, whose first name is to your petitioner unknown . . . Union Land and Grazing Company vs. Arce, 21 N.M., 115.

58. Undated Memorandum, Prince Papers, State Records Center, Santa Fe, New Mexico. Prince was a former governor of New Mexico.
59. Santa Fe, *New Mexican*, 22 Feb. 1916.
60. *Ibid.* According to the Abstract, the State Investment Company, headquartered in Las Vegas, New Mexico, was organized by George A. Flemming, William Shillinglaw, and Reeve Eagle of Las Vegas, New Mexico.
61. Margaret Meadors, "The Economy of Mora

County," *New Mexico Business*, vol. 20 (November 1967), 1-46.

62. Charles P. Loomis and Nellie H. Loomis, "Skilled Spanish-American War-Industry Workers from New Mexico," *Applied Anthropology*, 1:33-36.
63. In San Miguel County the population declined 23 percent from 27,910 to 22,751 in this same time period. In Guadalupe County the population fell 59.8 percent from 8,464 in 1940 to 4,496 in 1980; the Spanish American population in both counties suffered heavy land loss. (U.S. Bureau of the Census, Census of Population: 1950; vol. II *Characteristics of the Population*, part II, New Mexico; Census of Population: 1970, vol. I *Characteristics of the Population*, Part 33, New Mexico; Census of the Population; 1980; vol. II *Characteristics of the Population*, part 31, New Mexico).
64. "U.S. Bureau of the Census, Census of Population," Chapter C, *General Social and Economic Characteristics*, Part 33, New Mexico.

Clark S. Knowlton received his B.A. and M.A. degrees in Sociology from Brigham Young University and his Ph.D. degree from Vanderbilt University. He has taught in Georgia, New Mexico and Texas. He is now a professor of sociology at the University of Utah. He has one book published in Brazil, has written over 50 articles on the Spanish-Americans and Mexican-Americans in the Southwest, plus edited several publications of Human Adjustment to Arid Lands. Dr. Knowlton has also been instrumental in the development of several professional associations involved in the study of arid lands in the Southwest, and Spanish-American history and culture in New Mexico.

Law Books on the Hispanic Frontier

Joseph W. McKnight

The title page of the first volume of the 1653 edition of the Latin version of Juan de Solorzano's ***De Indiarum Iure,*** *first published in Madrid in 1629. From this work Solorzano's* ***Politica Indiana*** *(Madrid, 1648) emerged with additions, omissions and translation into Spanish. It was the later work that was commonly used on the frontier.*

As a private professional calling, law was not regularly practiced on the Spanish frontier of North America except in New Orleans. Even if entry into private legal practice had not been severely restricted, in most parts of the frontier legal practice would not have contributed significantly toward a practitioner's livelihood. At Mexico City, the capital of New Spain, and in Havana, Santo Domingo, and Guadalajara all grades of professional lawyers were available: advocates, counselors, notaries and pleaders. But in most of the frontier regions during the entire period of Spanish control there was a conspicuous absence of all of these. The exception was New Orleans, where private legal assistance was generally available.

New Orleans, which passed out of the Spanish domain in

1803, was the consistent exception to most of these general observations. At the capital of Spanish Louisiana, capable Spanish notaries were always available to draft any sort of legal document that a private individual might want, and there were several advocates and pleaders who would assist a claimant or a respondent in litigation.[1] Elsewhere, however, professional legal services were not available to private persons, or indeed to officials, most of the time.

Although a provincial governor was ordinarily entitled to a trained legal advisor on his staff, during the last half-century of Spanish rule an *asesor* was not assigned to assist a Spanish governor except in the coastal provinces of Louisiana and the Floridas. It was not until the Spanish governmental offices in New Orleans were closed that an *asesor* was supplied to West Florida by reassignment of the New Orleans legal officer to Pensacola, though an *asesor* was also assigned to St. Augustine. In the Western provinces (Texas, New Mexico, and Upper California), the officers of the crown lacked immediate legal assistance. For those regions the governor had to seek the advice of the *asesor* assigned to his superior further south. Deprived of first-hand legal advice, the governors of those regions rarely sought it, though some opinions sent to the governors have survived.[2]

Hence, except for the law which might be found in books, the Western frontier was virtually lacking in legal guidance under the Spanish regime, though there was some improvement in this situation during the period of Mexican rule which followed. To be sure, one of the first settlers of San Fernando de Bexar was designated as municipal notary, and he served in that capacity for 25 years. But his professional work was so unrewarding that in his petition to be relieved of his notarial duties in 1757, inadequate compensation was given as his principal reason.[3] When he was allowed to retire from his notarial calling, no one succeeded him. It was, therefore, not lawyers but law books to which the frontier population looked for guidance in formulating legal documents. Moreover, in a society in which most of the population could neither read nor write with any proficiency, reliance for legal guidance was put upon those who could use the books available. It is evident that a few of their fellow citizens and military officers assisted the settlers and soldiery in drawing papers and conducting trials.[4] In 1810, also at San Fernando, the governor designated four persons to act as pleaders.[5] Thereafter, however, political disturbances followed at such a rapid rate that there was little, if any, need for their services.

Although it may be supposed that each Spanish provincial governor would have had a few law books of his own, and in some cases, a few volumes of legal sources might have been on hand in the *casa real*, these conjectures cannot always be documented. The clergy, as the most literate members of frontier society, might have also been expected to have a book or two with some legal content, but this supposition can only be demonstrated in scattered instances. Law books which helped to maintain the continuity of Hispano-Mexican rules on the frontier were very thinly spread.

The first Spanish settlements on the northern frontier were in Florida during the late sixteenth century. In spite of a lack of evidence as to what law books the early governors of Florida had, it seems likely that they had a copy of the *Nueva Recopilación*[6] and probably Solórzano Pereira's *Politica Indiana*.[7] At any rate, in the mid-eighteenth century Governor Melchor de Navarrete proposed to his superior that, because of the lack of an *asesor*, he be allowed to give instruction to his military officers so that they could act as judges and prosecutors.[8] He would have needed a work comparable to that of Solórzano and a collection of laws in order to prepare his lessons. But nothing came of the governor's proposal.

As the Spaniards began to colonize the arid regions of New Mexico in the seventeenth century, it may be conjectured that the governor there included a few law books in the effects which he had transported hundreds of leagues overland. As in later times, the legal works on the frontier during the seventeenth century must be deduced from citations in reports and records. In the disputes between the governor and the Franciscans in the early 1640s, a number of legal works were referred to in dispatches. These included the *Nueva Recopilación*, Hevia Bolaños's *Curia Philippica*, Viladiego's *Instrucción Politica*, and canonical sources such as the decrees of the Council of Trent and writings of Martin Azpilcueta and Domingo de Soto.[9] In his reports, Governor Diego de Peñalosa (1661-1664) referred to Solórzano's *Politica Indiana*, Monterrosa's *Práctica Civil y Criminal*, and Hevia Bolaños's *Curia Philippica*,[10] another copy of which may have belonged to the governor's secretary.[11] Other references to legal authorities in the governor's dispatches were drawn from the notes in Hevia's treatise.[12]

There would have been a marked similarity in the books on law and administration that a frontier governor would have had whether he arrived on the frontier by land or by sea. In comparing the availability of books on the coastal frontier and the inland frontier, geography and climate were significant factors to be reckoned with, however. Books, like other fragile possessions, were easier to transport by sea than by land, and transportation (and hence communication) was far easier in the case of the provinces served by seagoing vessels. Hence, written sources would be expected to be more numerous and up to date on the coastal frontier than on the inland frontier. On the other hand, the geography of the eastern coastal provinces was also an enemy of the printed word. Whereas adequately protected books would last longer in the arid climate of the inland regions, the dampness of the eastern coasts and the danger of tropical storms were a constant threat to all perishable materials, particularly books. On the inland frontier of the West the danger of enemy attack was also a threat to perishables, and it seems likely that most written matter in mid-seventeenth-century New Mexico was destroyed during the Pueblo Revolt of 1680.

Following Spain's acquisition of Louisiana in 1762, and the establishment of Spanish law there in 1769, Lower Louisiana became the principal bastion of Hispanic law on the northern frontier. Without the maintenance of Spanish

The Cabiblo (city hall), built 1796-1799, New Orleans. (Courtesy the Historic New Orleans Collection.)

law in Louisiana, the survival of Hispanic principles elsewhere would have been far less marked. New Orleans became, and long remained, the fountainhead of Spanish legal institutions in North America. It was at New Orleans that the broadest collection of Spanish legal sources, and men knowledgeable in Spanish law, were congregated. The preeminence of New Orleans as a center of Spanish law was not significantly felt elsewhere along the Hispanic frontier, however, until sovereignty of Louisiana had passed into American hands. The event of greatest legal importance there was the enactment of the Digest of Laws of 1808. The Spanish elements in this otherwise Francophile code were of lasting importance to the maintenance of Spanish elements in the marital property law of Texas, California, and New Mexico and other aspects of the law in Texas. New Orleans was not, however, a significant source of law books, except to Texas, during the early nineteenth century. As a governmental center, New Orleans was important only to the other settlements of Lower Louisiana and West Florida and for the posts up the Mississippi River. Because the provincial administration (including access to the courts and notaries) was almost wholly centered at New Orleans, any need of law books elsewhere in the province was small.[13] As a consequence, Spanish law did not become well rooted in the remote parts of the province of Louisiana.

Most of the Spanish law books that anyone would have wanted to consult were available in New Orleans.[14] The services of notaries were readily at hand there, and the governor and the intendant were always advised by a university-trained *asesor* until the end of the Spanish regime.[15] This is compelling evidence that Spanish legal practice was firmly in place in New Orleans. Thus, in Lower Louisiana, Spanish law had put down deep roots that the American regime was unable to eradicate. To the east and west a slighter awareness of Spanish legal norms was maintained in the frontier regions, and maintenance of Hispanic rules in those areas was, in large measure, dependent on the availability of Spanish law books.

The Spanish were established on the Western frontier long before the acquisition of the province of Louisiana. After being ousted by the Pueblo Revolt, the Spanish began to reestablish themselves in the Santa Fe area in 1692. The earliest actual records of frontier Spanish law books come from New Mexico in the early eighteenth century. Governor Diego de Vargas had an impressive library of 33 titles of which four works (nine volumes) dealt with legal subjects. He owned two sets of the *Nueva Recopilación* (a two-volume set and a four-volume set), the two volumes of Solórzano's *Politica Indiana,* and Hevia's *Curia Philippica.*[16]

The settlment of the town of San Fernando in Texas began in 1731, and an earlier Spanish outpost had been maintained in East Texas. With the increasing Christian-missionary activity and the need of forts to protect the missionaries and the settlers, references to civil, ecclesiastical, and military law became more common in both New Mexico and Texas. The principal compilations of Spanish law covered all of these elements, and particular volumes dealt with specialized aspects of each of these subjects.

Because of their special interests, each segment of the frontier community tended to have recourse to particular types of books. For the governmental administrator (whether civil or military), works on governmental organization and general administration were deemed essential, along with manuals dealing with the adjudication of disputes. The treatises of Solórzano and Hevia were the works most often available. For the military contingent, a collection of military rules was deemed an integral part of a commander's regular equipment.[17] For the churchmen, some books on ecclesiastical law filled the same need.[18] For the civil population, recourse was most often found in legal manuals where forms were available for recording important transactions. After the statutes specifically applicable to the Indies were compiled as the *Recopilación de Indias* in 1680, that work was the source most relied upon in official documents and reports, along with the *Nueva Recopilación* (1567), which was almost wholly replaced by the *Novisima Recopilación* in the early years of the nineteenth century.

The law books that Governor Vargas of New Mexico had at the beginning of the eighteenth century are not dissimilar in nature from those owned by Governor Manuel Muñoz of Texas at the end of the century. Both governors had a copy of Hevia's standard work on judicial procedure. Although

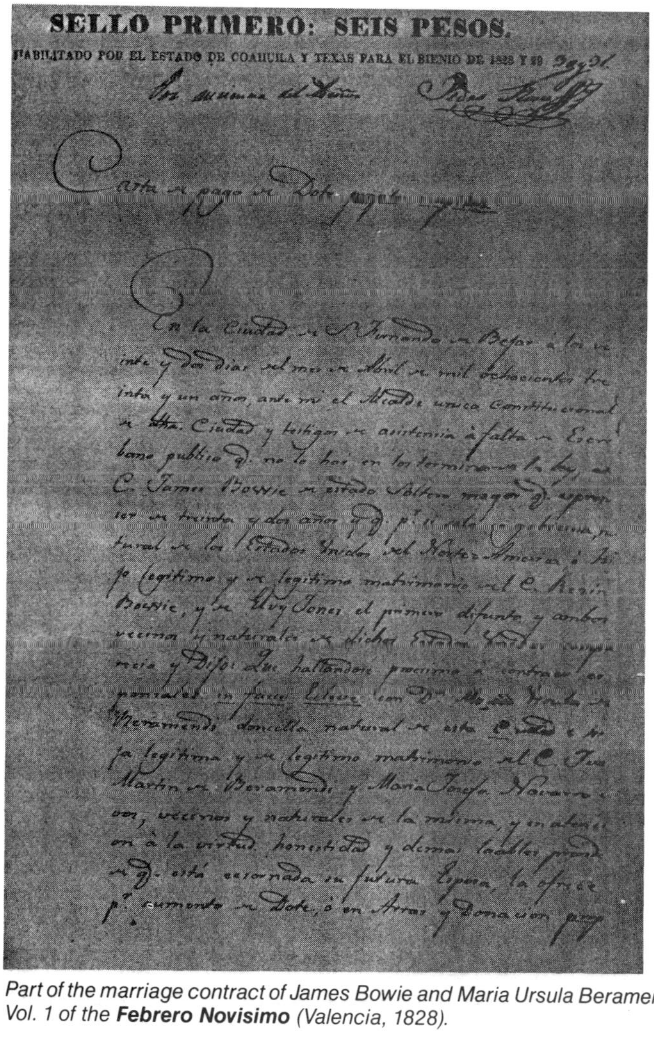

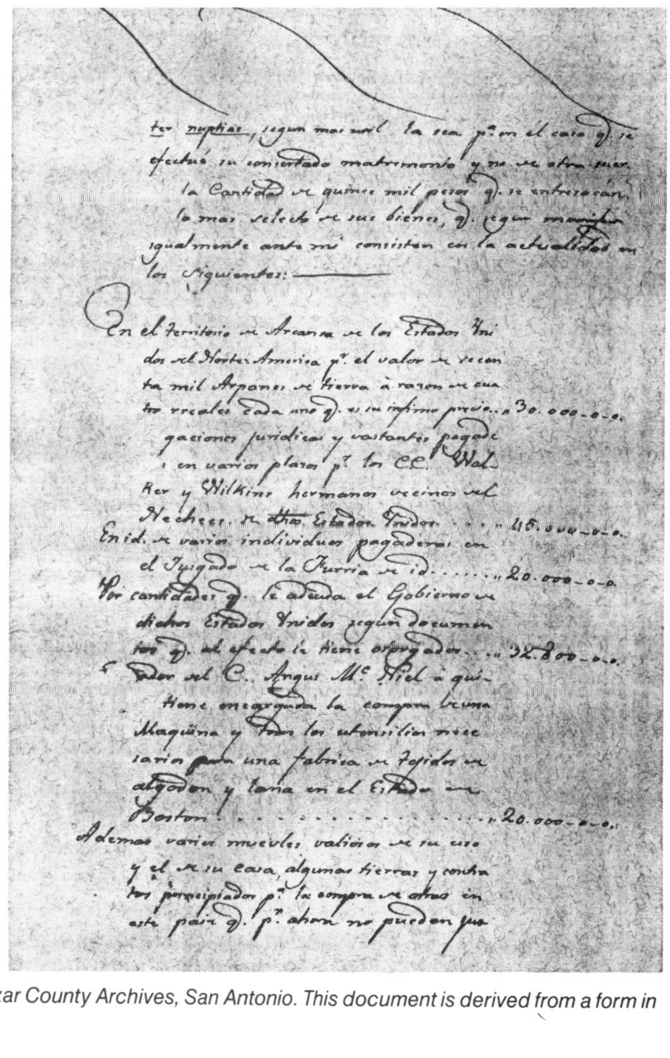

Part of the marriage contract of James Bowie and Maria Ursula Beramendi, Bexar County Archives, San Antonio. This document is derived from a form in Vol. 1 of the ***Febrero Novisimo*** *(Valencia, 1828).*

RECOPILACION DE LEYES DE LOS REYNOS DE LAS INDIAS. TOMO SEGUNDO.

EN MADRID. POR ANTONIO PEREZ DE SOTO. Año de 1774. TERCERA EDICION.

Title page of the Recopilación de Leyes de los Reyños de las Indias published at Madrid in 1774. This was probably the most commonly used law book on the frontier.

Muñoz had no copy of the *Nueva Recopilación*, there was a copy of the *Recopilación de Indias* at the *casa real*.[19] Muñoz's legal library included the *Instrucción de Intendentes* and several works on military law: *Ordenanzas Militares*, a *Prontuario* to accompany it, and Colón's *Juzgados Militares*.[20] Muñoz also had the professional civil-practice manuals of Colom and Febrero (eight volumes in all),[21] and these included forms covering the most common transactions of legal significance. In the liquidation of the estate of Governor Muñoz after his death in 1799, the civil-practice manuals were acquired by Antonio Gil Ybarbo, a retired captain of the militia and former Lieutenant Governor of East Texas, then living at San Fernando.[22] When he made his will a year later, Gil Ybarbo listed these works along with the legal works he already had: another work on judicial procedure (Gonzalo Suarez de Paz, *Praxis Ecclesiastica et Secularis*), Pedro Melgarejo's *Compendio de Contratos Publicos*, and a set of the *Recopilación de Indias*. It is evident from the municipal records of Bexar that Gil Ybarbo sometimes assisted the local townspeople in making their wills.[23] He may have supplemented his pension with an amateur legal practice of sorts.

In 1805 the Spanish crown promulgated its last compilation of the laws, the *Novisima Recopilación*, and on the basis of his citations of it, it can be concluded that Governor Salcedo of Texas had a copy of it before him in 1810.[24] As a result of the political and military turbulence in the ensuing years, however, it is hard to know what law books may have been in use in Texas and elsewhere on the Western frontier at the end of the Spanish regime. On the somewhat less turbulent Eastern frontier, some account can be made of the law books that survived the change of sovereignty from Spanish to American. In his pleadings and brief for a Pensacola litigant in 1821, Samuel Acre of Mobile cited the works of Hevia, Febrero, and Colom, as well as the *Partidas* and the *Recopilación de Indias*.[25] Thus, either at Pensacola or Mobile, these standard Spanish works were apparently continuously available at the end of the Spanish era. It is also evident that Ruperto Saavedra, the last *asesor* of East Florida, had a copy of the *Recopilación de Indias*.[26]

In addition to the civil and military authorities, churchmen also had some books on law among their possessions. In their periodic remonstrances to higher civil authority concerning treatment of the Indians and other matters, the missionaries of the central frontier and in faraway California sometimes invoked the authority of the *Recopilación de Indias*.[27] The 1785 inventory of Mission San José in Texas listed that collection of laws, Solórzano's *Politica Indiana*, the canonical encyclopedia *Biblioteca Ferraris*, which contained entries on various matters of law, and a work on the Council of Trent, which had generated much of the canon law then current.[28] These books had evidently been accumulated after a 1755 inventory of the mission which made no mention of books. In its library of 256 titles in 1788, the Mission of Santo Domingo in New Mexico had a copy of the work of Solórzano and three volumes on the Council of Trent.[29] Although law books of any kind were rare among the Spaniards in California, several missions had a copy of the *Recopilación de Indias*, and Mission San Antonio had a set of the *Biblioteca Ferraris*.[30] The missionaries of southern Arizona do not seem to have had any law books during the late eighteenth century.[31]

By treaty with Spain in 1795, the United States acquired a portion of West Florida, and that region became the Mississippi Territory in 1798. Although reliance was put on the work of Febrero in one dispute before the new American court,[32] there does not appear to have been much popular familiarity with the rules of Spanish law,[33] and the law of the territory was quickly and almost wholly Americanized.

The United States' next acquisition was the vast territory of Louisiana. In that part of the upper region of Louisiana which was organized as the Missouri Territory, the law was also Americanized with only modest subsequent reference to Spanish legal sources.[34] In the more extensively settled area of Lower Louisiana, however, resistance to Americanization of the law was registered within the first year after American annexation and culminated in the enactment of the Digest of

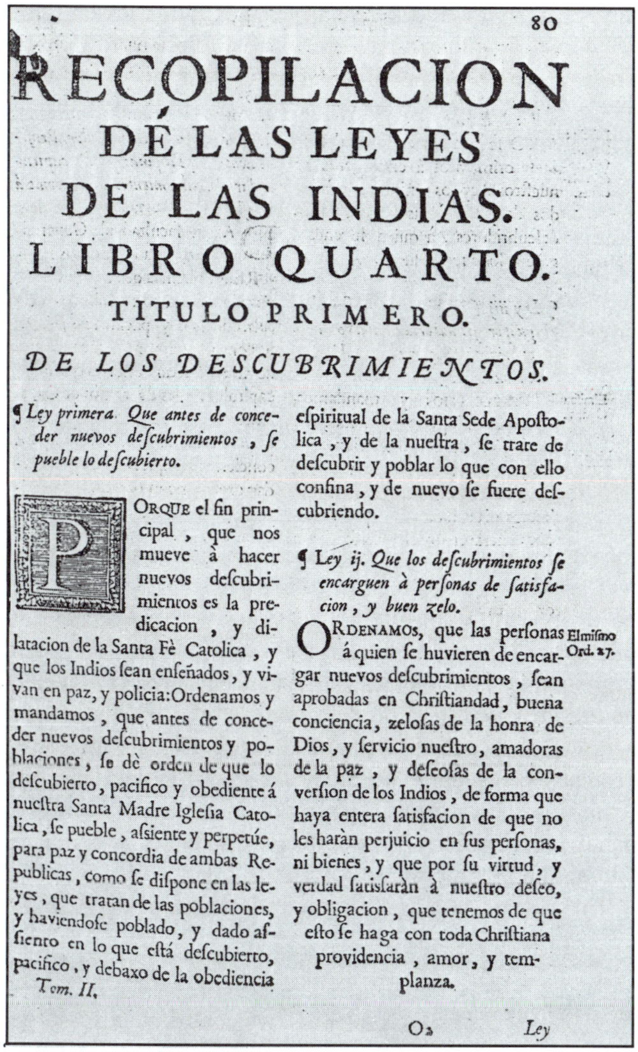

80

RECOPILACION DE LAS LEYES DE LAS INDIAS.

LIBRO QUARTO.

TITULO PRIMERO.

DE LOS DESCUBRIMIENTOS.

¶ *Ley primera. Que antes de conceder nuevos deſcubrimientos, ſe pueble lo deſcubierto.*

PORQUE el fin principal, que nos mueve à hacer nuevos deſcubrimientos es la predicacion, y dilatacion de la Santa Fè Catolica, y que los Indios ſean enſeñados, y vivan en paz, y policia: Ordenamos y mandamos, que antes de conceder nuevos deſcubrimientos y poblaciones, ſe dè orden de que lo deſcubierto, pacifico y obediente á nueſtra Santa Madre Igleſia Catolica, ſe pueble, aſsiente y perpetúe, para paz y concordia de ambas Republicas, como ſe diſpone en las leyes, que tratan de las poblaciones, y haviendoſe poblado, y dado aſsiento en lo que está deſcubierto, pacifico, y debaxo de la obediencia eſpiritual de la Santa Sede Apoſtolica, y de la nueſtra, ſe trate de deſcubrir y poblar lo que con ello confina, y de nuevo ſe fuere deſcubriendo.

¶ *Ley ij. Que los deſcubrimientos ſe encarguen à perſonas de ſatisfacion, y buen zelo.*

ORDENAMOS, que las perſonas á quien ſe huvieren de encargar nuevos deſcubrimientos, ſean aprobadas en Chriſtiandad, buena conciencia, zeloſas de la honra de Dios, y ſervicio nueſtro, amadoras de la paz, y deſeoſas de la converſion de los Indios, de forma que haya entera ſatisfacion de que no les haràn perjuicio en ſus perſonas, ni bienes, y que por ſu virtud, y verdad ſatisfaràn à nueſtro deſeo, y obligacion, que tenemos de que eſto ſe haga con toda Chriſtiana providencia, amor, y templanza. El miſmo Ord. 27.

Tom. II. O2 Ley

The beginning of Book IV of the Recopilacion.

Laws of 1808. Although this general codification of private law was verbally based in very large measure on the Code Napoléon, it embodied a large portion of the subsisting Spanish law, much of which was very similar to that laid down in the French Code. Other distinctively Hispanic provisions of the Digest, such as those relating to family property law and succession, differed significantly from the corresponding provisions of the French model.

Because the Spanish authorities continued to be relied on in the Louisiana courts before and after the enactment of the Digest, proposals were made for the publication of Spanish legal texts in English translation. Two such propositions were advertised in local newspapers. James Workman offered prospective subscribers a *Digest of the Laws of Castile and the Spanish Indies,* and Edward Livingston proposed a very ambitious ten-volume translation of the civil law for $100.[35] But neither suggestion garnered sufficient subscribers to justify completion of the project. In 1818, however, Louis Moreau Lislet, the principal draftsman of the Louisiana Digest of 1808, published a translation of those portions of the *Partidas* dealing with obligations,[36] and the Louisiana legislature subsequently agreed to sponsor an English translation of the whole, insofar as it was still the law in Louisiana. With the assistance of Henry Carleton, a collaborator on the earlier work, Moreau brought out a two-volume translation of the *Partidas* in 1822 that was widely distributed.[37] This work was used extensively in Louisiana and in Texas.

During the 1820s and early 1830s, several Anglo-American lawyers were among the settlers in Texas from the United States. Taking some of their models from Louisiana, from whence some of them had come, these lawyers attempted to conform their practices to what they supposed to be the Hispanic tradition. Although all but one of these Norte Americanos had no prior practical experience in Mexican law, they did the best they could with the very few legal materials at hand.[38] At San Felipe de Austin the *Novisima Recopilación* may have been available,[39] and one of the Louisianians had a copy of the 1820 English translation of the *Partidas*. Another had volume four of *Febrero Novisimo*, which he had borrowed from the set of a fellow settler in Anahuac. As the only practitioner's book available, the volume (devoted largely to judicial procedure) was in much demand by the local lawyers.[40] When the secretary of Austin's Anglo-American colony attempted to qualify as a notary, the lack of books with which to prepare himself must have been one of the principal reasons for his failure to meet the standards of qualification.[41]

The modest familiarity of the Anglo-Americans with Spanish rules of law during the Mexican period accounts for the persistence of Hispanic principles in the laws of the Texas Republic. The venue statute that was enacted in 1836, for example, was adapted directly from the language of the Louisiana translation of the *Partidas*.[42] Nevertheless, Spanish law books remained in short supply in Texas, and in 1843 Chief Justice John Hemphill commented judicially that he did not have access to the work of Febrero except through quotations in the Louisiana Reports.[43] A year later, however, the works of Febrero and Sala seem to have been available to the court.[44] By 1848, the Texas Supreme Court had also acquired Murillo's *Práctica de Testamentos* and Escriche's *Diccionario de Legislación*.[45]

Just prior to the outbreak of the war for Texas independence and again in the early years of the Texas Republic, Thomas Jefferson Chambers attempted to enlist subscribers for a publication of Spanish sources in translation, but like similar ambitious schemes of his Louisiana predecessors, his efforts failed.[46] The principal source of Spanish law cited in Texas during the 1840s and later was Joseph White's *New Collection of Laws*.[47] White was Florida's territorial delegate to the United States Congress and a commissioner for the determination of the validity of Florida's Spanish land grants. White's command of Hispanic sources is well illustrated by his use of the works of Colom, Elizondo, and Asso and Manuel in his brief to the Territorial Court of West Florida in 1831,[48] and in his successful representation of claimants of Spanish land grants before the Supreme Court of the United States during the 1830s.[49] White published a

John Hemphill (1803-1862) at age of 47 years, from oil portrait in old Supreme Court Room of State Capitol, Austin.

small collection of Spanish legal materials in English translation in 1828.[50] His much larger collection in two volumes was published in Philadelphia just after his death in 1839.[51] This heavily pirated work not only included a portion of John Kimball's English translation of the *Law and Decrees of the State of Coahuila and Texas*, which was published in Houston in 1839, but also the much more useful English translation of the *Instituciones* of Asso and Manuel which Judge Lewis Johnston of Trinidad had translated and published in London in 1825. The republication of the English translation of the treatise of Asso and Manuel gave frontier lawyers a general summary of the whole of Spanish private law, and it was cited frequently by the Texas courts as well as by those of New Mexico and California.[52]

Little is known of Spanish legal sources available in New Mexico and California during the early Mexican period, but New Mexico was served by an *asesor* in the early 1830s and California from 1830 to 1839.[53] The resident *asesor* of Santa Fe during 1831-1832 left an account of the state of the New Mexican judicial process of those times, but he did not mention the availability of printed legal works.[54] A trained lawyer also served as a district judge in New Mexico from 1832 to 1836 and another served in California from 1834 to 1836.[55] The introduction of a printing press into New Mexico in 1834 greatly advanced the dissemination of Hispanic legal literature. Legal books came to California by sea.

Father Antonio José Martinez set up a school for boys in Taos in the early 1840s. To provide a course book for his pupils, Martinez compiled and published the first law book printed in New Mexico in 1842. This work indicates what legal works were available to the author, as the book was drawn from the *Instituciones* of the Guatemalan scholar José Maria Álvarez and included legal forms from Murillo Velarde's *Cursus Juris Canonici* and Eugenio de Tapia's *Febrero Novisimo*.[56] A supplement on succession was added to these materials in 1843.[57] From the fact that Murillo's popular manual on succession was referred to in the Kearny Code of 1846,[58] it is apparent that Father Martinez advised the Anglo-American military draftsmen of that code, which was largely based on the law of Missouri. In 1850 the local need for Murillo's manual was supplied by a Santa Fe reprint of a recent Mexican edition of that work.[59] At the 1851-1852 session of the New Mexican territorial legislature over which he presided, Martinez drew from the works of Álvarez and Murillo in preparing a statute on succession, which was promptly enacted.[60] Thereafter, however, in spite of continued legislative requests for a further printing of Murillo's handy legal primer to supplement the statutory law, a later edition did not appear.[61]

There are no records of Hispanic law books on the Arizona

Thomas Jefferson Chambers. (Courtesy the San Jacinto Museum of History.)

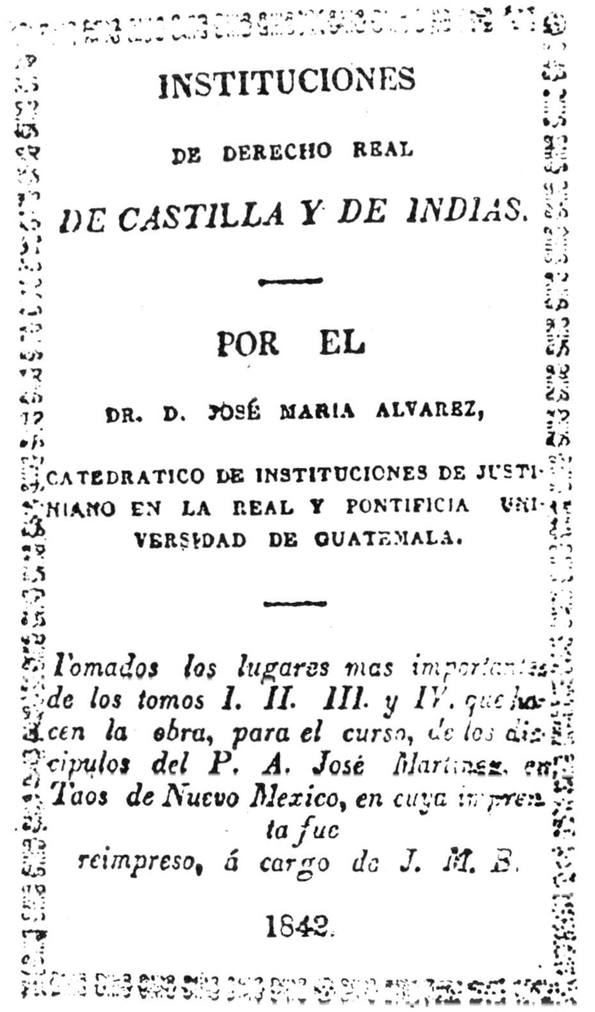

INSTITUCIONES

DE DERECHO REAL

DE CASTILLA Y DE INDIAS.

POR EL

DR. D. JOSÉ MARIA ALVAREZ,

CATEDRATICO DE INSTITUCIONES DE JUSTINIANO EN LA REAL Y PONTIFICIA UNIVERSIDAD DE GUATEMALA.

Tomados los lugares mas importantes de los tomos I. II. III. y IV. que hacen la obra, para el curso, de los discipulos del P. A. José Martinez, en Taos de Nuevo Mexico, en cuya imprenta fue reimpreso, á cargo de J. M. B.

1842.

Title page of the first law book published and printed in New Mexico by Father Martinez, Taos, 1842.

desert or in the mountainous region of eastern California, now called Nevada. Thus the survival of Spanish legal principles in those areas must be ascribed largely to borrowing from the laws of Texas and California.

Because the California settlements were supplied by sea, Spanish legal sources were comparatively more plentiful (in terms of the size of the local population) than in the interior provinces. Several sets of the *Recopilación de Indias* had reached Alta California during the Spanish period,[62] as well as other legal books.[63] After the mid-1820s legal sources became more available.[64] In 1840 the alcalde of Monterey, Salvador Vallejo, used the *Novísima Recopilación* and the *Collección de Decretos,* and he commented that he had purchased Galvan's *Ordenanzas de Tierras y Aguas* from a fellow alcalde who had an extra copy.[65] From the mid-1840s legal sources were even more plentiful. The 1845 inventory of the Court of First Instance at Monterey included a copy of the *Recopilación de Indias*,[66] and a layman's petition in a contested guardianship proceeding in Los Angeles in 1845 clearly demonstrates reliance on a legal treatise.[67] Commenting on what he had seen in California in 1846-1847, the traveler-poet Edwin Bryant mentioned two law books: ". . . a digested code of the laws of Spain and the Indies published in Spain about a hundred years ago and a small pamphlet defining the power of various judicial officers emanating down from the Mexican government since the revolution."[68] The "digested code," perhaps inaccurately described, is hard to identify,[69] but the pamphlet is recognizable as a copy of the Mexican law of 1837, frequently cited in the judicial records and later published in English by Halleck and Hartnell in 1849.[70] Walter Colton, the first Anglo-American alcalde of Monterey (1846), indicated some familiarity with the treatises of Febrero and Álvarez, which he described in 1847 as "works of remarkable comprehensiveness, clearness and facility of application."[71] Succession records of the time also show the use of legal formbooks.[72] In 1848 General Mason had a code of laws prepared, but political conditions changed so fast that he decided not to promulgate it.[73] These projected laws show some reliance on existing Hispano-Mexican sources.

At the Californian legislative session of 1849 there was some discussion of the comparative merits of a general perpetuation of the civil law (as advised by a group of lawyers in San Francisco) or the introduction of the Anglo-American system with which most of the new population was more familiar. With respect to the availability of sources of the two systems, it was reported to the California Senate's Judiciary Committee that books on Anglo-American law might be procured at moderate prices whereas books on Spanish law were not readily available but might be "procured by diligent search."[74] In addition to the various compilations of laws, works of Escriche[75] and Febrero were mentioned specifically. The California legislature opted for Anglo American law.

Gustavus Schmidt was the last of the compilers of Spanish law for frontier use. His *Laws of Spain and Mexico* was published as a synthetic code at New Orleans in 1851. It was widely cited in Texas, New Mexico, and California[76] for a number of years thereafter.

The various *Recopilaciónes* of statutes and the works of Solórzano and Hevia, which had been most relied on in the earlier period, were largely replaced in common use by the treatises of Asso and Manuel, Febrero, and Murillo. Once Anglo-American law had attained dominance on the former Hispanic frontier, occasional recourse continued to be made to Spanish sources in order to resolve disputes arising under the former legal regime or involving Spanish legal institutions. In time, as appellate judges began to examine such points, a better understanding of Spanish sources was achieved. Prior to the Civil War a substantial appreciation of the Spanish law and its sources had developed in most of the formerly frontier regions, but the continuity of much of that knowledge was swept away by the tumult of the war and its aftermath. In spite of this loss of historical continuity, the Hispanic influences already embedded in the statutes, judicial decisions, and local consciousness remained.

NOTES

1. As used here, the term *pleader* means an agent or attorney in fact, someone who acts for another in

a legal matter but who has no professional qualifications as an advocate.

2. For examples, see discussions of Asesor Pedro Galindo Navarro's opinions on various matters concerning wild livestock to Governor Domingo Cabello of Texas, 25 Oct. 1782, 30 Oct. 1782, and 22 Feb. 1786 in Jack Jackson, *Los Mestreños, Spanish Ranching in Texas 1721-1821* (College Station, 1986), 175-176, 241-244, and 297-300; Vsevolod Basanoff, "Dictamen of Pedro Galindo Navarro, Auditor de Guerra, of 7 Dec. 1795," *New Mexico Historical Review,* 8 (July, Oct. 1933): 183-200, 273-303. In this opinion to Governor Fernando Chacón of New Mexico, the *asesor* gave citations to the *Nuevo Recopilación* and *Reglamento de Presidios,* which he must have had before him. *Ibid.,* 185-187, 293-294. There was evidently some citation of laws in a 17 Apr. 1780 opinion of Galindo to Commandant Teodor de Croix, but Commandant Croix's letter of 20 Apr. 1780, which transmitted the opinion to Father Junipero Serra, did not mention the references. Antonine Tibersar, ed., *Writings of Junipero Serra 4* (Washington, D.C., 1966), no. 160 (Fr. Junipero Serra to Fr. Francisco Pangua, 24 Oct. 1780, quoting Croix's letter to Serra), 44-45; no. 155 (Fr. Serra to Commandant Croix, 20 July 1780), 20-21. Also see Galindo's opinion to Governor Juan Bautista Elguezábal of Texas, 31 July 1804, on disposition of livestock taken from smugglers. Jackson, *Los Mestreños,* 481-482.
3. Resignation of office by Francisco Joseph de Arocha, 13 Jan. 1757, Bexar Archives, University of Texas, Austin.
4. Although some persons acted for others in negotiations and in the resolution of judicial disputes, in the latter years of Spanish Texas no one had such a reputation as a pleader that caused him to be so identified in a Spanish census. Odie B. Faulk, *The Last Years of Spanish Texas 1778-1821* (The Hague, 1964) 94.
5. Ordinance of Governor Manuel Salcedo, 4 Mar. 1810, Bexar Archives, University of Texas, Austin.
6. This collection of laws was compiled in 1567.
7. Juan de Solórzano Pereira's work first appeared in 2 volumes (Madrid, 1629-1639), and it was reprinted in many editions thereafter.
8. John Jay Tepaske, *The Governorship of Spanish Florida, 1700-1760* (Durham 1964) 60-61.
9. Eleanor B. Adams & France V. Scholes, "Books in New Mexico 1598-1680," *New Mexico Historical Review,* 17 (1942): 226, 231-232, 257-259. Juan de Hevia Bolaños's *Curia Philippica* was first published in Lima in 1600 and remained a standard authority until the mid-nineteenth century. It is striking that many important Spanish legal treatises were the product of their author's ultramarine legal assignments. The works of Hevia and Solórzano are joined by those of Juan Matienço and Gregorio López in this regard.
10. Adams & Scholes, "Books in New Mexico 1598-1680," 252, 268-269.
11. Francisco de Anaya Almazán served as secretary for three governors.
12. The five additional legal works which are listed in Adams & Scholes, "Books in New Mexico 1598-1680," 269, were merely cited from Hevia's *Curia Philippica,* III.12.12 and 28.
13. See Amos Stoddard, *Sketches, Historical and Descriptive, of Louisiana* (Philadelphia, 1812), 273. McDermott found one unidentifiable Spanish law book in the possession of an eighteenth century resident of St. Louis. John Francis McDermott, *Private Libraries in Creole Saint Louis* (Baltimore, 1938), 111. He also found what may have been a copy of the *Coutume de Paris. Ibid.,* 81. In Ste. Genevieve in 1810 Henry Marie Brackenridge found a copy of the *Coutume de Paris* and used it to good effect. H.M. Brackenridge, *Recollections of Persons and Places in the West* (2nd ed. Philadelphia, 1868), 205-206.
14. Three New Orleans libraries illustrate the breadth of legal sources available. Irving A. Leonard, "A Frontier Library," *Hispanic American Historical Review,* 23 (Feb. 1943): 21, describing the very varied library of Manuel Gayoso de Lemos, commander of the Natchez district and later governor of Louisiana. Its six legal titles were compilations of laws and military regulations. Mitchell Franklin, "Libraries of Edward Livingston and [Louis] Moreau Lislet," *Tulane Law Review,* 15 (Apr. 1941): 401-414.
15. Eighteen *escribanos* and four *asesores* served in New Orleans during the period of Spanish rule (1766-1803).
16. Eleanor B. Adams, "Two Colonial New Mexico Libraries 1704, 1776," *New Mexico Historical Review,* 19 (Apr. 1944): 135, 137-138, 159-151.
17. See note 20, *infra,* and accompanying text. Two New Mexican succession records of the late Spanish period mention a set of military ordinances in three volumes among the possessions of military officers. Will of Lieutenant Francisco Trebol Navarro, Presidio de Santa Fe (no. 646, 1 Aug. 1785), SANM I, reel 4, fr. 234; Inventory of the estate of retired Captain Manuel Delgado, Santa Fe (no. 252, 29 Sept. 1815), SANM I, reel 2, fr. 365. In the earlier instance the testator also listed *un guia de forasteros con reglamento de Presidios.* In the other case, the inventory included a copy of *Práctica Criminal* and a collection of militia ordinances.
18. That there was periodic recourse to such books in New Mexico is evidenced by a letter from a friar in Albuquerque to Custos Mariano Sánchez Vergara at Sandia, 7 June 1802, no. 15, Loose Mission Documents, 1680-1850 in Angélico Chávez, *Archives of the Archdiocese of Santa Fe, 1678-1900* (Washington, D.C., 1957), 63.
19. In a report to Commandant Pedro Nava, Governor Muñoz cited *Recopilación de Indias* VI.4.6, Muñoz to Nava, 14 Aug. 1794. Carlos E. Castañeda, *Our Catholic Heritage in Texas,* 5 (Austin, 1942), 59. His predecessor, Governor Jacinto de Barrios y Jáuregui, had also cited the *Recopilación de Indias* in a letter to the Viceroy, 22 July 1756. Castañeda, *Our Catholic Heritage,* 4 (Austin, 1939), 69.
20. Inventory of the estate of Manuel Muñoz, died 27 July 1799, Bexar Archives, San Antonio, document WE-70, 17-18. The works listed are *Real Ordenanza para el Establecimiento é Instrucción de Intendentes de Exército y Provincia en el Reino de la Nueva España; Ordenanzas Militares Reglamento y Prontuario de Ordenanzas;* Félix Colón de Larriátegui, *Juzgados Militares de España y sus Indias.*
21. Josef Febrero, *Libreria de Escribanos, é Instruccion Juridica Theorico Principante,* 6 vols. (3rd ed., Madrid, 1783-1786) José Juan y Colom, *Instrucción Juridica de Escribanos,* 2 vols. (Madrid, 1787).
22. Joseph W. McKnight, "The Will of May 19, 1800 of Antonio Gil Ybarbo (1729-1809)," *El Campanario,* 8 (June 1977), 5, 8.
23. For example, the will of José Joaquin de la Garza, 19 May 1797, was written in Gil Ybarbo's hand and he was one of the witnesses to it. Document WE-46, Bexar Archives, San Antonio.
24. An ordinance on the making of mortgages, 4 Mar. 1810, quoted *Novisima Recopilación* X.16.3. Bexar Archives, University of Texas, Austin. See Hans W. Baade, "The Formalities of Private Real Estate Transactions in Spanish North America," *Louisiana Law Review,* 38 (Spring 1978): 655, 733 n. 343.
25. *Heirs of Vidal v. Innerarity,* 6 Oct. 1821, in Walter Lowrie & Walter S. Franklin, eds., *American State Papers: Miscellaneous,* 2 (Washington, D.C., 1834), 853, 865-866.
26. Opinion of Asesor Ruperto Saavedra to Governor José Coppinger of East Florida, 27 Oct. 1818, in Joseph M. White, *A New Collection of Laws, Charters and Local Ordinances of the Governments of Great Britain, France and Spain, Relating to the Concessions of Land in their respective Colonies together with the Laws of Mexico and Texas on the Same Subject,* 2 (Philadelphia, 1839), 282, 283.
27. For references to the *Recopilición de Indias,* see Carlos E. Castañeda, *Our Catholic Heritage in Texas,* 3 (Austin, 1938), 53, 56; Father Miguel Sevillano, President of the Rio Grande Missions, to Governor Carlos Franquis de Lugo of Texas, 22 Nov. 1736, and *Consulta Apolegética* of Father Sevillano to the Viceroy, 15 Feb. 1737, citing the *Recopilación de Indias,* III.16.7 in both instances. For a similar but much later example of reliance on legal authority by a missionary in California, see Zephyrin Engelhardt, *The Missions and Missionaries of California,* 3 (2nd ed., Santa Barbara, 1929), 136, citing Father Mariano Payéras of Mission Purisima Concepción to Governor Pablo Vicente Solá, 16 May 1821.
28. The 1785 inventory of Mission San José listed a set of *Recopilación de Indias* in 4 volumes, Solórzano's *Politica Indiana* (1 vol.), Ferraris's *Biblioteca Canonica, Juridica, Moralis, Theologica* (4 vols., Rome, 1766), and an octavo volume on the Council of Trent. The 1755 inventory listed no books. See Benedict Leutenegger & Marion A. Habig, *The San José Papers,* 1 (San Antonio, 1978), 107, 214 at 233-235.
29. Eleanor B. Adams & Angélico Chávez, *The Missions of New Mexico, 1776 . . . with other contemporary documents* (Albuquerque), 220-233.
30. Zephyrin Engelhardt, *San Antonio de Padua, The Mission of the Sierras* (Ramona, 1972), 71-72, referring to the 1836 inventory of the mission library. Also see Finbar Kenneally, ed., *Writings of Fermin Francisco de Lasuén,* 2 (Washington, D.C., 1965), no. 401 (Fr. Lasuén to Fr. José Gasol, 30 Mar. 1801) 186 at 187. By Nov. 1782, Mission Santa Clara at Monterey had a copy of the *Recopilación de Indias,* and it was still in use in 1796. Fr. Junipero Serra requested a copy of the *Recopilación de Indias* on 15 Aug. 1779, but it had not arrived by 24 Oct. 1780. Tibesar, *Writings of Serra,* 3 (Washington, D.C., 1956), no. 141 (Fr. Serra to Fr. Rafael Verger, 15 Aug. 1779), 334-335 at 352-353; Tibesar, *Writings of Serra,* 4:44-45 at 50-51, (Fr. Serra to Fr. Pangua, 24 Oct. 1780); Tibesar, *Writings of Serra* 4:397 (Frs. Murgia and Peña at Mission Santa Clara to Governor Pedro Fages, 1 Nov. 1782), 4:398, 400 (Frs. Murgia and Peña to Fr. Serra, 1 Nov. 1782); Kenneally, *Writings of Lasuén* 1:no. 41 (Fr. Lasuén's report of judicial proceedings, 28 June

1786), 199 at 132; 1:no. 243 (Fr. Lasuén to Governor Diego de Borica of California, 12 Nov. 1796), 405. Also see note 62, *infra*.

31. See John L. Kessell, *Mission of Sorrows; Jesuit Geuvavi and the Pimas, 1691-1767* (Tucson, 1970). Four documents of transfer of the southern Arizona missions (two in 1737, one in 1761 and another in 1765) give extensive lists of articles, including a few ritualistic books, but no legal books.
32. William Baskerville Hamilton, *Anglo-American Law on the Frontier: Thomas Rodney & His Territorial Cases* (Durham, 1953), 134, 136, 172-173, 176-77.
33. The Natchez records for the 1790s give some insight into the somewhat elastic but nonetheless efficient handling of successions without any apparent participation of a trained lawyer, and William Dunbar, a British resident of Baton Rouge, has left a very favorable report of the quality of civil justice meted out to creditors under District-Governor Gayoso. J.F.H. Claiborne, *Mississippi, as a Province, Territory and State*, 1 (Jackson, 1880), 137. A precis of Natchez records is found in May Wilson McBee, *The Natchez Court Records, 1767-1805* (Greenwood, 1953).
34. The records of Upper Louisiana support a greater popular familiarity with French customs than with Spanish law, but in a few later disputes arguments were based on earlier Spanish law in force. See *Picotte v. Cooley*, 10 Mo. 312 (1847); *Riddick v. Walsh*, 15 Mo. 519, 536-537 (1852); *Childress & Mullamphy v. Cutter*, 16 Mo. 24, 41-43 (1852); *Cutter v. Waddingham*, 22 Mo. 206 (1855).
35. Hamilton, *Anglo-American Law on the Frontier*, 194.
36. Louis Moreau Lislet & Henry Carleton, *A Translation of the Titles on Promises and Obligations and Sale and Purchase, and Exchange, from the Spanish Las Siete Partidas* (New Orleans, 1818).
37. Louis Moreau Lislet & Henry Carleton, *The Laws of Las Seite Partidas Which Are Still in Force in the State of Louisiana*, 2 vols. (New Orleans, 1820). Although the title page was dated 1820, the work was not ready for distribution until 1822.
38. Hans W. Baade, "Law and Lawyers in Pre-Independence Texas," in *Centennial History of the State Bar of Texas* (Austin, 1981) 240, 243-254, gives a brief sketch of these lawyers. Luke Lessasier and Hosea H. League came from Louisiana. Thomas Jefferson Chambers was admitted to practice by act of the Congress of Coahuila y Texas in 1834 and served successively as *Asesor General* of the state and then as Chief Justice of Texas in 1834-1835.
39. Baade, "Law and Lawyers in Pre-Independence Texas," 250.
40. George Fisher in Matamoros to Robert M. Williamson in San Felipe de Austin, 4 Aug. 1834, Eugene C. Barker, ed., *The Austin Papers*, 2 (Washington, D.C., 1928), 1071; Robert E. David, ed., *The Diary of William Barret Travis* (Waco, 1966), 7-8 (entries of 3, 6 Sept. 1833).
41. Margaret Swett Henson, *Samuel May Williams, Early Texas Entrepreneur* (College Station, 1976), 23. Also see H.H. League to Samuel M. Williams, 9 February 1831, Rosenberg Library, Galveston; Baade, "Law and Lawyers in Pre-Independence Texas," 246.
42. See Joseph W. McKnight, "The Spanish Influence on the Texas Law of Civil Procedure," *Texas Law Review*, 38 (Nov. 1959): 24, 27-40.
43. *Scott & Solomon v. Maynard*, Dallam 548, 550 (1843).
44. See *Smith v. Townsend*, Dallam 569, 571-572 (1844).
45. See *White v. Gay's Executors*, 1 Texas 384, 389 (1847); *Heir of Holliman v. Peebles*, 1 Texas 673, 715-716, 719 (1848).
46. Thomas Jefferson Chambers, *Prospectus for Translating into English and Publishing a Compilation of the Laws in Force in the State of Coahuila and Texas . . . to be interwoven with a Compendium of the Spanish Code* (San Felipe de Austin, 1832); Thomas Jefferson Chambers, *A Sketch of the Spanish and Mexican Laws, Affecting Rights in Texas as presented in a Proposition made to the Second Legislature of Texas* [in 1848] (Austin, 1850).
47. See note 26, *supra*.
48. *Le Sassier v. Alba*, Florida Territorial Court of Appeals Records (1830-1831). The works cited were Colom, *Instrucción Juridica de Escribanos*, 2 vols. (Madrid, 1787); Francisco Antonio de Elizondo, *Practica Universal Forense de lost Tribunales de España, y de las Indias*, 8 vols. (Madrid, 1788); and Ignacio Jordan y Asso & Miguel de Manuel y Rodriguez, *Instituciones del Derecho Civil de Castilla*, 2 vols. (7th ed. by Joaquín Palacios, Madrid, 1806).
49. This representation spanned the years 1832-1836 and included such cases as *United States v. Arrendondo*, 31 U.S. 691 (1832); *United States v. Percheman*, 32 U.S. 51 (1833); *Mitchel v. United States*, 34 U.S. 711 (1835); *United States v. Sibbold*, 35 U.S. 313 (1836).
50. Joseph M. White, *Private Land Claims* (Washington, D.C., 1828).
51. White, *New Collection of Laws*.
52. Judicial citations were usually given to the first volume of White's work, but the page references indicate reliance on the translation of Asso and Manuel. *Hill v. M'Dermot*, Dallam 419, 423 (1841); *Garret v. Nash*, Dallam 497, 499 (1843); *McMullen v. Hodge*, 5 Tex. 34, 80 (1849); *Paschal v. Perez*, 7 Tex. 348, 370 (1851); *Parker v. Parker*, 10 Tex. 84, 94 (1853). For represenative New Mexican and Californian citations, see *von Schmidt v. Huntington*, 1 Cal. 55, 59 (1850); *Macondray v. Simmons*, 1 Cal. 393, 395 (1851); *Chavez v. McKnight & Gutieres*, 1 N. Mex. 147, 155 (1857); and *Jaremillo v. Cruz Romero*, 1 N. Mex. 190, 196 (1857).
53. Licenciado Rafael Gómez arrived in California as her first *asesor* in 1830 and was succeeded in 1834 by Licenciado Cosme Peña who served until 1839. Hubert H. Bancroft, *History of California 1825-1840*, 3 (San Francisco, 1886), 46; David Langum, *Law and Community on the Mexican California Frontier* (Norman, 1987) 45, 63. Another trained lawyer served as secretary of the appellate court and as substitute judge of a small community. *Ibid.* 46. As *asesor* in New Mexico in 1831, Licenciado Antonio Barreiro succeeded Eleuterio Maria de Lagarza who had declined the appointment. H. Bailey Carroll & J. Villasana Haggard, *Three New Mexico Chronicles* (Albuquerque, 1942), xx; Lansing Bartlett Bloom, "New Mexico Under Mexican Administration, 1821-1846," *Old Santa Fe* 1 (Oct. 1913), 269, 271.
54. Antonio Barreiro, *Ojeada* (Puebla, 1832), 38-39.
55. Langum, *Law and Community*, 34, 46.
56. José Maria Álvarez, *Instituciones de Derecho Real de Castilla y de Indias . . . L'omados los lugares mas importantes de los tomos I. II. III. y IV. que hacen la obra, para el curso, de los discipulos del P.A. Jose Martinez, en Taos de Nuevo Mexico* . . . (1842). Álvarez's treatise was first published in Guatemala in 1818-1820. The forms are from Pedro Murillo Velarde, *Cursus Juris Canonici* and Eugenio de Tapia, ed. *Febrero Novisimo*, 10 vols. (Valencia, 1830), 3:347-348, 4:316-317.
57. This second book was much briefer than the first and had no formal title page, merely a heading: *De Lib. 2 de Alvarez*. It included a form of will (somewhat edited) from Murillo's *Cursus Juris Canonici*, III.26.
58. 1846 New Mexico Gen. Laws (Kearny Code) 3, § 1 at 17.
59. Pedro Murillo Velarde, *Práctica de Testamentos* (Santa Fe, 1850).
60. 1851-1852 New Mexico Gen. Laws, 352-371.
61. In 1861 the New Mexican legislature urged the Territorial Secretary to have Murillo's handbook on the law on wills translated and published. 1860-1861 New Mexico Gen. Laws, 1181 (English text), 1211 (Spanish text). In 1884 the legislature went further in appropriating funds for the distribution of 150 copies of Murillo's *Práctica de Testamentos* to local authorities. 1884 New Mexico Gen. Laws, 191, ch. 79, § 1. Nothing seems to have come of these efforts.
62. Both Governor Neve (1779) and Governor Borica (1796) had the *Recopilación de Indias* at hand, as did Mission Santa Clara by November 1782. Tibesar, *Writings of Serra*, 3:334-335, 352-353 (1779); Kenneally, *Writings of Lasuén*, 1:405-406 (1796); Tibesar, *Writings of Serra*, 4:397-398 (1782). Also see J.N. Bowman, "Libraries in Provincial California," *Quarterly of the Historical Society of Southern California*, 43 (Sept. 1961): 426, 433. The copies of the *Recopilación de Indias* at Mission Dolores, Theodore Hittell, *History of California*, 2 (San Francisco, 1885), and at Mission Purisima Concepción, Englehardt, *Missions and Missionaries*, 3:136, probably date from the Spanish period.
63. The will of Governor José Joaquin de Arrillaga, 15 July 1814, Englehardt, *Missions and Missionaries*, 3:8-9, and the will of retired Sergeant José Maria Ortega, Mission Santa Inez, 18 June 1821, *Los Angeles Judicial Records*, A:1071-1076, seem to be drawn from a formbook. Also see note 30, *supra*, and accompanying text.
64. *Monterey Archives*, 2:143-182 (1835) (reference to the *Recopilación de Indias*); *Monterey Archives*, 15:497 (1838) (apparent reliance on a treatise to show a defect in a bill of exchange); Langum, *Law and Community*, 125-126 (use of the *Novisima Recopilación*, and a copy of Mexican statutes and decrees by the *juez de paz* in Sonoma in 1839); *Archives of California*, 38:412-422 (1840), *Monterey Archives*, 6:467 (1842) (two instances of apparent reliance on a treatise in asserting minority as a defense to a contract); *Los Angeles Judicial Records*, A:155-170 (1843) (reference to a treatise).
65. Bowman, "Libraries in Provincial California," 433; Langum, *Law and Community*, 126.
66. *Monterey Archives*, 8:5 (1845), but there were no law books listed in the inventory of 1843. *Monterey Archives* 11:301-304 (1843); Langum, *Law and Community*, 125-126.
67. The litigant made an exceptionally terse and accurate statement of his right to be appointed as legitimate guardian of a minor, but the source of his phraseology is not identifiable. *Valdez v.*

Bouchet, 5 Nov. 1845, *Los Angeles Judicial Records,* A:213-218. Another layman, Abel Stearns in Los Angeles, had a copy of the *Ordenanzas de Bilbao* in 1845. Langum, *Law and Community,* 221.

68. Edwin Bryant, *What I Saw in California* (New York, 1848), 436.
69. Langum thinks it was a copy of the *Recopilación de Indias.* Langum, *Law and Community,* 125. There does not, however, appear to be an edition of the *Recopilación de Indias* of the appropriate approximate date. See Antonio Palau y Dulcet, *Manual de Librero HispanoAmericano,* 15 (Barcelona, 1962), 301.
70. J. Halleck & W.E.P. Hartnell, *Translation and Digest of Such Portions of the Mexican Laws . . . As Are . . . in force and adapted to the present condition of California* (San Francisco, 1849). The first printing press arrived in California in 1833. The first book was published in 1834: a pamphlet of 16 pages devoted to a governmental regulation of the local legislative assembly. Bowman, "Libraries in Provincial California," 433.
71. Walter Colton, *Three Years in California* (Cincinnati, 1850), 249.
72. See inventory of the estate of José Antonio Yorba, 30 May-22 June 1844, *Los Angeles Judicial Records,* 2:189, 192-203; will of William E.P. Hartnell (1798-1854), Susanna Bryant Dakin, *The Lives of William Hartnell* (Stanford, 1949), 291-292.
73. *Laws for the Better Government of California during the Military Occupation of the Country by the Forces of the United States* (San Francisco, 1848), the contents of which are summarized in Lindley Bynum, "Laws for the Better Government of California, 1848," *Pacific Historical Review,* 2 (no. 3, 1933): 279, 285-291.
74. Committee on the Judiciary, California Senate, *Report on Civil and Common Law,* 1 Cal. 588, 603 (1850).
75. Joaquín Escriche, *Diccionario Razonado de Legislación Civil, Penal, Comercial y Forense.* Also see text accompanying note 45, *supra.*
76. Gustavus Schmidt, *The Civil Law of Spain and Mexico* (New Orleans, 1851). For some instances of judicial reliance on Schmidt's work, see *Leitensdorfer v. Webb,* 1 N. Mex. 34, 71-72 (1853); *Trevino v. Fernandez,* 13 Tex. 630, 655 (1855); *Martinez v. Lucero,* 1 N. Mex. 208, 214-216 (1857); *Moore v. Davey,* 1 N. Mex. 303, 305 (1859); *Noë v. Card,* 14 Cal. 577 (1860).

Joseph W. McKnight is professor of law at Southern Methodist University in Dallas and a member of the Executive Council of the Texas State Historical Association. The author is grateful to David Langum and Malcolm Ebright for their suggestions and criticism.

Mexican Colonial Land Law

Guillermo F. Margadant S.

Mexican colonial land law is a branch of the Spanish colonial legal system, the "*Derecho Indiano*" (law of the Indies). Within this system however, in spite of the unifying tendencies springing from the *Consejo de Indias*, many local differences existed. So in the evolution of the land law of New Spain we find some specifically New-Spanish features (though always against the general background of Spanish colonial law and doctrine), but within this New-Spanish colonial land law, we must allow for some regional differences. Especially between the rules for the territory corresponding to the jurisdiction of the Viceroyal *Audiencia* in Mexico City, and those for the regions that fell under the jurisdiction of the *Audiencia de Guadalajara* (to which most of the regions now belonging to the United States correspond), we observe these regional differences, in terminology and otherwise.

This New Spanish land law — and water law, so intimately related to it — sprang from several sources: part of it can be traced back to Castilian law; in other cases we find survivals of the pre-Cortesian indigenous customs; many aspects came from laws enacted especially for the Indies or parts thereof; and finally, customs that developed in New-Spanish administrative practice account for some features.

Castilian Influences on New Spanish Land Law

Although during the four and a half centuries that have passed since the conquest of Mexico uniformity of law increased in Spain, without reaching total territorial unity until very recently, it is better to speak of "*Castilian* law" instead of "*Spanish* law," especially for the time of the initial, gradual formation of the general administrative and legal structure of the Indies. We must remember that the Conquest had been an adventure, started by the Castilian crown: Castilian colonizers enjoyed a preference over other Spaniards, and Castilian law was used as a supplementary system for the laws specifically issued for the Indies.[1]

Castilian influence is visible in the following aspects of New Spanish land law.

Land grants used for rewards

The heroes of the reconquest of Islamic territories by Christian troops were rewarded with large amounts of land, and this tradition continued in the Americas. The feudal spirit, still so visible in Renaissance Castile, also provided that with such grants of land several public powers were implied (for example, jurisdiction in civil and criminal cases, the privilege to appoint several public officers, and some fiscal powers).[2]

The Adelantado

The figure of a promotor (*adelantado*), in charge of creating a new settlement, had precedents in the late-medieval Castilian practice of repopulation of the often depopulated frontier regions between the Christian and the Islamic territories of the Iberian peninsula. An *adelantado* was a person who furnished the capital for discovering and pacificying a certain part of the Indies, and who, for the purpose of settling the new area, handpicked his followers, and received from the Crown wide discretion as to land distribution within his group.

The Encomienda

The *encomienda*, another institution popular during the first generations of the conquest of the Indies, had a typical neo-feudal flavor. It received, however, a fatal blow from the *Nuevas Leyes* in 1542, and was then suject to erosion until its liquidation at the beginning of the Bourbon regime. Though this institution belonged to the field of public law, it granted the *encomendero* great local influence which often allowed him to accumulate considerable land holdings. For this reason the institution of the *encomienda* is mentioned in relation to the evolution of land ownership in New Spain.

Castilian Rules of Private Law as to Land Ownership

For many aspects of Mexican colonial land law, we have to look to private Castilian law. Thus for the transfer of land, easements and profits *a prende*, mortgages, acquisition of title by prescription, or the statute of limitations, the New Spanish rules must be looked for in the Castilian *Siete Partidas* (a general code from the middle of the thirteenth century), the *Leyes de Toro* (1505), and other Castilian enactments. These codes were complemented by commentaries published by Castilian interpreters, which frequently link the codes with Justinian law[3] and Canon law, twin currents of legal thinking that received the common label "Ius Commune."

Pre-Cortesian Indigenous Customs

The official tolerance of indigenous legal customs that did not infringe upon the interests of the Crown and the Church,[4] caused a long survival of these customs as to land tenancy. The original dichotomy of Spanish settlements and Indian Pueblos made such survival easier.

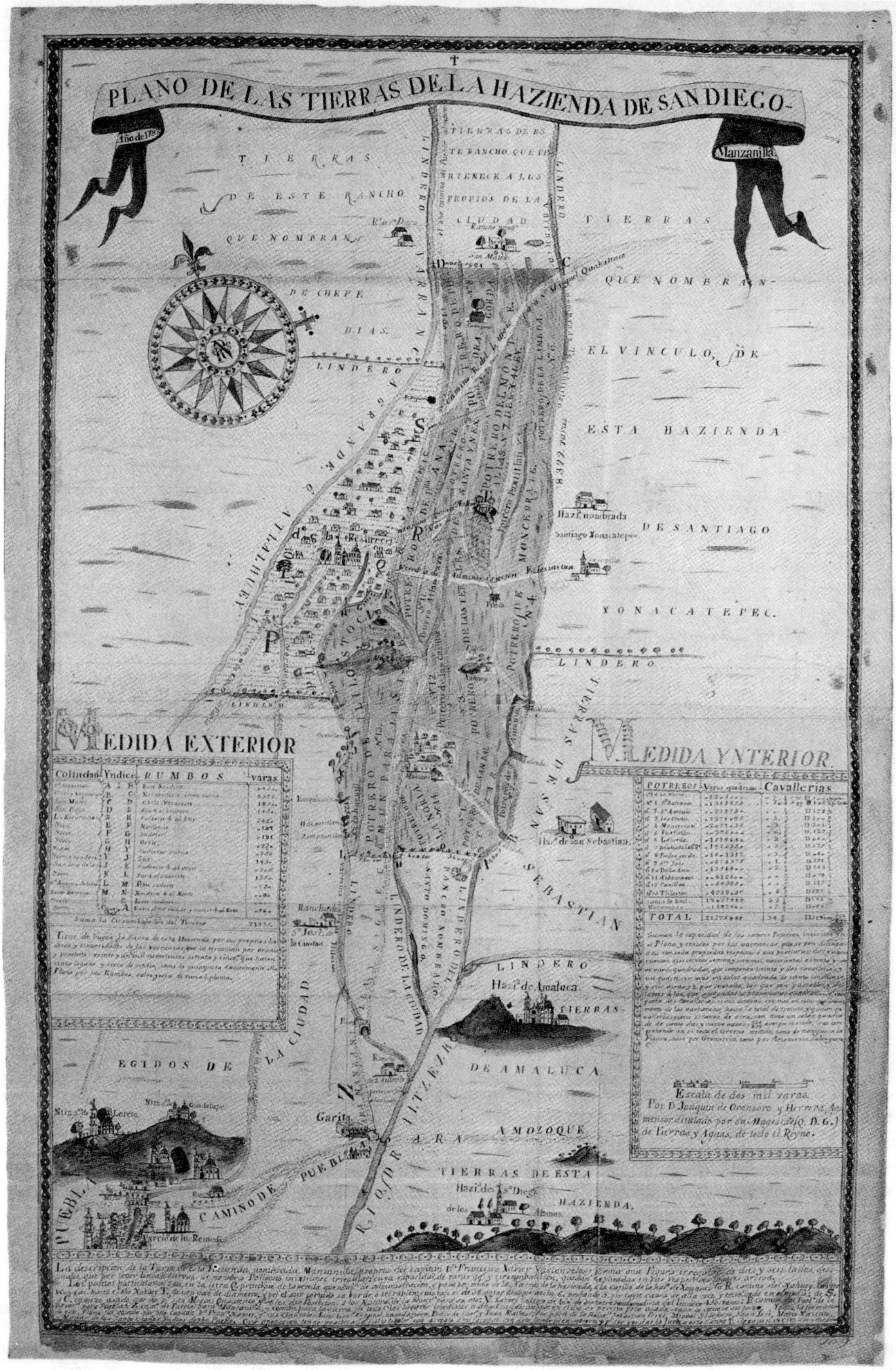

This 1787 map of the lands of the Hacienda de San Diego was made by Joaquin de Oronsoro y Herrera in connection with a lawsuit between the ***Pueblo de la Resurrección*** *and the* ***Marqués de Monserrat****. The Indians claimed the right of free passage along a road crossing the hacienda lands in accordance with their customary usage of the road from time immemorial. (From* ***Cartografía Mexicana Tesoros de la Nación Siglos XVI a XIX****, México, D.F.: Archivo General de la Nación, 1983, 90-91.)*

Laws Enacted Specifically for New Spain

Several underlying principles relating to the special enactments for the Indies (*Derecho Indiano*) influenced land distribution in the Indies.

First of all, we find the clearly expressed idea that the Castilian Crown was the fundamental owner of all land (including the subsoil), and water in the Indies. Thus, all land in the Indies was originally *realengo* (public domain), though the Crown did not press this point too strongly in relation to land worked by the Indians at the time of the Conquest, and the water used for such land.

The Crown adopted a clear paternalistic policy as to the Indians, which implied its willingness to treat them in a privileged way in relation to land and water.

This meant that land worked by the Indians at the time of the Conquest could not, theoretically, be taken away from them. This was in spite of the abrupt diminishment of the indigenous population on account of epidemic diseases, especially from the beginning of the Mexican Conquest to the first third of the seventeenth century, which often left Indian communities with more land than was necessary for them. This policy even expressed itself in first-refusal rights, given to Indian settlements as to land, close to their pueblos and applied for by Spaniards.[5] However, wild tribes (*barbaros chichimecas, indios de guerra*), were not favored in this respect.[6] Sale of private land by Indians was placed under certain controls, so that there would not be a wholesale transfer of land from the Indian world to the Spanish settlers.

The separation of Spaniards and Indians, incorporated in the Theory of the two Republics, led to separate Spanish and Indian settlements,[7] which made more feasible this protection of Indian lands.[8] However, in relation to such privileges granted to the Indians, some negative factors should be mentioned.

In the first place, the Indian population decreased (perhaps in proportion from five to one), on account of epidemic diseases, and weakened their will to defend Indian common land against encroachments. In additon, the lumping together of several Indian settlements into medium-sized towns, though in theory not depriving the Indians of their original holdings, led to abuses as to indigenous land.[9]

In spite of the specially appointed protectors of the Indians, the rather efficient *Juzgado de Indios*,[10] favorable laws, and the activity of certain idealistic friars, the *caciques*[11] would often collaborate with the local Spanish elite to deprive Indian settlements of their common lands

In addition, the original halo of untouchability around Indian land vanished by and by. We find that regularization of *de facto* situations by way of *composiones* was extended to land occupied by Indians, although still in an atmosphere of special tolerance for aboriginal possession.[12] And, at least in 1735[13] (and perhaps before), the investigation of Indian land titles was placed on the same level as the investigation of Spanish holdings.

Continuing with the basic principles applied by the Crown to land distribution, we must mention the originally favorable disposition of the Crown towards the creation of property rights for the benefit of Castilians (or eventually other Spaniards), in order to permeate New Spain with Spanish civilization, and to root to the soil the many Spanish adventurers, who were reluctant to settle down.[14]

This granting of land to Spanish individuals or settlements was handled in the following ways.

Land Granted for Merits

Initially, this transfer of land from the Crown to a limited form of private property, in which no title in fee simple was given because a *dominium eminens* or *directum* was retained by the Crown, was often the result of rewards the Crown had to grant to *conquistadores*

Once the first dust cloud of the boisterous *Conquista* had settled down, we find *capitulaciones*[15] which granted important privileges to promotors (*adelantados*), as to land distribution among their followers. Apart from distributing land among his men in accordance with their merits, an *adelantado* was generally allowed to claim greater allotments of land for himself, and could assure for his family a permanent place in the first ranks of New Spain by holding such land in a form of a perpetuity called "*mayorazgo*." The *adelantado's* followers normally received fair amounts of property, but generally not sufficiently extensive to become the beginning of the enormous *latifundia* (landed estates), which the promoters themselves were allowed to create. Factors taken into account in the distribution of available land were social differences, economic contributions, active participation in the risks and labors of the venture,[16] and physical characteristics of the land, including fertility and watering circumstances. The effective possession of land and water by Indians was always to be respected.

Land Granted in the Light of General Social Policy

If, after the pacification of a region, it seemed that for lack of Spanish settlers, the region could return to pre-pacification conditions, the Crown would give out land in fair amounts, in order to establish a firm substratum of Spanish settlers in the colony. In the *Plan of Pitic* we find a good example of such a grant, bestowed upon a new settlement. In general, the individual *suertes* so granted were smaller than the ones the followers of the *adelantados* would receive, since these later grantees had no special social or military merits. However, the importance of such individual lots was enhanced by access the new owners had to the use of important common lands (*ejidos, dehesas*, etc.).

In a case like the foundation of Puebla, the Crown decided to offer good land freely in a safe part of New Spain, in order to absorb the many Spanish adventurers, the *vagamundos* or *vagabundos*, who, during the first generation of New Spain, had become a danger to morals and public order.[17]

It was a requirement for the acquisition of ownership of such land that the grantee should take possession, build a

POLITICA INDIANA,

COMPUESTA POR

EL DOCT. D. JUAN DE SOLORZANO PEREYRA

CAVALLERO DEL ORDEN DE SANTIAGO, DEL Conſejo del Rey Nueſtro Señor en los Supremos de Caſtilla, y de las Indias.

DIVIDIDA EN SEIS LIBROS.

EN LOS QUALES CON GRAN DISTINCION, Y ESTUDIO SE trata, y reſuelve todo lo tocante al Deſcubrimiento, Deſcripcion, Adquiſicion, y Retencion de las meſmas Indias, y ſu Govierno particular, aſsi cerca de las perſonas de los Indios, y ſus Servicios, Tributos, Diezmos, y Encomiendas, como de lo Eſpiritual, y Ecleſiaſtico cerca de ſu Doctrina: Patronazgo Real, Igleſias, Prelados, Prebendados, Curas Seculares, y Regulares, Inquiſidores, Comiſſarios de Cruzada, y de las Religiones. Y en lo Temporal, cerca de todos los Magiſtrados Seculares, Virreyes, Preſidentes, Audiencias, Conſejo Supremo, y Junta de Guerra de ellas con inſercion, y declaracion de las muchas Cedulas Reales, que para eſto ſe han deſpachado.

OBRA DE SUMO TRABAJO, Y DE IGUAL IMPORTANCIA, Y utilidad, no ſolo para los de las Provincias de las Indias, ſino de las de Eſpaña, y otras Naciones (de qualquier profeſsion que ſean) por la gran variedad de coſas que comprehende, adornada de todas letras, y eſcrita con el metodo, claridad, y lenguaje, que por ella parecerà.

CON DOS INDICES MUY DISTINTOS, Y COPIOSOS, UNO DE LOS LIBROS, Y Capitulos, en que ſe divide: y otro de las coſas notables, que contiene.

SALE EN ESTA TERCERA IMPRESSION ILUSTRADA POR EL Licenc. D. Franciſco Ramiro de Valenzuela, Relator del Supremo Conſejo, y Camara de Indias, y electo Oidor Honorario de la Real Audiencia, y Caſa de la Contratacion de Cadiz: y en dos Tomos.

CON LICENCIA. EN MADRID: Por Matheo Sacriſtan. Año de 1736.

The title page of Juan de Solórzano Pereira's ***Politica Indiana****, one of the most important early treatises about the Indies and the laws governing them.*

The city of Guaymas in the state of Sinaloa, Mexico. (Photo no. 8495, Sally Wagner Collection. Courtesy State Records Center & Archives, Santa Fe, NM.)

stone house, fence the property, and live and work on the new land for four, or sometimes five years.[18] In all these cases, the creation of private ownership was subject to the condition that Indian interests should be respected, and that other persons with prior rights should not be injured. In matters of land, these restrictions were more rigidly applied than in relation to water. With respect to water, redistributions (*nuevos repartimientos*), which had become advisable in the light of new circumstances, were more easily authorized than was the case with land.

Land Sold by the Crown to Individuals

Around 1581, in the pacified parts of New Spain, gratuitous distribution of land was superseded by the sale of Crown land, whereby interested individuals (Spaniards, *criollos*, and even *mestizos*) could acquire land by way of public auctions.[19]

For acquisition of title the same requirements stated above would apply. Important officers[20] found themselves generally excluded from the possibility of buying land (either from the Crown or from previous owners), in the region where they exercised their functions. For the *Provincias Internas*, a royal cedula of 14 February 1805 established the procedure for *denuncios* of free land by applicants, and the prices for different categories.[21]

Land Ownership from Composiciones

Land distribution at the beginning of the New Spanish period was handled in a haphazard way, so that due attention was not always paid to correspondence between grants and taking of possession, between *mercedes* and the de facto situations that sprang from them.[22] After 1591 the Crown began to regularize the situation through *composiciones*. For a payment based upon an appraisal, or upon other circumstances (Solano speaks of "agreed fines"), a landowner would receive clear title from the Crown.[23] We see, for instance, that the legal quality of seemingly valid, but in reality invalid, titles could be taken into account as a factor in determining the price.[24] Part of the amount finally agreed upon (including the expenses of the procedure), could be paid in installments.[25] As a result, such corrections by *composiciones* became another avenue to ownership of land and even of water rights.

The law of 1591 led to the first wave of *composiciones* from 1592 to 1625.[26] New series of individual *composiciones*, initiated in 1631 and 1635 by Viceroy Cadereita, and in 1640 by Viceroy Escalona, produced only modest results. But in 1643, Viceroy Salvatierra started the system of *composiciones colectivas*, in which group bargaining between the viceregal authority and local communities of Spanish settlers took place for large amounts of money. Such local groups of beneficiaries (*compuestos*) would

This map was made by Ignacio Castera as part of the inventory of the estate of Manuel de Fraga y Neira in a 1787 insolvency proceeding. Although the mapmaker did not include a survey showing the bearings and distances of these properties, he does include a revealing drawing in the lower right corner, showing the surveyor's tools used at the time to make such a survey. (From ***Cartografía Mexicana Tesoros de la Nacion Siglos XVI a XIX,*** *México, D.F.: Archivo General de la Nación, 1983, 88-89.)*

then distribute the burden of the payment among themselves. Between 1648 and 1650 the wave of this new brand of *composiciones* produced some 125,000 pesos for the royal treasury. By the middle of the eighteenth century, these *composiciones* still yielded annually several thousand pesos, sometimes more than ten thousand, and a few times more than twenty thousand (in 1746: 42,551 pesos).[27]

As a result of these *composiciones*, the panorama of land titles was eventually cleaned up in the regions of initial settlement, and the impact of these regularization measures was gradually directed to the more recent zones of colonization. So the general picture was: first a quick, rather careless distribution of land (which had a relatively low value), soon followed by lawless encroachment on royal land around the formally granted properties, and then gradual corrections by *composiciones*, especially under the influence of increasing land prices, and the ups and downs of the needs of the Treasury.[28]

Indian Holdings

Indian holdings were comprised of private and common land, and the intermediate form of family lots within the common lands, that would be cultivated perpetually by the same family, but would revert to the community for redistribution, in case the family died out or left. Private Indian land was subject to special legal requirements that attempted to protect the Indians against the danger of a general stream of Indian land sales to the Spanish settlers. The Crown also paid attention to the need to stimulate Indian agriculture, to assist in the task of assuring a reasonably stable food supply to the towns of New Spain.

At the time the *composición* system was introduced, Indian private land was already subject to it,[29] but Indian community land was screened off from this system.[30] However, after 1746 Indian commons were subject to the *composición* system. A complication in relation to Indian holdings, private or collective, sprang from the policy of *congregación* or *reducción* of the Indians into middle-sized towns of 300-400 Indian families, for reasons of fiscal control, Christianization, and protection against their returning to ancestral ways.[31] This policy, which was initiated around 1500 on the Caribbean Islands and suddenly pushed rather dogmatically by the end of the sixteenth century by Viceroy Monterrey, caused special hardships, and regularly met with important obstacles, mostly from the Indians, but sometimes from the *encomenderos*. Usually such a *congregación* forced the Indians to abandon their original villages, but if the new settlement was not too far away from the original Indian land, the Indians could continue to cultivate it. Normally the new land was of much better quality than the land the Indians had to abandon,[32] and apart from their cemeteries, the Indians generally lost interest in their previous holdings.

Once the location of the new place had been established, first the land for the church building was determined, and from there the *fundo legal* [33] would be measured out. This *fundo* provided for the urbanized part of the settlement, and around it, for the individual lots forming the horticultural and agricultural belt. As mentioned, families would have the perpetual use, but not the ownership of such lots. Though some authors believe so, it is doubtful that the *fundo legal* also contained the *ejidos*.

In New Spain in the strict sense, i.e. the territory that was subject to the jurisdiction of the viceregal *audiencia* in the city of Mexico, this *fundo legal* was 500 varas[34] measured from the church to the four cardinal directions, as Viceroy Peralta had ordered on 26 May 1567.[35] For the territory subject to the *Audiencia* of Guadalajara, at least by the end of the eighteenth century, the *fundo legal* was one *legua en cuadro* considerably more than in the rest of the colony.[36]

Most probably, the *ejido* did not form a part of the *fundo legal*, because the word *ejido* was often not used in the technical sense defined by the *Recopilacion*,[37] but in the general sense of commons. As the agricultural and horticultural belt, designated as *fundo legal*, contained lots cultivated by individual families, but belonging to the Indian community,[38] there is some confusion in this respect, and knowledgeable contemporary authors disagree about whether the *ejido* was included within the *fundo legal*.[39]

From the end of the *fundo legal* on,[40] a protection zone of 1,000 varas (from 1687 on, 1,100 varas) would be measured to keep the Spanish *haciendas* and *estancias* at a certain distance. This buffer zone is later mentioned as one league which is not at all the same length; a league (roughly the distance one walks in one hour) contained 5000 varas![41] Another feature of the Indian settlements was the special *tierra del cacique*, on which some person-

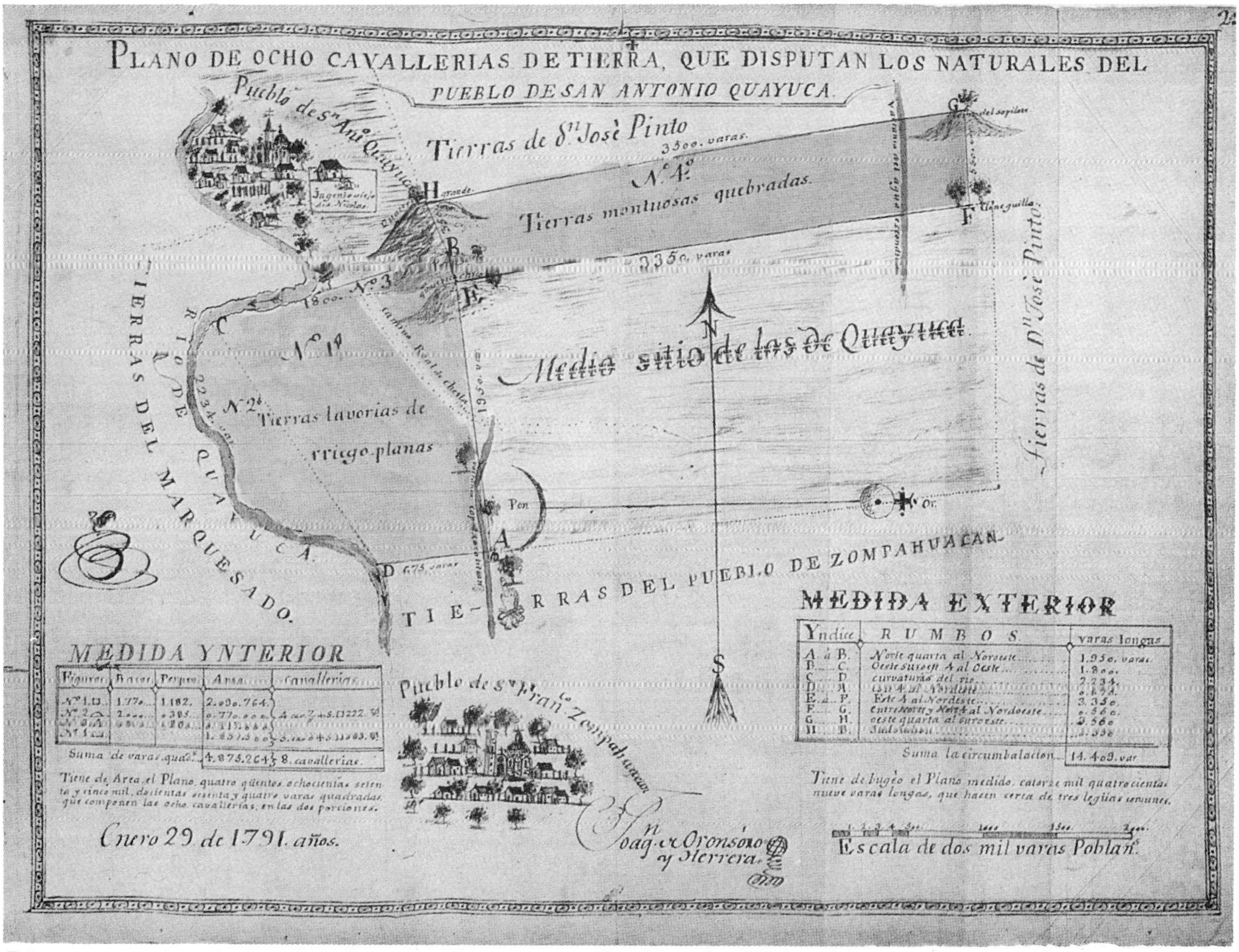

This survey map, drawn by Joaquín de Oronsoro y Herrera, was used in evidence in a 1791 lawsuit between the Indians of San Antonio Quayuca and Jose Pinto del Aguila in the State of Puebla. The map shows distances, measured with a cordel, as well as bearings. It describes the boundary between the lands of the Pueblo and the lands of Jose Pinto, as well as the mountainous lands and the irrigated farm lands of the Pueblo. (From ***Cartografía Mexicana Tesoros de la Nación Siglos XVI a XIX,*** *México, D.F.: Archivo General de la Nación, 1983, 92-93.)*

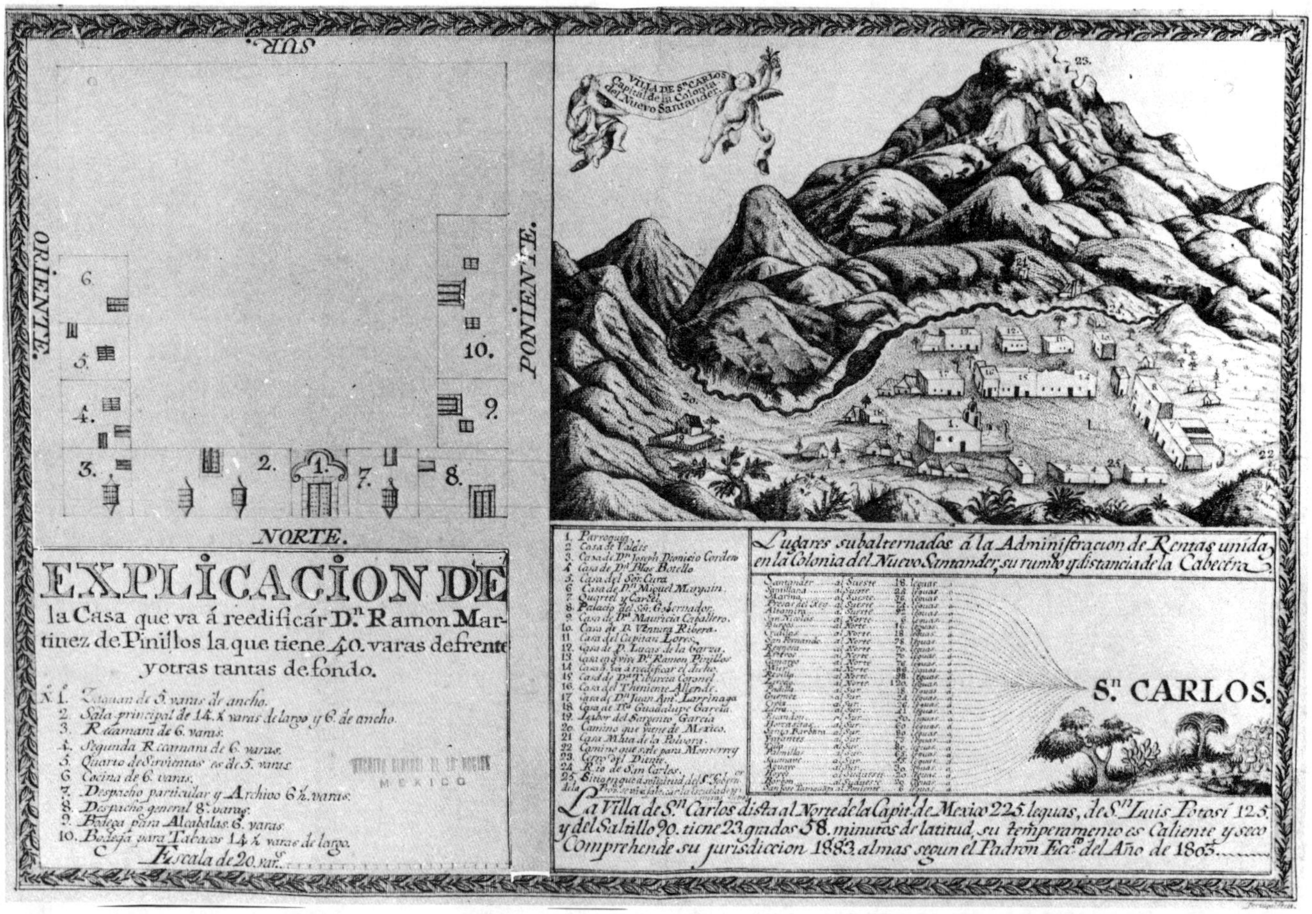

This 1803 pen drawing of the villa of San Carlos in the state of Nuevo Santander (now Tamaulipas), by Bernardo de Portugal, records the topography of the area, as well as census data, the houseplan of a leading citizen, and distances to other communities. (From ***Cartografía Mexicana Tesoros de la Nación Siglos XVI a XIX****, México, D.F.: Archivo General de la Nación, 1983, 126-127.)*

al services by the local Indians had to be performed, sometimes for a certain remuneration, sometimes not.[42]

Classification of Land, in Accordance to its Function

Many terms bewilder the scholar who enters the labyrinth of old documents on land questions. In the following pages, we shall try to bring some degree of order into this matter. However, official and popular terminology diverge, and as the authors of the documents generally were not trained lawyers, often the popular use of words prevailed. Local differences complicated the matter, and the rules themselves changed without always being clear as to what exactly the territorial extent of the change would be.

Tierras Realengas. This is land belonging to the Crown and available for later distribution by the way of grants.

Solares. These are individual lots of land, given in the part of a grant that will be settled, for the purpose of building a house with its kitchen garden.

Suertes. These are individual lots of land for agricultural purposes which, as the name indicates (*suerte* means luck), were distributed by some aleatory system. They were measured out in a part of the land granted to the community that was especially suited for agricultural purposes. In the Spanish settlements, as distinct from the *pueblos de Indios*, such individual lots were private property. Irrigation rights would spring from special water grants, or would be implied by special terms used for the land.[43]

Propios. These lots were normally in the same region of the settlement as the *suertes*, but were reserved by the municipal authority as a source of communal income. Such revenue producing land could be leased to members of the community, or worked collectively.

Ejido. This is a term that often leads to confusion. The *Recopilacion* gives a definition, in Book IV, title 7, law 13, from which we see that its original purposes were the assembling of cattle of individual owners in the morning, for the cowboys to take them to the collective meadows, and for recreation. However, Book VI, title 3, law 81, of the *Recopilacion* tells us something quite different, and this terminology is confirmed, at least for Indian Pueblos in 1713, but contradicted by the differentiation between *ejido* and *dehesa* made in 1579 by the New Spanish

Viceroy in relation to an Indian Pueblo. Modern authors have described the *ejido* as the growing edge of the urbanized part of the community.[44]

However, one gets the impression from the documents that the line between the general term of "commons" (which also includes the *dehesa,* the *monte,* or the *baldios*) and the specific concept of *ejido* was not always observed.

Dehesa. This is a common meadow.

Monte. This is wasteland, covered by a grant to a settlement, and at the disposal of the members of the community for hunting, collecting wood for the fire, reeds for weaving, etc. In one document we find the term used in the sense of useful land, surrounded by good houses, which is not claimed by anyone.[45]

Baldio. The term *baldios* is often used in the sense of *tierras realengas*, and indeed, much of the royal land not yet claimed was wasteland, but not all wasteland had remained royal land.

Defense of the Commons

As might be expected, private land was generally better defended against encroachments than was common land. In this respect, the *Archivo General de la Nación* shows a curious imbalance among the commons of the Indians and of the Spanish settlers. In the sections called *Tierras,* and *Indios,* one finds many cases in which Indians fight for the recovery of common lands, usurped by Spanish settlers. However, one must search for quite some time to find cases of commons belonging to Spanish settlements, that are defended against encroachments. Why?

In the first place, the *pueblos de indios* by far outnumbered the Spanish settlements, known as *lugares, villas,* and *ciudades*. Moreover, it is not likely that a Spanish *hacendado,* or owner of an *estancia,* would illegally occupy part of the commons of some Spanish settlements easily: an immediate reaction could be expected! On the other hand, an *hacendado*, with the help of some members of the Indian elite, could more readily occupy Indian commons, first in a provisional way and then claiming immemorial possession.[46] Since the Indians were often rather subservient to their *caciques* and *principales* (especially in the first half of the New Spanish period when epidemics had reduced the Indian population to such an extent that many Pueblos had more land than they could use), a Spaniard would often use an Indian *cacique* as an intermediary. Still, the Indians became increasingly litigious, and in response to many encroachments on their commons, we eventually find a flood of claims for recovery.

When we do find a case in which Spanish settlers defend their commons against Spanish *hacendados*, it often springs from rather peculiar circumstances. For instance, by the beginning of the eighteenth century Valladolid (the present Morelia), had suffered a long crisis in its municipal structure, but by 1718 things were normalized, and a regular munici pal council (*cabildo*) had come into power again.[47] The new municipal officers knew that during the municipal disorganization, several *hacendados* had occupied the municipal common lands. For the time being, the *cabildo* tried to at least prevent the occupants from enclosing the land. In the course of the next decades, they were less and less successful in this respect. This was evidenced by the fact that some *barrios,* where the Indians were allowed to live outside the Spanish town but within the land granted to Valladolid, were deserted for lack of common meadows and water for the *huertas*

A drawback for the town was that during the chaotic period of municipal confusion, essential documents had disappeared from its archive. The *cabildo* announced that all citizens should deliver official documents in their custody, needed to prove the legal structure of the community, and money was collected from the Indians and *arrieros* to finance a lawsuit.[48] The *regidores* themselves contributed funds, and in 1747 a claim was presented to the viceroy against certain *haciendas*, for the recovery of *ejidos* (common meadows), and *propios*, and also for freedom of passage. With laudable speed, a favorable partial result was obtained that same year. However, enforcement of this decision was difficult, and since the *cabildo* wanted a more complete victory, it applied to the viceregal administration for copies of some of the lost foundation documents and went on with the case.

The *hacendados* claimed immemorial possession, but an abundance of witnesses — mostly offering hearsay evidence — were presented by the *cabildo* to the contrary. Suspicion against the *haciendas* was increased by proof that one of the *hacendados*, when selling an *hacienda*, had made the buyer waive any claims for legal defects of the property.[49] This would not have been necessary if the seller had a good conscience concerning clear title to his land. The *hacendados* were reluctant to present their titles, and when finally subpoenaed to do so, they tried to appeal. Here, in December of 1754, unfortunately the documents have a considerable chronological gap. But later, we see that Charles IV decided, on 14 July 1790, to do justice to Valladolid, and recognize the right of the city to its common lands.

This case was long, taking more than 40 years. The problem sprang from quite unusual municipal circumstances at the beginning of the century. Otherwise the *hacendados* probably would have been stopped by the *cabildo* at their first attempts to encroach upon the com mons.

Privatization of Commons

As the idea of collective property, or common lands, went against the principles of economic liberalism of the eighteenth century, progressive authors of that period proposed the privatization of all common land, and later, of the *realengas* in general, as far as they could be of any economic use.

The Cadiz legislation refers to this topic, especially in

The city of Morelia (formerly Valladolid), with the spires of the beautiful seventeenth century cathedral on the left. (Photo no. 8511, Sally Wagner Collection. Courtesy State Records Center & Archives, Sante Fe, NM.)

the Decrees of 9 September 1812 (which only affects common land in exceptional cases), and of 4 January 1813, which attempts to abolish all common land. Curiously enough, King Ferdinand II, who was so prone to delete the legislative effect of the preceding liberal period, was by 1815 still interested in the fulfillment of this last decree.[50] However, a *Bando* of Viceroy Apodaca in 1820, after the wholesale reestablishment of the Cadiz legislation of the 1810-1814 period,[51] seems to return to the less drastic text of the Decree of 9 September 1812.[52]

Land Belonging to the Church

Church land, not intimately connected with spiritual functions (e. g. the cemetery), was frowned upon by the Crown, as it was — fiscally speaking — almost sterile because it was not taxed, and was probably also undesirable from a spiritual, social, and political point of view.[53] Accordingly, in creating individual property by way of grants, the granting authority would generally stipulate that the land should never be turned over to the church.

Discovered irregularities as to these restrictions were not always forgiven and sometimes became subject to the normal *composición* policy.[54] Besides, the expulsion of the Jesuits in 1767 led to important deamortizations,[55] which continued in 1804 on account of the short-lived consolidation policy by which the state forced the church to sell property and to invest the cash in state bonds. Still, the church emerged from the colonial period as the main landowner in new, independent Mexico, and the necessary deamortization of such "amortized land"[56] would be one of the central political and economic problems of the next generations.

The increase of church property did not spring from royal grants, but from the stream of Spanish wills which contained gifts of real estate to the church (*mandas y herencias*,) or from gifts by rich Spaniards or *criollos*. Let us also remember in this respect the "dowries" certain convents received at the occasion of the entrance of new nuns into the convent. Of course, each item of real estate that came into the hands of the regular clergy threatened the financial interest of the secular clergy, because of the exemption from tithes (*diezmos*) attached to such a transfer.

These transfers to the church had lasting effects due to the traditional principle of ecclesiastical administration, though not rigorously observed, that the Church always acquires but never alienates.[57]

Land Granting Authorities

At first the municipal councils (the *cabildos*) and, within the limits of their *capitulaciones*, the *adelantados*, would decide on land distribution. But after 1531 the requirement of ratification by the *Consejo de Indias* — the *Real Confirmación* — was added to the formalities, with the purpose of increasing central control and uniformity. This confirmation was not an empty formality, for we find cases in which it was refused, so that the land had to be returned to the Crown.

DON ALEJO GARCIA CONDE, CABALLERO GRAN CRUZ DE LA MILITAR Y NACIONAL ÓRDEN DE SAN HERMENEGILDO,

Mariscal de Campo de los Ejércitos Nacionales, Gobernador Comandante general y Gefe superior político de estas cuatro Provincias internas de occidente de Nueva España, &a.

Por el Exmó. Sr. D. Antonio Porcel Secretario de Estado y del Despacho de la Gobernacion de Ultramar se me han dirigido con Real órden de 19 de Julio último, diferentes Reales Decretos, entre los cuales se comprende el que sigue:

"Las còrtes generales y extraordinarias, considerando que la reducion de los terrenos comunes á dominio particular es una de las providencias que mas imperiosamente reclaman el bien de los pueblos y el fomento de la agricultura e industria; y queriendo al mismo tiempo proporcionar con esta clase de tierras un auxilio á las necesidades públicas, un premio á los benemeritos defensores de la Patria, y un socorro á los ciudadanos no propietarios, decretan:

ARTICULO. 1.° Todos los terrenos baldios ó realengos, y de propios y arbitrios, con arbolado y sin èl, así en la Peninsula é Islas adyacentes, como en las provincias de Ultramar, excepto los ejidos necesarios á los pueblos, se reducirán á propiedad particular, cuidandose de que en los de propios y arbitrios se suplan sus rendimientos anuales por los medios mas oportunos, que á propuesta de las respectivas Diputaciones provinciales aprobarán las Córtes.

ART. 2.° De cualquier modo que se distribuyan estos terrenos será en plena propiedad y en clase de acotados para que sus dueños puedan cercarlos, sin perjuicio de las cañadas, travesias, abrevaderos y servidumbres, disfrutarlos libres y exclusivamente, y destinarlos al uso ó cultivo que mas les acomode; pero no podrán jamás vincularlos, ni pasarlos en ningun tiempo ni por título alguno á manos muertas.

ART. 3.° En la enagenacion de dichos terrenos seràn preferidos los vecinos de los pueblos, en cuyo tèrmino existan y los comuneros en el disfrute de los mismos baldios.

ART. 4.° Las Diputaciones provinciales propondrán á las Córtes por medio de la Regencia el tiempo y los términos en que mas convenga llebar á efecto esta disposicion en sus respectivas provincias, segun las circunstancias del pais, y los terrenos que sea indispensable conservar á los pueblos, para que las Córtes resuelban lo que sea mas acomodado à cada territorio.

ART. 5.° Se recomienda este asunto al zelo de la Regencia del Reyno y de los Secretarios de la Gobernacion, para que lo promuevan é ilustren á las Córtes siempre que les dirijan las propuestas de las Diputaciones provinciales.

ART. 6.° Sin perjuicio de lo que queda prevenido se reserva la mitad de los baldios y realengos de la Monarquia, exceptuando los ejidis, para que en el todo ó en la parte que se estime necesaria sirba de hipoteca al pago de la deuda nacional, y con preferencia al de los créditos que tengan contra la Nacion los vecinos de los pueblos á que correspondan los terrenos; debiéndose entre estos créditos el primer lugar á aquellos que procedan de suministros para los Ejércitos nacionales, ó prestamos para la guerra, que ayan hecho los vecinos desde 1.° de Mayo de 1808.

ART. 7.° Al enagenarse por cuenta de la deuda pública esta mitad de baldios y realengos, ó la parte que se estime necesario hipotecar, serán preferidos para la compra los vecinos de los pueblos respectivos, y los comuneros en el disfrute de los terrenos expresados; y á unos y á otros se admitirán en pago por todo su valor los créditos competentemente liquidados que tengan por razon de dichos suministros y prestamos, y en su defecto cualquier otro crédito nacional lejitimo con que se hallen.

ART. 8.° En la expresada mitad de baldíos y realengos debe comprenderse y computarse la parte que ya se haya enagenado justa y legalmente en algunas provincias para los gastos de la presente guerra.

ART. 9.° De las tierras restantes de baldíos y realengos, ó de las labrantías de propios y arbitrios, se dará gratuitamente una suerte de las mas proporcionadas para el cultivo, à cada capitan, teniente ó subteniente, que por su abanzada edad, ó por haberse inutilizado en el servicio militar, se retire con la debida licencia, sin nota y con documento legitimo que acredite su buen desempeño; y lo mismo á cada sargento, cabo, soldado, trompeta y tambor, que por las propias causas ó por haber cumplido su tiempo obtengan la licencia final sin mala nota, ya sean nacionales ó extrangeros unos y otros, siempre que en los distritos en que fijen su residencia haya de esta clase de terrenos.

ART. 10. Las suertes que en cada pueblo se concedan á oficiales ó á soldados serán iguales en valor con proporcion à la cabida y calidad de las mismas, y mayores ó menores en unos paises que otros, segun las circunstancias de estos, y la poca ò mucha extension de las tierras; procurandose que à lo menos, si es posible, cada suerte sea tal, que regularmente cultivada baste para la manutencion de un individuo.

ART. 11 El señalamiento de estas suertes se hará por los Ayuntamientos Constitucionales de los pueblos á que correspondan las tierras, luego que los interesados les presenten los documentos que acrediten su buen servicio y retiro, oyendose sobre todo breve y gubernativamente á los procuradores sindicos, y sin que se exijan costos ni derechos algunos. En seguida se remitirá el expediente á la Diputacion provincial, para que esta lo apruebe y repare cualquier agravio.

ART. 12. La concesion de estas suertes, que se llamarán premio patriótico, no se estenderá por ahora á otros individuos que los que sirvan o hayan servido en la presente guerra, ó en la pacificacion de las actuales turbulencias en algunas provincias de Ultramar. Pero comprehende á los capitanes, tenientes, subtenientes y tropa, que habiendo servido en una y otra, se hayan retirado sin nota y con legitima licencia por haberse estropeado é imposibilitado en accion de guerra, y no de otro modo.

ART. 13. Tambien comprehende á los individuos nó militares, que habiendo servido en partidas, ó contribuido de otro modo á la defensa nacional en esta guerra ó en las turbulencias de Amèrica, hayan quedado ó queden estropeados é inutiles de resultas de accion de guerra.

ART. 14. Estas gracias se concederán a los sugetos referidos, aunque por sus servicios y acciones señaladas disfruten otros premios.

ART. 15. De las mismas tierras restantes de baldios y realengos se asignarán las mas apropósito para el cultivo, y á todo vecino de los pueblos respectivos que lo pidan y no tenga otra tierra propia, se le dará gratuitamente por sorteo, y por una vez, una suerte proporcionada á la extension de los terrenos, con tal que el total de las que asi se repartan en cualquier caso no exceda de la cuarta parte de dichos baldíos y realengos: y si estos no fuesen suficientes, se dará la suerte en las tierras labrantías de propios y arbitrios; imponiéndose sobre ella en tal caso un cánon redimible equibalente al rendimiento de la misma en el quinquenio hasta fin de 1807, para que no decaigan los fondos municipales.

ART. 16. Si alguno de los agraciados por el precedente artículo dejase en dos años consecutivos de pagar el cánon, siendo de propios la suerte, ó de tenerlo en aprovechamiento, será concedida á otro vecino mas laborioso que carezca de tierra propia.

ART. 17. Las diligencias para estas concesiones se harán tambien sin costo alguno por los Ayuntamientos, y las aprobarán las Diputaciones provinciales.

ART. 18. Todas las suertes que se concedan conforme al articulo 9, 10, 12, 13 y 15, lo serán tambien en plena propiedad para los agraciados y sus sucesores en los términos y con las facultades que expresa el articulo 2; pero los dueños de estas suertes no podràn enagenarlas antes de cuatro años de como fuesen concedidas, ni sugetarlas jamas á vinculacion, ni pasarlas en ningun tiempo ni por titulo alguno á manos muertas.

ART. 19. Cualquiera de los agraciados referidos ó sus sucesores que establezca su habitacion permanente en la misma suerte, serà exento por ocho años de toda contribucion ò impuesto sobre aquella tierra ó sus productos.

ART. 20. Este Decreto se circulará no solo á todos los pueblos de la Monarquía, sino tambien á todos los ejércitos nacionales, publicandose en estos de manera que llegue á noticia de cuantos individuos los componen.

Lo tendrá entendido la Regencia del Reyno, y dispondra lo necesario á su cumplimiento, haciendolo imprimir, publicar y circular.=Francisco Ciscar, Presidente.=Florencio Castillo, Diputado Secretario.=Juan Maria Herrera, Diputado Secretario.=Dado en Cádiz á 4 de Enero de 1813.=A la Regencia del Reyno."

Y para que tan benefica soberana disposicion llegue á noticia de todos los habitantes de las provincias de mi cargo, como Gefe superior político de ellas, mando que se publique por bando en toda su comprension, á cuyo fin se remitirán los competentes exemplares á los Señores Magistrados, Ayuntamientos Constitucionales, y demas Autoridades que corresponde. Dado en Chihuahua á 21 de Abril de mil ochocientos veinte y uno.

Alejo Garcia Conde

*Copy of the 4 January 1813 decree of the **Spanish Cortes** issued by Comandant General Alejo Garcia Conde. (SANM I, No. 1133. State Records Center & Archives, Santa Fe, NM.)*

In 1538, the *cabildos* — no monuments to fairness and objectivity in this respect — lost their land distribution privilege, and the viceroy, or the president of the *Audiencia de Guadalajara* in the north of the colony, took over their role (though the *cabildos* still had to give opinions as to land grants within their jurisdiction).[58] After 1656 only sales valued at more than 500 pesos had to be confirmed in Spain itself.

From 1692 till 1754, land matters were directed from Spain by the *Superintendencia del Beneficio y Composición de Tierras,* a body under the *Consejo de Indias*, presided over by one of the members of this *consejo*, the *superintendente*. As *subdelegados* of this *superintendencia* we find the *oidores* of the Indian *audiencias* who in turn appointed, district by district, land officers who, by personal inspection (*visitas a la tierra*), had to build up a *catastro*, a land register.

Then, in 1754, an important *real instrucción* transferred the basic decisions concerning land again, from Spain to the Indies, where the *Juzgados de Tierras* initiated a general review of property titles, with corrective *composiciones* as to abuses committed after 1700. The confirmation of grants and *composiciones* was given in the Indies, in the form of a marginal notation by the *Juzgados de Tierras.*

After 1776, when the *Comandancias* were established for new settlements, a special *Comisionado*, representative of the *Comandante*, had great powers regarding the distribution of residential or agricultural land,[59] and in 1786 the intendency system gave wide powers in land matters to the *Intendentes.*[60] After 1798, for sales of less than 200 pesos, the requirement of confirmation could be waived by payment of a 2% surtax.[61]

The Cadiz liberalization measures gave a central role to the *ayuntamientos* (under supervision of the *diputaciones provinciales*) as to the privatization of land (in which respect, not much went from paper into three-dimensional reality, during the colonial period).

New Spain transferred to Mexico, in 1821, a land situation with rather well defined boundaries in the center, and more vague contours in the outer regions. The form of land holding showed wide variation, from great expanses of public land — the former Crown land — often of little practical value, large *haciendas* and *estancias*, enormous church holdings, small agricultural lots, which were often augmented by access to common lands (*ejidos, dehesas, montes,* and *baldios*), and some land, used for municipal fiscal purposes (*propios*). From a social and economic point of view, the flaws of this system in the light of the *Zeitgeist* were mainly the existence of the *latifundia* of the *hacendados*, and the "dead hand" of perpetual ownership, especially as to church property.

Then, in the 1850s, church property was deamortized[62] but at the same time the commons of Indian communities were jeopardized by this policy. However, during the Mexican Revolution (1910-1920), a basis was laid for the splitting up of the big *haciendas*, and the commons of villages received the legislative support that had been weakened since the Cadiz period. Besides, the land holding panorama was enriched by two creations of the revolution: the *ejido* (a term now used in a new sense), and the protected, private *pequeña propiedad* — not necessairily very small, as it could reach 250 acres of the best agricultural soil, or grazing land for up to 500 head of cattle.

The *ejido* led to a new form of amortization, and has not always come up to economic expectations. Additionally, in some cases the *pequeña propiedad* was allegedly used for speculation, and its maximum limit seems high in the light of growing land scarcity. In today's Mexico interesting discussions are going on about the future of both the *ejido* and the *pequeña propiedad*.

Abreviations: UNAM: Universidád Nacionál Autónoma de Mexico; Encinas stands for: Diego de Encinas, Cedulario Indiano, 1596 edición facsimilar, Madrid, 1945. FS stands for: Francisco de Solano, Cedulario de Tierras, Compilación de Legislación Agraria Colonial (1497-1820), Mexico D.F., UNAM, 1984; Konetzke stands for: Colección de Documentos para la Historia de la Formación Social de Hispanoamérica, Madrid, 1956-1962, 5. vol.; MM stands for: Julio Cesar Méndez Montenegro, *444 Años de Legislación Agraria, 1513-1957*, Guatemala, 1960; RI stands for: the *Recopiloción de Leyes de los Reinos de las Indias*, Madrid, 1681, 4 vol. There are several later editions, without amendments, and modern facsimilar editions. The latest one of these was published by MA. Porrúa, Mexico D.F., 1987, and is accompanied by a fifth volume with modern comments.

1. After 1614, however, new Castilian enactments needed a special *pase* (approval) in order to be applicable to the Indies.
2. In the unique merced granted to Cortés on 29 July 1529 we can observe very clearly this medieval Castilian spirit. *Cedulario Cortesiano*, Arteaga Garza and Perez San Vicente (Mexico D.F., 1949), doc. 32, 125-130.
3. Not Justinian law in its pure, original form of the Corpus Iuris from the 6th. Century A.D., but seen through the comments by Glossators, Postglossators, Mos Gallicus, Iurisprudentia Elegans, and other interpreters, belonging to the "second life of Roman Law."
4. See RI, II.1.4; V.2.22, and V.15.83, and J. Manzano y Manzano, "Las Leyes y Costumbres Indígenas en el Orden de Prelación de Fuentes del Derecho Indiano," 18 *Revista Levene* (1967), 65-71.
5. See Konetzke, III, 25, No. 12.
6. FS, doc. 205.
7. Magnus Moerner, *Estado, Razas y Cambio Social en la Hispano-América Colonial*, (Mexico D.F., Sep-Setenta 128, 1974).
8. In the terminology used in this respect, referring to a *República de Indios*, as distinct from the *República de Españoles*, one should remember that the term "República," in that period, was used as a general equivalent of political community or state, not in the sense of a structure of the state, different from the tradition of monarchy.
9. See G.F. Margadant, *La política de congregación de indios en su fase mas áspera (1598-1605),* in Estudios en Honor del Dr. L. Recasens Siches, (Mexico D.F., UNAM, 1980), 626-649.
10. See Woodrow Borah, *Justice by Insurance: The General Indian Court of Colonial Mexico and the Legal Aides of the Half-Real* (Berkeley, 1983), passim.
11. *Caciques* were the elite of the Indian world, springing from pre-Cortesian nobility, as maintained in power by the Castilian Crown.
12. MM 21/5.
13. FS doc. 201.
14. Norman S. Martin, *Las Vagabundos en la Nueva España* (Mexico, D.F., 1987), passim.

15. *Capitulaciones* were agreements between the crown and prospective promotors, interested in the discovery, and then conquest, pacification, and settlement of the discovered region or later just the population of some region, already discovered but not yet settled by Spanish colonists.
16. *Caballerías*, i.e. lots given to followers who owned a horse, were bigger than the *peonías*, i.e. lots awarded to footsoldiers. The exact proportion between the *caballería* and the *peonía* is difficult to ascertain, as the basic rule for this (June 18, 1513; see RI.IV.12.1) is expressed partly in terms of area and partly of produce (*fanegas*), but the proportion was roughly four or five to one.
17. These peopele, on account of their participation in such colorful events as the *Conquista* (and, sometimes, before, in the *Siege of Granada*), did not feel anymore the attractions of a stable, rooted, family life, and had to be lured back into an orderly existence.
18. FS, p. 17.
19. Encinas, I.74; FS doc. 155 (see also RI IV.12.16). The procedure "*a vela y pregón*" literally, "by candle and herald," was a colorful procedure announced by a herald, where a candle was lit, and a public auction held, during which the bidding could continue until the candle burnt out. This procedure gets a more pragmatic profile in 1631 (FS 168; see also RI IV.12.15). It was not necessary to pay the whole price at once: part of it could take the form of a *censo a quitar* (quit rent).
20. Viceroys, Oidores, Fiscales, and since 1604, even Alcaldes Mayores, as well as their close family members, paid different prices for land acquired through *denuncias*.
21. FS, doc. 226.
22. Especially the "lost lots," left between grants, became a real invitation to illegal occupancy by neighbors.
23. FS, 22.
24. For example, a grant by a *cabildo*, after these municipal councils had lost the power to grant land.
25. After 1636 the system did not require a confirmation of such regularization by authorities in Spain (for normal grants, this confirmation was still required, though in special cases it could be granted by the Viceroy).
26. For the financial results of these *composiciones* within the jurisdiction of the viceregal *Audiencia* of New Spain, see J. J. Te Paske, and José & María Luz Hernandez Palomo, *La Real Hacienda de Nueva Espana: la Real Caja de Mexico (1576-1816)* (Mexico D.F., INAH, 1976). A complete and realistic view on these matters, however, is hampered by the fact that this study only refers to the territory covered by the viceregal *Audiencia* (not to the *Audiencia* of Gaudalajara), and especially from 1692 to 1730 the amounts paid for *composiciones* often seem to fall under the heading of "*donativos*" and not "*composición de tierras*."
27. Since the beginning of this policy, several authorities got involved in these *composiciones*. From 1692 till 1754, they were handled by the *Superintendencia del Beneficio y Composición de Tierras*, in Spain, and their subordinate *Tribunales* in New Spain.
28. Generally, the *composición* money was earmarked for the construction of a fleet that would maintain Spanish power in the Caribbean Sea: the *Armada de Barlovento*.
29. Doubt is provoked, in this respect, by a *Real Cedula* of 1661 (Konetzke, II.2.487/8), which mentions exemption of Indian property from *composición*, but this probably only refers to Indian commons.
30. In this respect, the *Instrucciones Generales* of 24 November 1735 can be interpreted both ways, but the *Instrucción* of 1 July 1746 leaves no doubt anymore: FS, doc. 201 and FS, doc. 209.
31. See FS, pp. 79-84, with reference to many documents reproduced in the later part of the book, and Encinas, IV.272.
32. FS, p. 83.
33. The term *fundo legal* came into unofficial use, probably by the end of the eighteenth century, when the institution itself had already developed.
34. Later 600 varas, FS, doc. 181.
35. In 1687 the point of departure for these measurements changed from the church — or the cemetery cross — to the edge of the urbanized part of the settlement, and then in 1695 came back to the church.
36. FS, doc. 223.
37. RI, IV. 7. 13, and RI, VI. 3. 81.
38. Lots on this land could not even be leased to Spaniards. RI, VI.15.17.
39. See FS, p. 86, where Solano takes the position of Wistano L. Orozco, against Mendieta y Núñez. The wording of the Cadiz decree of 4 January 1813, art. 1, offers arguments for the position of Solano and Orozco.
40. FS, doc. 114.
41. FS, doc. 117.
42. Charles Gibson, *The Aztecs Under Spanish Rule* (Stanford, 1964), 264-267.
43. See William B. Taylor, "Land and Water Rights in the Viceroyalty of New Spain," 50 *New Mexico Historical Review* (July 1975), 207; and Michael Meyer, *Water in the Hispanic Southwest, A Social and Legal History, 1550-1850* (Tucson, AZ, 1984), 126-131.
44. FS, doc. 195, for reference to Indian Pueblos in 1713. For the *ejido* as the growing edge of the community, see Daniel Tyler, "Ejido Lands in New Mexico, pp. 25 and 29 of this book.
45. FS, doc. 178.
46. In accordance with the *Normativa de Blanes* (FS, doc. 223, art. 18), this is possession for over forty years.
47. The volumes 713, 714, 715, and 716 of the section *Tierras* refer to this case. However, as so often happens, the documents are filed in a chronologically haphazard way, rather carelessly — occasionally one even finds a page bound upside down — and the *expedientes* within the volumes are often incomplete, finishing in the middle of a sentence.
48. These were mule drivers who needed common meadows for their animals.
49. The buyer purchased *con sus tachas buenas o malas* (with its good and bad qualities), folio 54 (reverse).
50. See his *Real Orden* of 8 June 1815; *Condumex*, XLI.I.10.804.
51. Royal decree of 11 April 1820.
52. *Condumex*, 351.72, Na. 34.348.
53. For this reason, the claim of church organizations to pre-Cortesian temple lands was not favorably received by the Crown. FS, 92.
54. At least since 1735. FS, doc. 201.
55. For an impressive list, see FS, doc. 214.
56. The term "amortized land" is used for land that is not in free commercial circulation, but in "the dead hand;" other types of amortized land were the perpetuities (*mayorazgos*) of aristocratic Spanish and Indian families, the *fundos legales* of Indian puebles, and the *dehesas, baldíos* and *ejidos*.
57. William B. Taylor found that his principle of ecclesiastical mortmain was not so encompassing for Colonial Oaxaca as had been supposed. Taylor, *Landlord and Peasant in Colonial Oaxaca* (Stanford, 1972), 194.
58. RI, IV.12.8.
59. See, for example, art. 17 of the *Plan de Pitic*.
60. See art. 81 of the New-Spanish *Ordenanza de Intendentes*.
61. FS, doc. 222.
62. *Ley Lerdo*, 1856; Reforma law of 1859.

Chronology

1519-1521-The Spanish army under Cortes defeats the Aztecs.

During the first few generations of New Spain, until about 1600, there was a generous and gratuitous distribution of land by *Adelantados, Cabildos,* and *Audiencias*.

1531 Distribution of land was put under supervision of the *Consejo de las Indias.*

1538 — The *Cabildos* lost their powers with respect to the distribution of land; thereafter only the Viceroy, the *Presidente* of the Guadalajara *Audiencia*, and the governors, had the power to distribute land.

1581 — Sale of Crown land (instead of gratuitous distribution), became the prevailing land distribution system. Measures were also taken against sales of Indian land to Spanish colonists, to the extent that such sales could cause damage to the Indian economy, but the epidemic disease suffered by the Indian population frustrated these attempts to protect the Indians.

1591 — The system of *composiciones* was organized to correct the errors committed during the initial period of liberal land distribution, and subsequent abuses. The result was the first long wave of *composiciones*, continuing until 1625.

1600-1700 — Sandwiched between the two mining centuries (the 16th and the 18th centuries), is the 17th century, one of quiet economic growth, springing mostly from agriculture. The New-Spanish economy of this period profited from a gradual increase in the Indian population (who now regretted the loss of their land during the *cocolixtle* period).

1612, 1617, and especially 1631 — The system of public sale of *realengas* was improved (*subasta a vela y pregon*).

1631, 1635, and 1640 — Minor *composición* regulations paved the road to the short but efficient *composición* period of 1648-1650, with the new system of collective *composiciones.*

1692 — The *Superintendencia del Beneficio y Composición de Tierras* was created in Spain, with *Juzgados de Tierras* in the Indies. They had remarkable success in building up of the *catastro,* or land register. Until 1754, this *Superintendencia* produced a constant flow of *composiciones*.

1695 — More flexibility is introduced in the *mayorazgo* system.

1735 — Extension of land title investigation to Indian land.

1738 — Reform under which *vecinos* received a say in the valuation of granted land.

1754 — A land reform which included a general review of land titles to cure any irregularity that originated after 1700, with a transfer of the control by *confirmación* from Spain to the Indies, where the *Juzgados de Tierras* took care of this aspect of land law. Deamortization of Church property received an interesting prelude in the way Jesuit property was handled after their expulsion in 1763.

1786 — The Intendency system was extended in New Spain, and the *Intendentes* were given a central role in the land distribution process.

1800-1821 — Mexico's pre-Independence years are characterized, as far as land law is concerned, by the deamortization of part of Church property by means of the consolidation system, which from 1804 to 1810 was affecting New Spain, and by the liberalization movement, which flourished in the *Cortes* of Cadiz from 1810 to 1814, and then again from 1820 till 1821. These *Cortes* tended towards the privatization of common lands of Spanish and Indian settlements, including municipal *propios* (but with the exception of "necessary *ejidos*"), *baldíos,* and *realengos*. They also abolished *mayorazgo*, for the institution had too aristocratic a taste, and went against the French Revolution's principle of free economic circulation of all forms of wealth.

These broad lines of development are surrounded by a myriad of minor measures, often of a regional nature (as were the several rules, enacted by the powerful *Visitador,* José de Galvéz, for parts of northwestern New Spain).

Bibliography

I. Legislative and administrative colonial materials

As to the basic laws, a first approach is offered by the *Recopilación de Leyes de los Reinos de las Indias* (RI), of 1681.

The several comments by "*notistas*" (Zurita, Cuervo, Ayala, and P.A. de Palacios), that accompany this basic compilation, should never be neglected.

For the generations which preceded the *Recopilación*, the *Cedularios* by Puga (1563), and by Encinas (1596), are important, as are the *Nuevas Ordenanzas de Descubrimiento y Población*, of 1573 in relation to land distribution by promoters of settlement ventures. Their text can be consulted, with certain discrepancies, in VI *Boletin del AGN (May-June 1935):* 3, 321-360; *Colección de Documentos Inéditos relativos al Descubrimiento, Conquista y Organización de las Antiguas Posesiones en America y Oceanía*, vol. VIII, 484-537; ibid. vol. XVI, 142-187; and FS, doc. 91.

The material found in the above important sources, has been supplemented by many later enactments, which can be found (often together with administrative decisions), in older publications, such as:

Galván, Mariano, *Ordenanzas de Tierras y Aguas* (Mexico), several editions available, the third edition of 1849 was used here).

Hanke, Lewis and Rodríguez, Celso, *Los virreyes Españoles en América durante el gobierno de la Casa de Austria*, 5 vol. (Mexico and Madrid, 1976-1978). A rich source of documentary data.

Matraya y Ricci, J.J., *Catálogo Cronológico etc.* (Lima, 1819). Pérez y López, A. X., *Teatro de la legislación universal de España e Indias* (Madrid, 1791-1798).

Colección de Documentos Inéditos relativos al Descubrimiento, Conquista y Organización de las Antiguas Posesiones en América y Oceanía, 42 vol. (Madrid, 1864-1884).

Colección de Documentos Inéditos relativos al Descubrimiento, Conquista y Organización de las Antiguas Posesiones Españoles de Ultramar, 25 vol. (Madrid, 1885-1932). Includes interesting materials — legislative, administrative and other kinds.

II. Treatises on the Indies, written during the colonial period

Avendaño, Diego de, *Thesaurus Indicus.*

Escalona Aguero, Gaspar de, Gazophilatium Regium Perubicum (Madrid, 1675).

León Pinelo, Antonio de, *Tratado de las confirmaciones reales de encomiendas, oficios y casos en que se requiere para las Indias Occidentales* (Madrid, 1630).

Saenz de Escobar, Joseph, *Tratado de Agrimensura,*

Medidas de Agua y Medidas de Minas (never printed, but available in manuscript copies and in their photostatic reproductions).

Solórzano Pereira, Juan de, *De Iure Indiarum* (Madrid, 1629, 1639)

______________, *Política Indiana* (Madrid, 1646).

III. Compilations of legislative and administrative materials, published after the colonial period

Disposiciones Complementarias de las Leyes de Indias, 3 vol. (Madrid, 1935).

Dublán y Lozano, *Legislación Mexicana*, 42 vol. (Mexico, 1876-1912).

Colección de los Decretos y Ordenes que han expedido las Cortes Generales y Extraordinarias (Madrid). Some of the Cadiz enactments can be found in a more complete form here than in Dublan y Lozano (except for the last months of the New-Spanish period). The discussions on the land topics can be consulted in the corresponding *Actas*.

Fabila, Manuel Montes de Oca: *Cinco Siglos de Legislación Agraria (1493-1940).*

Konetzke, Richard, *Colección de Documentos para la Historia de la Formación Social de Hispano-America,* 5 vol. (Madrid, 1956-1962).

Méndez Montenegro, Julio César, *444 años de legislación agraria, 1513-1957* (Guatemala, 1960).

Muro Orejón, Antonio, *Cedulario Americano del siglo XVIII, 3* vol., (Sevile, 1956-1977).

Solano, Francisco de, *Cedulario de Tierras: Compilación de Legislación Agraria Colonial, 1497-1820* (UNAM, 1984). A valuable recent publication with a fine introduction.

It is in these compilations that we find the important post-*Recopilación* regulations, such as the *Superintendencia del Beneficio y Composiciones de Tierras* (1692), the land reform decree of 1754, and the *Ordenanza de Intendentes* for New Spain (1786); also local regulations, like the *Plan de Pitic,* or the Gálvez rules for settlements in Baja California (FS, doc. 211).

IV. Bibliographies

López Rosado, Diego G., *Fuentes para el estudio de la propiedad de la tierra y colonización* (Mexico, D. F., 1979).

Martínez Rios, Jorge, *Tenencia de la tierra y desarrollo agrario de Mexico* (Mexico, D. F., 1970).

In Francisco de Solano's *Cedulario de Tierras* at pp. 39-40, there is a list of treatises written in colonial times for use by surveyors, which often present legal information in passing.

V. Monographs and treatises

a) Older works

Enríquez Molina, Andrés, *Los Grandes Problemas Nacionales* (Mexico, D. F., 1909). Though now outdated in many respects, this work makes important contributions to our vision of New-Spanish land law.

Orozco, Wistano Luis, *Legislación y Jurisprudencia sobre Terrenos Baldíos,* 2 vol. (Mexico, D.F., 1895). This work is still worthwhile. Though it is true that the comments added to the legislative material often seem superficial to modern readers, one should not forget that this is a pioneering work.

b) Contemporary literature

Chevalier, François, *La formation des grands domaines au Mexique* (Paris, 1952). Translated as *Land and Society in Colonial Mexico* (Berkeley and Los Angeles, 1963).

Gibson, Charles, *The Aztecs Under Spanish Rule* (Standford, 1964). Translated as *Los aztecas bajo el dominio español*, 1510-1820 (Mexico, 1967).

Mariluz Urquijo, José María, *El régimen de la tierra en el Derecho Indiano* (Buenos Aires, 1978).

Méndez Montenegro, J. C., *Aspectos legales del problema de la tierra en la época colonial* (Mexico, 1978).

Morales Padrón, F., "Descubrimiento y toma de posesión," XII *Anuario de Estudios Americanos* (Sevile, 1955), 321-380.

Ots Capdequí, J. M., *España en América: El régimen de las tierras en la America españa* (Ciuidad Trujillo, 1946).

Solano, Francisco de, *Tierra y sociedad en el reino de Guatemala* (Guatemala, 1977).

Guillermo F. Margadant S. is a professor of Roman law and legal history at the *Universidad Nacional Autónoma de México* in Mexico City, where he received his doctorate in law in 1960. He has written several books and numerous articles on Roman law, Mexican law, and general legal history. Professor Margadant serves as a consultant and expert witness for the New Mexico State Engineer in water rights adjudication lawsuits, and is a Visiting Professor of Law at the University of Texas Austin School of Law.

Index

John J. Vander Velde
Special Collections Librarian
Kansas State University Libraries